# LOVE IN THE PROMISED LAND

# LOVE IN THE PROMISED LAND

*The Story of
Anzia Yezierska and John Dewey*

## MARY V. DEARBORN

THE FREE PRESS
*A Division of Macmillan, Inc.*
NEW YORK

Permission has generously been granted to include in this volume quotations of or concerning Anzia Yezierska and John Dewey from: Boston University, Mugar Memorial Library; *Bread Givers* by Anzia Yezierska, copyright © 1925, renewed 1952 by Anzia Yezierska, transferred to Louise Levitas Henriksen in 1970, reprinted by permission of Persea Books, Inc., 225 Lafayette Street, New York, N.Y. 10012; The Center for Dewey Studies, Southern Illinois University, Carbondale, Illinois; Collection of American Literature, The Beinecke Rare Book and Manuscript Library, Yale University; John Jacob Coss Papers and John Dewey Papers, Rare Book and Manuscript Library, Columbia University; Dorothy Canfield Fisher Papers, University of Vermont Library; Zona Gale Collection, The State Historical Society of Wisconsin; *Hungry Hearts and Other Stories* by Anzia Yezierska, copyright © 1985 by Louise Levitas Henriksen, reprinted by permission of Persea Books, Inc.; ''The Man Who Made Us What We Are'' by Search-Light (Waldo Frank), *The New Yorker*, May 22, 1926, reprinted by permission, © 1926, 1958 The New Yorker Magazine, Inc.; *The Open Cage* by Anzia Yezierska, copyright © 1979 by Louise Levitas Henriksen, reprinted by permission of Persea Books, Inc.; Charles Olson Papers, Literary Archives, University of Connecticut Library; *The Poems of John Dewey* and *John Dewey: The Early Works*, Jo Ann Boydston, ed., vols. 1, 4, and 5, Southern Illinois University Press; *Red Ribbon on a White Horse* by Anzia Yezierska, copyright © 1950 by Anzia Yezierska, copyright renewed 1978 by Louise Levitas Henriksen, reprinted by permission of Persea Books, Inc.; unpublished letters of Anzia Yezierska quoted by permission of Louise Levitas Henriksen.

Copyright © 1988 by Mary V. Dearborn

The Free Press
A Division of Macmillan, Inc.
866 Third Avenue, New York, N.Y. 10022

Collier Macmillan Canada, Inc.

Printed in the United States of America

printing number
1   2   3   4   5   6   7   8   9   10

*Library of Congress Cataloging-in-Publication Data*

Dearborn, Mary V.
    Love in the Promised Land: the story of Anzia Yezierska and John Dewey/Mary V. Dearborn.
        p.   cm.
    Bibliography: p.
    Includes index.
    ISBN 0-02-908090-8
    1. Dewey, John, 1859–1952—Friends and associates. 2. Yezierska, Anzia, 1880?–1970—Relations with men—John Dewey. 3. Philosophers—United States—Biography. 4. Authors, American—20th century—Biography.  I. Title.
B945.D44D38  1988
191—dc19
[B]
                                                                        88–359
                                                                          CIP

*For Eric*

# Contents

# Acknowledgments

I have run up sizable professional and personal debts while writing this book. Chief among them is my debt to members of Anzia Yezierska's family, who were of great help in reconstructing the life of this complex woman. First I must thank Yezierska's daughter, Louise Levitas Henriksen, who was extremely generous with her time and resources even while busy with her own book about her mother. *Anzia Yezierska: A Writer's Life* appeared while this book was in production; Louise Henriksen and I have not read each other's work, but we have discussed our views many times. Without her kind and insightful assistance I could not have written *Love in the Promised Land*. Other Yezierska relatives who have been helpful include Shana Alexander, Laurel Bentley, Richard Goldberg, Edwin Margolius, Marjorie Mayer, Steven Rubenstein, Ruth Shaffer, Louise Tamotzu, and, especially, Victor Rubenstein. Nicholas Goldberg kindly introduced me to his extraordinary uncle, Jonathan R. Goldberg, who provided much interesting information and advice.

I am also grateful to many friends, acquaintances, and students of Yezierska. Joshua F. Greenberg kindly provided me with a thesis written by his uncle, Dr. A. Herbert Greenberg. Jim Tuck's enthusiastic recollections were a great encouragement; Arthur Zipser was helpful regarding details about Rose Pastor Stokes; and Henry Grinberg provided information about Yezierska's old age. Florence Zunser Saltz was an invaluable source concerning Yezierska's relationship with her mother, Miriam Shomer Zunser. Steve Siegel, the curator of New York City's 92nd Street YM-YWHA, along with Nancy Sinkoff, a historian of Jewish culture then working in the Y's archives, uncovered much valuable information about Yezierska's stay at the Clara de Hirsch Home. Zona Gale's biographer, Virginia Cox, has been generous in recounting her findings about Gale's friendship with Yezierska, and Sylvia Grider helped in similar ways concerning Dorothy Scarborough. Frederic Cornell gave me useful information about the history of the Rand School. Jules Chametzky contributed, in addition to his warm support, his file of notes and correspondence about Yezierska. Thanks also to Wilma Breit, Roberta Matthews, Marina Seevak, and Phyllis Weglein.

As far as John Dewey is concerned, my greatest debt, in addition to the libraries and archival sources listed below, is to Jo Ann Boydston, director of The Center for Dewey Studies in Carbondale, Illinois. It was she who edited Dewey's poetry and who in so doing recovered the connection with Yezierska, and it was she and Gipsey Hicks at Southern Illinois University Press who have allowed me to quote from Dewey material. Various intellectual debts to other Dewey scholars are, I hope, covered in the notes to this book.

Without the generous cooperation of librarians and curators this enterprise would have been impossible. I am grateful to the staff of the Columbia University Libraries, especially Kenneth A. Lohf in the Rare Book and Manuscript Library, and the staff of the New York Public Library, especially that of the Jewish Division. Others who were particularly helpful include Kevin McElvey and Margaret R. Goostray at the Mugar Memorial Library, Boston University, where the largest collection of Yezierska material is housed; Betty Weneck at the Milbank Memorial Library, Teachers College, who helped reconstruct Yezierska's college and teaching careers; Connell B. Gallagher at the Bailey/Howe Library, University of Vermont, who answered repeated requests about Dorothy Canfield Fisher and Dewey material; Sara S. Hodgson at The Huntington Library, who graciously scoured that collection's holdings for more traces of Yezierska; Harold Miller at The State Historical Society of Wisconsin (Madison), an important source for Zona Gale material; Ellen Kuniyuki Brown of The Texas Collection, Baylor University, where Yezierska's correspondence with Dorothy Scarborough is located; Saundra Taylor and Cheryl Baumgart at the Lilly Library, Indiana University, who helped with inquiries about both Dewey and Yezierska; Carolyn A. Sheehy at The Newberry Library; Gene de Gruson at the Leonard

H. Axe Library, Pittsburg (Kansas) State University; George F. Butterick at the University of Connecticut Library; Odessa Ofstad at the Pickler Memorial Library, Northeast Missouri State University; and Dione Miles at The Walter P. Reuther Library, Wayne State University. I must also thank the National Archives, New York branch; the Bentley Historical Library at the University of Michigan; the Beinecke Rare Book and Manuscript Library at Yale University; the Tamiment Library at New York University; the Western Jewish History Center; the Library of Congress; the Alderman Library at the University of Virginia; and the YIVO Institute for Jewish Research.

My friends and colleagues at Columbia University have helped my work in diverse ways. In the Department of English, I am grateful to Joseph Ridgely and Carole Slade, among many others. The contribution of Jack Salzman, director of the Center for American Culture Studies, is difficult to articulate but no less substantial for that. Doris Getzler, Joy Hayton, and Elnora Johnson fully deserve their customary tributes. Columbia's Society of Fellows in the Humanities has aided the publication of this book by awarding me a two-year Mellon Fellowship for research and teaching. I am extremely grateful to the Society's director, Loretta Nasser, for her friendship, support, and insights. Many members of the Society contributed to this work, but I should single out Richard Andrews, who clarified some key historical points; Walter Metzger, who helped me understand why I was doing what I was doing; and Gauri Viswanathan, conversations with whom have forced me to clarify my thinking in several important areas. My Humanities students in 1986–1987 played an undefinable but essential role in the writing of this book.

Among the friends who have sustained me throughout this project, I have to identify the usual suspects: Meryl Altman, Nat Austern, Allan M. Brandt, Laura Henigman, Warren Johnson, and Beth Langan, for contributions as diverse as checking references and making dinner. Special thanks are due to Martin Hurwitz and to Joe Markulin.

The fine insights and instincts of my agent, Maxine Groffsky, helped at every stage of this work. My editor, Erwin A. Glikes, convinced me that the story I wanted to tell was not just that of Anzia Yezierska but that of Yezierska and John Dewey. His faith in me has buoyed me at crucial points; throughout the progress of this work he has been all that an editor should be. Other individuals at The Free Press provided generous and sometimes crucial assistance: Susan Llewellyn, the copy editor, improved the manuscript immeasurably, as did Edith Lewis, while Eileen DeWald gave useful advice. Thanks also to Noreen O'Connor and to photo researcher Toby Greenberg.

Finally, I must cite two major creditors. My father, Richard W. Dearborn, functioned as my ideal reader—carefully reading and editing early drafts, and steering me back on course several times. Both he and Eric Laursen were extremely influential in helping me unlearn bad writing habits. Eric applied his considerable intelligence and excellent editorial skills to every page of every draft, and his enthusiasm for my subject made writing this book a genuine pleasure. It is to him I owe my greatest debt, for his persistent and loving support.

# Introduction

One night in 1958 eleven men gathered in an apartment overlooking the Hudson River on New York City's Riverside Drive. Corliss Lamont, the founder of the American Civil Liberties Union, had summoned them there, informing them in advance that their mission was to reminisce, for posterity, about a dead friend.

The eleven men included the author of *Studs Lonigan*, the president of Sarah Lawrence College, a number of Columbia University professors, the former director of the League for Industrial Democracy, a Columbia University librarian, and one of the founders of the New School for Social Research. The subject was John Dewey. To some, Dewey had been professor and mentor; to others, a colleague. At least one had considered himself Boswell to Dewey's Dr. Johnson. Each of the eleven would have claimed John Dewey as a friend.

But for a gathering of intimates, the occasion was remarkably solemn—though drinks were served, and the "Dewey cocktail" ("a species of rather strong Old-Fashioned") was ritually recalled. The quality of the talk was tentative and reverential, although a repeated motif in the group's talk was a plea to avoid excessive "pietism." The men retold some well-known Dewey anecdotes but referred mainly to Dewey's more noted accomplishments. This talk was for the record, as those present well knew—Lamont taped the evening and would later publish it as *Dialogue on John Dewey*—and the subject was the public man. At least one of the eleven, however, may have remembered more of the private John Dewey than the record was to show.

Conversation had turned to Dewey's appreciation of art and the influence on his work of the inventor and art collector Albert Coombs Barnes. Harold Taylor, the president of Sarah Lawrence, asked, "Is it true that Barnes was the chief instrument for

1

getting John interested in and working on aesthetics?'' Herbert W. Schneider, who had begun his Columbia career in 1917 as Dewey's assistant, replied, ''Painting, but not poetry. Dewey had a—'' John H. Randall, Jr., cut him off: ''Dewey was always interested in poetry.'' Corliss Lamont: ''And actually wrote some himself.''[1]

There the matter was left. What Schneider alluded to Dewey ''having'' was not pursued. Nobody present showed interest in Lamont's tantalizing reference to Dewey's poetry—somewhat remarkable in light of the hagiographical preservation of Deweyana already under way in the late fifties (and only one observer, Paul Levy, has noted this key moment since). And, in fact, this poetry would shatter conventional versions of the Dewey story. For the great bulk of it is love poetry, written to a then unknown writer about twenty years his junior: the Polish immigrant Anzia Yezierska, with whom Dewey had an intense relationship in 1917 and 1918. Dewey's involvement with Yezierska, a passionate younger woman, was a threatening undercurrent on that Riverside Drive evening.

One of the men present that night in 1958, Milton Halsey Thomas, knew more than he let on. For Dewey's poetry would never have seen the light of day—and his relationship with Yezierska would have remained unknown—were it not for Thomas's self-described ''Boswellizing.''[2] Dewey scribbled his love poems on scraps of paper, never intending them to be seen. Thomas salvaged the scraps from Dewey's wastebasket and the cubbyholes of his desk and preserved them in Columbia's archives.

Even then, the poems would have gathered dust had not rumors begun to surface among Dewey scholars about the existence of the material. When a pirated copy appeared, the John Dewey Foundation at Southern Illinois University, which had received the poems in the early 1970s, undertook publication. In 1977, *The Poems of John Dewey*, edited by Jo Ann Boydston, appeared, complete with textual emendations, lengthy footnotes, and appendices analyzing typewriter faces and Dewey's use of the apostrophe. The volume disappeared into the limbo that is the fate of many scholarly books, attracting almost no notice, even among Dewey scholars.

Why has Dewey's poetry received so little attention? It would seem to constitute invaluable new information about this important man who has remained consistently elusive to biographers and historians. Dewey was arguably the most influential figure in twentieth-century America. He has been called the father of the Progressive movement, thought to be responsible for the sweeping social reforms that characterized the early years of this century. Pragmatism, the school of philosophy he founded, became, according to many observers, virtually the official American philosophy. His educational innovations changed the face of American schooling and, by extension, the very course of American life. During his lifetime, he was elevated to the status of a national hero. (Of course, a man of such stature excites equally vigorous criticism, and Dewey has been blamed for everything from juvenile delinquency to antiintellectualism to, most recently, widespread cultural illiteracy.)

Yet Dewey the man, cloaked in all the praise and condemnation, is elusive. This great humanist, commonly remembered as warmly helpful to students and colleagues and open-minded in all encounters, has nevertheless emerged as a curiously flat figure in biographies and historical studies. It is possible that Dewey's poetry has been ignored because his official image cannot accommodate it. This very public man led a rich, if hidden, private life. There is a living, breathing man behind the monumental image, a man who was, for a time, passionately in love.

And while Dewey never allowed his emotions into his work except in verse he intended no one to read, Anzia Yezierska, the woman he addressed in his poetry, put her emotional life—in particular, her love for Dewey—at the center of her work. The counterpart to Dewey's poetry is Yezierska's fiction, six volumes of stories and novels about immigrant life. Widely read and critically acclaimed in the 1920s, her books fell into oblivion for the next four decades; only recently has she been rediscovered and her works made available again. And, though the circumstances in each case are entirely different, it is interesting that the record both writers left concerning their relationship nearly disappeared. The reasons are as curious in Yezierska's case as they are in Dewey's. The critical and popular disfavor into which her works fell raises questions about America's response to a writer whose sole subject was the immigrant and whose single theme was the immigrant's passionate desire to find her place in the

New World. Was there something in her very intensity that ultimately drove readers away?

Yezierska brought to every experience—not just her stories and novels—a vibrancy that transfixed all who met her. It is not hard to imagine what Dewey saw in her. She was, by all accounts, a physically striking and emotionally passionate woman, with brilliant red hair, creamy white skin, and violet-blue eyes.[3] Dewey, in contrast, was almost sixty, gray-haired and spectacled, gentle and kindly in demeanor but thought by many to be self-possessed to the point of aloofness. Something sparked between them, and an intense relationship ensued, a relationship that profoundly affected the careers and thinking of both. Equally arresting is the anomaly of their meeting, the fact that two people seemingly so different in background and temperament found each other and fell in love, which makes their meeting a rich cultural moment. When Anzia Yezierska met John Dewey, the immigrant met America, and America the immigrant.

Their relationship was not brought to light until the recent discovery of Dewey's poetry and the rediscovery of Yezierska's fiction. These records reveal the explosive impact the meeting had on both. For Yezierska, who became famous as the "sweatshop Cinderella" when her first book of stories was sold to the movies in 1920, the relationship was to become an obsessive subject in her stories and novels of immigrant life. Her passionate immigrant heroines, who "think with the heart rather than the head"—as she often writes—are locked in intimate confrontation with native-born American men who are all reason and no passion.

Yezierska saw in their relationship an insistent paradigm of the division between immigrant and native-born America, a paradigm Dewey took up as well. Dewey saw in Yezierska a natural counterpart to his own intellectualism, the infusion of emotion he felt immigrants could bring to himself and to America; his poetry, lines from which appear verbatim in Yezierska's fiction, documents his intense response to the potential she represented. Both saw their encounter as emblematic. To Yezierska, Dewey was no less than America incarnate; in union with him, she saw the realization of all her hopes and dreams, all the possibilities held out by the "promised land." For Dewey, Yezierska was the archetypal "other," the immigrant he sought so desperately to understand.

The relationship of these two figures, at once diametrically opposed and felicitously juxtaposed, draws attention to some of the most significant themes in American history since the Civil War. Among these are the rise of progressivism in education, the social development of liberalism, the rise of a reforming elite, and the changing roles of men and women as Victorian America gave way to our urbanized and industrialized modern culture. Because, taken together, their lives constitute an important chapter in cultural history, I discuss in detail several of these themes—among them, for instance, the rise of scientism in the nineteenth century, so significant to Dewey's choice of vocation, and the strange new discipline of domestic science, so vexed a feature of Yezierska's career.

To understand why Dewey responded as he did to Yezierska, it is necessary to read their lives concurrently, as stories set against each other. During Dewey's early years, while he developed his monumental philosophy and emerged as a social thinker and actor of great impact, Yezierska struggled to find her own vocation, climbing out of the ghetto by becoming a teacher. As Dewey became a public figure in the early years of this century, Yezierska forged her independence as a "new woman," partaking of the heady intellectual atmosphere of bohemian Greenwich Village.

Their lives—outwardly so different—ran along distinctly parallel lines. After his move to Columbia University from the University of Chicago in 1904, for example, Dewey became increasingly involved in specifically social issues—issues that were of concern to Yezierska as well. A friend of Jane Addams, Dewey actively supported the settlement house movement in New York and was an active participant in the exciting, radical "downtown" scene. In fact, Yezierska benefited from the very social and educational reforms Dewey wrote about and taught. Dewey, for example, supported vocational education for the immigrant—the same kind of education that lifted Yezierska out of the ghetto, winning her a scholarship to study domestic science, which she went on to teach. As Yezierska lobbied with her friend Henrietta Rodman for the rights of teachers, Dewey worked for organization of teachers' unions. And, when Yezierska grew frustrated at the roadblocks that in 1917 made it impossible for her to teach at a higher level, their lives finally intersected.

The divergence of their lives after their encounter is as significant as their earlier points of contact. As Yezierska seemed to lapse into silence, Dewey's career continued on its vigorous course. His long life spanned the years between the Civil War and the Cold War, and he must be understood in the context of the great changes that have characterized American life in the modern age. The private life of this public man has never received proper attention. His politics also need closer examination, for Dewey rightly saw himself as, like Hegel, a political philosopher. He was, of course, a social philosopher as well—it is not incorrect to call him the philosopher of democracy—and he needs to be studied in a social context.

Yezierska's life and reputation provide a rich and telling counterpoint to Dewey's. During her lifetime she was seduced and betrayed by her public, as she was by John Dewey, and yet she remained idealistic and courageous, a true American heroine. Strangely enough, it has been Dewey, the figure of such stature, who has fallen into eclipse since his death in 1952. The official image of him has taken over, and his books remain largely unread. But Yezierska has been rediscovered with enthusiasm since her death in 1970. Contemporary readers have found in Yezierska a powerful model of female identity and authorship in the twentieth century, and are moved by her portrayals of the attempt to mediate between immigrant and native-born America. Set against Dewey's, Yezierska's life presents a female and immigrant version of the American experience. If one did, indeed, think with the heart and the other with the head, their stories, taken together, tell an important American story.

# 1

## Dewey: The Making of the Philosopher

"The ice of his New England heart"—so Anzia Yezierska phrased her chief complaint about John Dewey. The idea of "Anglo-Saxon coldness" was central to her image of Dewey, to the mythological terms in which she cast their relationship. Indeed, Dewey's New England beginnings are an essential component of our national image of our national philosopher. His "homespun" pragmatism, his "New England" reticence, his exposure to the democratic values of his home town of Burlington, Vermont (a town that could boast not only "Yankee" neighborliness but 100 prostitutes, there to service the merchants visiting this lumber-trading center)—all are cited as features that contributed not only to Dewey's philosophy but to his personality. It speaks perhaps to a national nostalgia for our country's beginnings that we so fondly cling to Dewey's Yankee birth to explain what we do not know about this man.

It is indeed true that Dewey's Vermont years were intellectually and emotionally formative, but in ways that go beyond stereotypes of what we think of as "Yankee." And it is indeed fitting that this man whom many have held up as America's national philosopher should hail from New England, which had been since the nation's birth the seat of American culture. But by Dewey's birth this had begun to change; and by 1893, when John Dewey was on the verge of his fame, Frederick Jackson Turner announced that the frontier was closed. The nation was settled. Just as the New England preacher gradually relinquished his role as arbiter of social and cultural mores, so too did New England cease to be the center of American intellectual life. And, too, the

7

small town was no longer the social unit that governed the everyday life of the individual; the late nineteenth century was characterized by massive urbanization that shifted the whole focus of everyday life.[1]

Appropriately, John Dewey too made his way from New England to the new Midwestern intellectual centers in Michigan and Chicago and from there to New York City, which during his long years there emerged as the intellectual capital of the nation if not the world. Dewey was to become an inveterate New Yorker who vacationed in Key West and Nova Scotia, features that his official image cannot readily accommodate. On the centennial of Dewey's birth, a colleague remembered that Dewey often said he didn't see why "you fellows want to go back to summer places in Vermont. I got out as soon as I could."[2] John Dewey came from Vermont, but when he left it, he left it for good.

On October 26, 1949, six days after Dewey turned ninety, he and his wife did return briefly to Vermont—for a birthday celebration, which they made a day trip, returning home on a sleeper that night. The town had planned a modest birthday celebration—a tour of the town and the campus of the University of Vermont, a dinner on the campus, and a memorial address. When the procession arrived at the house in which he was brought up, he was asked if he wanted to come in and take a look around. No, Dewey said, "it would tear my heart out to go in."[3]

Few times in his life would Dewey use terms as emotional as these—he is not incorrectly known for what might be called bloodless prose. He used the language of tearing, of laceration, at one other important point, when, in his intellectual autobiography "From Absolutism to Experimentalism" (1930), he again spoke of visceral violence referring to his New England heritage:

> . . . the sense of divisions and separations that were, I suppose, borne in upon me as a consequence of a heritage of New England culture, divisions by way of isolation of self from the world, of soul from body, of nature from God, brought a painful oppression—or rather, they were an inward laceration.[4]

Dewey's childhood in Vermont was on the surface as bucolic as a Currier and Ives print, but, as with Dewey himself, the real experience was somewhat more complex.

Archibald Sprague Dewey, John's father, was descended from

a long line of New England farmers. His grandfather had moved in the 1780s from New York State to Bennington, Vermont, where he married a Bennington girl, Jerusha Hopkins. Together, they moved to Fairfax, a town a little north of Burlington, where Archibald was born in 1811.[5] In the 1830s, Archibald Dewey left the family farm for Burlington, where he opened a grocery store. At the age of forty-four, he married the twenty-four-year-old Lucina Artemisia Rich, whose ancestors were farmers but also congressmen and lawyers. Archibald and Lucina Dewey had four sons, the eldest of whom died in childhood. John Dewey was their third son, born on October 20, 1859, the year in which Charles Darwin's *The Origin of Species* was published.

When Dewey was still a baby, his father volunteered for the Union Army and became a quartermaster of the First Vermont Cavalry; he was cited for "coolness and decisiveness under fire."[6] Young John was himself a witness to events of the Civil War, as his mother and her sons followed her husband to the Union headquarters in northern Virginia for the last winter of the war. It is difficult to say what precipitated her move—such moves were rare, especially over so great a distance—but it seems fair to say that if Lucina's move evoked a sense of her dependence on her husband, it also bespoke considerable bravery. John Dewey's daughter, in relating this piece of family history, wrote: "This was an almost heroic move for a woman of those days."[7]

By all accounts, Lucina Dewey was a remarkable person. She was a pious woman who had troubled her father by undergoing an adolescent conversion at a revival meeting. By the time of the birth of her children, she had come around to the liberal evangelicalism of the day and raised her sons in that tradition. Dewey remembered her asking her sons daily whether they were "right with Jesus," and the petition necessary for the eleven-year-old John to join the Burlington Congregational Church was written not in his handwriting but his mother's: "I think I love Christ and want to obey Him. I have thought for some time I should like to unite with the church. Now, I want to more, for it seems one way to confess Him, and I should like to remember Him at the Communion."[8]

While Dewey was spared the "crisis of faith" that afflicted so many of his contemporaries, born at a time in which Darwin's evolutionary findings necessarily challenged the faith that had characterized America since the Puritans, he had nevertheless to come to terms with his mother's influence. But this would come when he was older, beyond Vermont and her reach. By 1886 he was able to write, "Religious feeling is unhealthy when it is watched and analyzed to see if it exists, if it is right, if it is growing."[9] When Lucina came to live with her son and his young family in Chicago years later, Dewey resisted her efforts to see that her grandchildren attended church and Sunday school; he had gone enough as a child, he said, so that his children would not have to go at all.[10] This resistance, however, reflected a confidence that had been, as we shall see, won only after considerable struggle.

The Dewey family was deeply involved in Burlington social life and especially that of Burlington's University of Vermont. Dewey's closest childhood friends, John Wright and James Buckham, were sons of Matthew Buckham, who was to become a president of the university. Students lived as boarders in the Dewey home. Lucina was well known for her solicitude with students—she served them hot chocolate and wedges of pie, listened to their troubles and counseled them on "right living" and good study habits. A Burlington neighbor, Jessie Whitcomb, immortalized Lucina's role as dispenser of tea and cookies in her 1899 *Freshman and Senior*, written under the pseudonym Elvirton Wright. There, as Mrs. Carver, Lucina Dewey is portrayed as holding "little gatherings . . . of a most impromptu, strictly college kind" and as fretting about the moral progress of her current student boarder.[11]

In Lucina's friendliness to college boys we can see the beginnings of John Dewey's lifelong kindness to his students, the root of the sort of impulse that would lead him, for instance, to have his student Max Eastman to dinner every Sunday during Eastman's graduate years at Columbia.[12] But if Lucina was solicitous of Burlington youth, she was not overly protective of her own sons—one modern commentator notes that she was the type who often didn't catch rips or tears in her children's clothing—and if she did, as often as not she would put off their mending.[13] The woman had a higher calling.

More influential still, perhaps, were Lucina's charity activities. Burlington was no small New England town—it had grown from a village of three or four thousand to a city of fourteen thousand

and was the second largest lumber center in the country.[14] It had its own slum quarter, where Lucina busied herself with charity work. Generations of New England women, of course, had considered helping the poor part of their daily round of moral duties; charity was often institutionalized as part of the neighborhood church's agenda. But Lucina seems to have approached her work with a verve that anticipated that of the Progressive reformers who were to be so central to Dewey's rise to fame. Vermont novelist Dorothy Canfield Fisher, in an anecdotal essay on Dewey, writes of her, "Much of her time was spent, often against jeering misunderstandings from the toughs she was trying to help, in the typical, fumbling, amateur, lion-hearted effort to help the underprivileged by which the best of the nineteenth-century 'good women' prepared the way for modern social welfare work."[15] While John Dewey's "democratic" upbringing has been overemphasized—it is likely that his world's limits were home, school, the church, and the outdoors where he played and explored with his brother and the Buckham boys, and did not extend to the town's slums—his mother's well-meaning efforts to improve the plight of others must have left a deep impression. Hers seems indeed to have gone beyond the cheerful "Sunday visitor" impulse of many Victorian women; reform for her was a deeply held conviction.

Set against Lucina's intensity and drive were her husband's geniality and tolerance. He was widely liked around Burlington, not only by university and church society but by those who visited his grocery store and, later, his cigar and tobacco store. He ran the liquor dispensary for the temperance town, a position of some importance; he was also one of the first treasurers of the Burlington Savings Bank. Townspeople watched for his ads in the daily papers. One, advertising salt fish in 1859, read:

### TURNED UP

*Not the sea serpent with fabulous tale [sic]*
*but the veritable mackerel without any head,*
*has both been seen and caught and is now on*
*exhibition at*

### DEWEY'S

His "Hams and Cigars—Smoked and Unsmoked" is well known, as is his red wheelbarrow painted "Stolen from A. S. Dewey."

Another salesmanlike verse read:

> *Lives there a man with soul so dead*
> *Who never to himself has said*
> *"Give me, to wet my daily bread*
> *A cup of Dewey's coffee!"*[16]

Archibald read Shakespeare, Milton, Lamb, and Thackeray to his sons and regaled them with Civil War stories; John Dewey later said that his happiest childhood memories centered around his father.[17]

Lucina's demanding moral exactitude showed itself in Davis and John's shyness; both were self-conscious, quiet boys. But from his father John gleaned a healthy good humor, and he, the Buckham boys, his brother Davis, and their cousin John Rich (who had become part of the family after his mother died), seem to have led happy, active childhoods.

Yet no one in the Dewey family—or the Burlington community—had any idea of what they expected of the next generation, their children. When asked, Archibald said that he would like it if one of his sons became a mechanic.[18] Lucina never stated her preference, but one imagines that she might rather have liked one of her sons to become a clergyman. Just as it was unclear in the 1870s and 1880s which way New England culture was going, it was also not clear which direction the Dewey offspring might take. As, with increased communications and industrialization in general, horizons broadened beyond the New England town, so too did a once perfectly respectable position like Archibald Dewey's become unthinkable for a young boy of brains and any ambition whatsoever. The Deweys must have vaguely realized, too, that there was nothing tying their sons to Burlington; in fact, their sons were of a new generation, one that left the small town for the wider world.

John Dewey acknowledged his lack of direction in later years, stating that "he probably would not have gone to college if there hadn't been a college right there in Burlington to slide into."[19] This step, then, seemed natural enough, and, with his brother and his cousin, Dewey entered the University of Vermont; he was then fifteen. The issue of vocation was temporarily put aside.

Dewey enrolled for the classical course, which entailed classes in Greek, Latin, ancient history, geometry, and calculus. Under H. A. P. Torrey and Matthew Buckham, John studied political and moral philosophy. Moral philosophy, the dominant influence in American colleges at the time, concentrated on moral development and character building, seeking to preserve traditional moral values in a changing society. Based on Scottish commonsense philosophy, moral philosophy charted a course through the theologically difficult waters of the late nineteenth century.[20] Philosophically, the legacy of men like Torrey and Buckham in Dewey's development was great; he struggled to accommodate and later to reject their ways of thinking. Practically, however, they provided no real direction for him. "Teachers of philosophy," Dewey wrote later, "were at that time, almost to a man, clergymen."[21]

The problem was that the more John Dewey read, the evermore untenable did the ministry become as a chosen profession. By his junior year Dewey had discovered Thomas Huxley, whose impact he recalled even sixty years later.[22] He read Matthew Arnold's critiques of religious orthodoxy and numerous English and American periodicals, including the *Journal of Speculative Philosophy*, the *North American Review*, and the *Edinburgh Review*. His favorite author was the evolutionist Herbert Spencer. With the evolutionists, Dewey began to see all ideas in terms of growth and progress, life itself as a great experiment.[23] In such a context, the fixed ideas of theology were impossible.

For John Dewey, life itself was to be a great experiment. And, though he was spared a crisis of faith, he suffered instead a very modern crisis of vocation. Had he been born two decades earlier, he would almost certainly have become a clergyman. And that avenue was by no means entirely closed off; Dewey's boyhood friend John Buckham, for instance, went on to become a theologian—albeit of the most ecumenical and progressive sort.[24] But for John Dewey, who graduated from the University of Vermont in 1879, twenty years after Darwin's discoveries had done no less than to question the very existence of God, that route was not possible.

The crisis of vocation was not uncommon among educated men in late Victorian America. As they discovered, in Darwin's words, that there was no more design in nature "than in the course in which the wind blows,''[25] it became necessary to concentrate on the empirical, on what was known. Science was the new religion; scientific inquiry would reveal the lost design. Moral philosophy gave way to the social sciences, and the disciplines of anthropology, psychology, economics, sociology, and political science were born in its place. It was believed that science could produce revolutionary progress in other spheres than that of nature—in understanding the mind, in educating children, even in running a household. Frederick Taylor conducted the first of his time and motion experiments in 1882—experiments that led to his formulation of "scientific management," by which it was hoped that not only the workplace but ultimately society itself would be transformed. *Popular Science Monthly*, whose first issue appeared in 1872, introduced all manner of new "scientific" thought to a wide audience. A whole class of women were actively engaged in creating the discipline of "domestic science," seeking to elevate the role of woman by elevating the nature of her work to the realm of science. Moreover, such scientific and technological developments as the telegraph, the statistical survey, and the railroad network led many thinkers to envision grand schemes for social change in all spheres. Dewey's contemporary, Thorstein Veblen, imagined an entire working society overseen by tomorrow's experts—engineers.[26] By 1899, John Dewey could write that as science developed and was

> progressively applied to history and all the social sciences, we can anticipate no other outcome than increasing control in the ethical sphere—the nature and extent of which can be best judged by considering the revolution that has taken place in the control of physical nature through a knowledge of her order.[27]

In understanding John Dewey's life, it is impossible to overstate the importance of the growing scientism in every area of American life. To a young man searching for his vocation, however, it was one thing to believe in science and another to set out to be, for instance, a sociologist—especially when entering that profession meant developing the discipline.

Though not strictly speaking a contemporary, psychologist George Stanley Hall, an important influence in John Dewey's life, provides a useful example of a learned young man in search of his vocation. Hall was to become a renowned psychologist and the president of Clark University, but in his youth he had no clear idea of what direction his life might take. He was twice forced to travel to Germany, not simply for exposure to the exciting new ideas in German universities but also to find some way to incorporate these new ideas into earning a living. Writing home to his mother that he wished to stay in Germany to earn a Ph.D. in philosophy caused his mother to write back with bewilderment: "Now Stanley wherein is the great benefit of being a Ph.D. I think a *preacher* should be D.D. Just *what is* a Doctor of Philosophy? and wherein would it give you *credit, influence,* or usefulness?"[28]

Hall did earn a D.D. from Union Theological Seminary, but he was frustrated by his failure to secure a position teaching philosophy with a divinity degree. He returned to graduate school at Harvard to study with William James (another philosopher who was to make his mark in psychology) and received a doctorate from the department of philosophy in psychology, the first doctorate awarded by Harvard's philosophy department and the first in the field of psychology to be given in the United States.[29] Yet Hall continued to face difficulty in finding an academic position. He worried that "neither psychology or philosophy would ever make bread" and considered taking a medical degree.[30] Eventually, of course, Hall became an enormously influential and respected scholar and public figure, but he made his start by narrowing his focus to child study and pedagogy, just as, interestingly, would John Dewey. Both men had noted the increased attention paid to education in German academic circles as well as growing interest in the life of the child in their own country, and both sensed that scientific method could legitimize pedagogy, which would in turn enrich their respective fields, philosophy and psychology.

Understanding Dewey's crisis of vocation provides an interesting lens through which to view his subsequent career. For he was not simply a philosopher. He was a teacher of philosophy, a psychologist, a social critic, a reformer, an educator: what we in the twentieth century would call, most broadly, an intellectual. As, with the rise of the American university, more and more Americans were earning their Ph.D.'s—doctorates of "philosophy," after all—Dewey himself realized that philosophy was simply a catchall term for what he did: "Very much of what has been represented as philosophic reflection is in effect simply an idealization, for the sake of emotional satisfaction, of the brutely given state of affairs.''[31]

It is, in fact, more accurate to describe Dewey's eventual profession as that of a university professor than that of a philosopher. The founder of the American Association of University Professors, Dewey was one of the first higher education professionals; his career developed congruently with what historian Laurence Veysey, in a book of the same title, calls the emergence of the American university. And, in fact, it is not surprising that the vocational crises of men like Hall and Dewey bore a distinct resemblance to those of the men who were to become the presidents of the largest of the growing American universities. Charles Eliot, later the president of Harvard, thought he might become a businessman or scientist; he wrote at age twenty-four, "What a tremendous question it is—what shall I be?''[32] James B. Angell was a civil engineer, a journalist, and a professor of modern languages before becoming president of the University of Michigan. William Watts Folwell, later president of the University of Minnesota, tried being a lawyer, a civil engineer, and a mathematics teacher, writing to his mother in 1861 with some urgency: "According to the best of my knowledge I am *twenty eight* years old today. *Twenty eight!* And *nothing done*. My education unfinished—no immediate expectation of being 'settled in life'—rather a sorry picture.''[33]

What the examples of Hall and the university presidents suggest is the important fact that in the nineteenth century (and perhaps the same holds true today) it was not possible to set out to become an intellectual. So, for the time being, John Dewey became a teacher: "Like many other young graduates uncertain about their life career he wanted a teaching position," wrote Dewey's daughter.[34] He could find none for months after his graduation, until his cousin Affia Wilson, the principal of a high school in Oil City, Pennsylvania, wrote that a position had opened there. Dewey seized this temporary solution. He taught for two years in Oil City and the following year in Lake View Seminary back in Vermont.

The man who was to become the single most influential figure in the history of American education, then, began his career by teaching school. And, by all accounts, he did so rather indifferently. Oil City was no laboratory school; there was no sculpturing in clay or weaving textiles or performing scientific experiments in John Dewey's classroom. Like those of most of his fellow teachers, his job was mainly disciplinary, though he did his best to teach Latin, algebra, and the natural sciences, using the traditional methods of his day—the "three Rs" of rote, reward, and the rod. And, like most of his fellow teachers, he did his job with only moderate success. His shy manner made it difficult for him to maintain order in his classroom. One of his students remembered two things in particular about his teaching: "how terribly the boys behaved, and how long and fervent was the prayer with which he opened each school day."[35]

It is not remarkable that John Dewey made no real innovations in his own classroom; his later innovations were made only after sustained study and in a climate in which educational reform had become almost a fad. What is interesting is that he made no reference to his teaching years in his later writing on education; the experience seems to have left little impression on him. And, in fact, he seems to have been quite unhappy in these years, trying to keep alive his interest in philosophy and to nurture his ambitions while working in an ignominious profession first, in what must have been a depressing little city, and then, later, back in Vermont on his own turf, hardly the conquering hero. Teaching in Victorian America was a feminized profession; it was thought that women were best suited to the raising of children and therefore to teaching, and they could be paid considerably less than men.[36] Not coincidentally, the profession was not highly regarded. Catherine Beecher in 1846 had commented on "the contempt, or utter neglect and indifference, which has befallen this only noble profession open to women. . . . The employment of teaching children is regarded as the most wearying drudgery, and few resort to it except from necessity."[37]

All this was, of course, to change, and education was to become a focus of attention for all reformers and intellectuals in the twentieth century, with Dewey himself rising to prominence through his educational reforms. In the very year in which he began teaching in Oil City, in fact, signs of the elevation of the field were in the air: the University of Michigan established a chair in the History, Theory, and Art of Education. By 1889, B. A. Hinsdale, commenting on such chairs, could write in the National

Education Association's *Journal of Addresses and Proceedings*, "Education is more than a great and difficult art; it is a noble science. Back of its methods, processes, and systems, are facts, principles, and theories—in fact, whole systems of philosophy."[38] Thus the "art" of education was gradually elevated to a "science."

Dewey's elevation of the status of education could be classed as part of a wider trend—the growing professionalization of his day. His was an age that saw the birth of the sanitation engineer, a time when undertakers became embarrassed by their previous association with cabinetmakers and liverymen and became "morticians." In every sphere, new standards of professional behavior and knowledge were set. The American Medical Association and the American Bar Association were transformed from loosely fraternal clubs into enormously powerful bureaucratic institutions; the American Historical Association, the American Economics Association, the American Political Science Association, and the American Sociological Society all spun off from their parent group, the American Social Science Association, during these years. Not coincidentally, the rise of professionalization encouraged the development of a professional elite—and, indeed, Dewey and his fellow reformers were to be accused (not entirely incorrectly) of social engineering of the most elitist and socially conservative sort.[39]

That the elevation of education corresponded with John Dewey's days as a schoolteacher suggests the confusing complex of circumstances in which he struggled to find his vocation. He did not know how to make his living—and yet he would become a member of a new professional class. Today's idea of "the professional," in fact, came into being because of people like Dewey. John Dewey the schoolteacher was to become, over the next two decades, something very different: John Dewey the educator. The change in his status corresponded exactly with the growing professionalization in almost every area of American life.

As Dewey the schoolteacher struggled with his future, so too did he struggle with his past. In Oil City, he was later to say, he underwent a "mystic experience," brought on by that old question, "whether he really meant business when he prayed." The experience was not dramatic; what he felt was a sublime peace, "just a supremely blissful feeling that his worries were over," as he later described it to Max Eastman. He later said that the thought that came to him was, "What the hell are you worrying about, anyway? Everything that's here is here, and you can just lie back on it." He could say later, "I've never had any doubts since then—nor any beliefs. To me faith means not worrying."[40]

This can be interpreted in two ways: First, it suggests that Dewey felt some respite from his uncertainty about the future. And he was, indeed, increasingly set on becoming a philosopher, having received encouragement from W. T. Harris's acceptance of two articles for the *Journal of Speculative Philosophy*. It also suggests a coming to terms with his own past. He later wrote that while the conflict between his early religious beliefs and his new convictions was "the source of a trying personal crisis, it did not at any time constitute a leading philosophical problem."[41]

When religion poses no philosophical problems, the crisis of faith becomes instead a "personal" crisis, a coming to terms with one's self. Dewey must have felt that some of the "inward laceration" caused by the dualisms of his New England upbringing ("isolation of self from the world, of soul from body, of nature from God") had healed over. Of course, he was looking forward philosophically to his own Hegelianism, which held that mind and nature have an essential unity and that in studying nature man is studying the true underlying nature of reality. Dewey's Hegelianism helped him resolve troubling dualisms intellectually, but he was probably wrong in feeling that he had conquered them in his own life. As we will see, dualisms were to continue to plague him, culminating, in part, in his meeting with Anzia Yezierska and the writing of his poetry. For the moment, however, he had learned to suppress troubling emotional doubts.

Determined to continue his search for his vocation, Dewey took up private study in the philosophic classics upon his return to Vermont, working under H. A. P. Torrey, the chairman of intellectual and moral philosophy at the University of Vermont. He later characterized Torrey as a Scottish commonsense realist and a moral intuitionalist, calling him "constitutionally timid."[42] But Torrey schooled him well in the classics, and Dewey later credited Torrey with convincing him to pursue graduate study at Johns Hopkins University. Still nervous about his decision—as he later wrote, it "was something of a risk; the work offered there was almost the only indication that there were likely to be any self-supporting jobs in the field of philosophy for others than clergymen''[43]—he must have been made more so by the university's rejection of his application for a scholarship. Luckily, an aunt stepped forward with a loan of five hundred dollars, and John Dewey set out to pursue his chosen vocation.

At Johns Hopkins, Dewey became a Hegelian. He was always a man in search of a system, something like George Eliot's Casaubon's key to all mythologies. To some extent, of course, all philosophers are. But Dewey's easy embrace of Hegelianism under G. S. Morris at Johns Hopkins suggests how eager he was to resolve troubling dualisms, to find a rational structure for his innate idealism. Morris's neo-Hegelianism influenced him profoundly over the next decade. As Neil Coughlan, the biographer of Dewey's early years, points out, he would eventually replace his early Hegelianism with instrumentalism, or what we now know as pragmatism, but he could not shed the impulse that brought him to it originally, which was the need for a system translated in philosophical terms to ''a notion of philosophy as the expression and defense of an ethos.''[44]

At Johns Hopkins, Dewey was exposed to the new psychology as well. With G. Stanley Hall, he studied physiological psychology, which he admired for its organicism, its insistence on the unity of psychic life; unlike Hall, who soon recognized that psychology could not be understood in merely a physiological sense, Dewey complacently embraced the new psychology because it promised that the study of physiological processes like reflex actions would bear out the unity of consciousness between mind and nature, the unity he always sought between seeming dualisms. Moreover, he did not really understand what psychology meant at this point; he understood it to be simply a more ''scientific'' way of studying how we think. Though he was to make important contributions to the field, like his 1896 essay ''The Reflex Arc in Psychology,'' he continued to value psychology primarily as a tool, writing in ''From Absolutism to Experimentalism'': '' . . . in the present state of men's minds the linking of philosophy to significant issues of actual experience is facilitated by constant interaction with the methods and conclusions of psychology.''[45]

In opening his mind to psychology in these earlier years, however, Dewey looked forward to the years when he would integrate the methodologies of other disciplines in formulating his social thought.

We can understand Dewey's interest in psychology in another light as well. Hall was an influential member of the department, and Dewey, having set his mind on becoming a philosopher like his teachers, was eager to please. (In Hall's case, this backfired: Hall, feeling that Dewey's talents were less than outstanding, recommended in one year that Dewey's fellowship not be renewed, and a few years later rejected Hopkins president Daniel Gilman's suggestion of Dewey for a teaching appointment, declaring Dewey incompetent.[46]) Moreover, Dewey was increasingly caught in a dilemma: Philosophy as it was then defined was largely theistic, and what Morris expected from Dewey was that he continue in this classical tradition. Though he was attracted to the methods of men like Hall, and though he was intrigued by the possibility of applying philosophy to history and to what he then called ''social ethics,'' his decision to become a philosopher dictated that he keep to the straight and narrow. His dissertation was on Kant—hardly a Dewey favorite, but certainly a safe topic. Dewey in these years had not overcome his boyhood timidity; he was an eager young graduate student as yet unwilling to make waves. We can perhaps better understand his relative complacency at Johns Hopkins if we understand that his years there were like other young men's college years. At the University of Vermont, Dewey was still an adolescent and he lived at home; at Johns Hopkins he was coming of age. Part of his business there was putting behind him his own emotional past.

When in 1890 he wrote a piece on what should be expected of a college education, he clearly referred to his years at Hopkins and not those at Vermont:

> The voyage one takes in entering college life is a voyage to a far part, and through many countries foreign in space, in time, in manner of speech and thought. If such travelling of the spirit does not remove the narrow and small cast of one's opinion and methods it is failing of its aim. . . . And when one gives up his provincialisms let him make the renunciation complete.[47]

The shy, self-effacing young Dewey was working on renouncing his provincialisms and becoming a solid professional scholar. As his self-confidence grew, he became less reluctant to question traditional tenets of the classical philosophy he had been schooled in and to develop a philosophical approach all his own, at the same time turning his attention to the practical application of philosophy in social affairs—and social thought was, after all, the area in which he was to leave his real mark.

When he graduated from Johns Hopkins in 1884 and joined the department of philosophy at the University of Michigan, Dewey began an apprenticeship that was to last until about 1900, when he began to turn his interest more fully to social ideas and education. More than that, Dewey enjoyed in these years a rise in status and reputation; they were years of growth. He arrived in Michigan as a poorly paid professor, shy, tentative, and still very much dependent—philosophically and emotionally—on Morris. But in his Michigan years he was promoted to assistant professor, then to full professor, and finally to chairman of the philosophy department. His 1886 *Psychology*, which tried to fit psychology into his wider Hegelian scheme, found a wide audience; intellectually, he was a figure to be reckoned with. Moreover, he met and married Harriet Alice Chipman, who influenced his thinking tremendously.

The woman who became Dewey's wife, known to all as Alice, was a small-town girl, born and raised in Fenton, Michigan. But hers were not small-town values. She was raised by her mother's parents, Frederick and Evalina Riggs. Frederick was an unconventional man, a supporter of American Indian rights, and he encouraged independent thinking and sensitivity to social issues in his granddaughter. His lessons seem to have taken hold; Alice entered the University of Michigan in 1882, at a time when university education for women was still hotly debated. Once there, she entered the world of ideas with vigor; she was a charter member of the Philosophical Society and read a paper at one of its early meetings—philosophy was very much a male province at the time—and as a member of the Samovar Club, studied the "back-to-the-people" Russian movement as expressed in the works of Turgenev. Her daughter later credited Alice with widening Dewey's awareness of social conditions and social injustice: "Things which had previously been matters of theory acquired through his contact with her a vital and direct human significance." In a sense, she was an active agent in the creation of Dewey as social thinker and activist, instrumental in his shift from absolutism to pragmatism. Moreover, she aided in his conversion from dogmatic religious thought to a social gospel; her daughter writes that she had ''a deeply religious nature but had never accepted any church dogma. Her husband acquired from her the belief that a religious attitude was indigenous in natural experience, and that theology and ecclesiastic institutions had benumbed rather than promoted it.''[48] Alice Dewey was as important an influence as any of his philosophic reading or activity.

Moreover, Dewey's marriage had a profound maturing effect. Upon his arrival in Michigan, he was a shy young man, hardly a figure of authority for the young men and women he was to teach. He had no real home but lived in a local boardinghouse (where, in fact, he met his wife). This was a man to whom home life and family were to become important to an unusual degree. His wife became an active partner in his work, and they were for the time extremely happy together; Dewey later remarked to Max Eastman, ''No two people were ever more in love.''[49] The six children they bore over the next ten years were a constant source of inspiration. Those who study Dewey always readily approve Max Eastman's memory of Dewey being happiest at work with one child hanging on his pants leg and another with his finger in the inkwell.[50] When asked to come up with telling memories of the man, the novelist James Farrell, a close friend of Dewey's, cited another fatherly image. Farrell remembered his son Kevin sitting on Dewey's lap and tugging on his mustache. Dewey started talking about George Bernard Shaw and concluded, somewhat pensively, that Shaw didn't like growing things and he didn't like children. Farrell remarked, ''Again and again one saw that John had a feeling for growing things. He thought of things in terms of growth.''[51]

In these years, too, we get a sense of Dewey's emerging personality. He was congenial and well liked by students; active in many student organizations, a frequent contributor to the school newspaper; and he and his wife often entertained students in their home. His shyness, perhaps, gave him a reputation of reticence and reserve, which in turn was misinterpreted as coldness—a reading of his character totally at odds with his openness and tolerance. Because of his geniality, students were not afraid to poke fun at him, but the quality they most often singled out was his reserve. One student poem quipped: ''Dewey, with countenance changeless as stone,/Ever recalling the north frigid zone." A "Sophster's Dictionary" coined a new word, "Dew(e)y," and gave the following definition: "Dew(e)y.—Adj. Cold, impersonal, psychological, sphinx-like, anomalous and petrifying to flunkers."[52]

Already, then, the Dewey image was emerging—a contradictory, enigmatic image, presenting as it does a man who was genuinely liked and open and encouraging to all manner of individuals, yet at the same time cold, impersonal, immovable.

Dewey's years at Michigan divide neatly into two periods, with the dividing point a brief stint at the University of Minnesota in 1888. In the early years, he continued his refinement of a Hegelian system, though he found it difficult to account for new social realities within a framework so implicitly idealistic. It is important to note that Christianity continued to hold a place in Dewey's and Morris's system, with the result that the philosophy department—where Hegelianism was recognized as the "official" philosophy—had a decidedly religious tone. A Latin professor said that the department was "pervaded with a spirit of religious belief, unaffected, pure and independent." He added, however, that a student taking courses there would encounter "the skepticism of the age" more than he would if he were to take "the more dogmatic lessons inculcated in those institutions which, for particular reasons, feel obliged to advertise the teaching of religion as a specialty."[53]

So Dewey "allowed" a place for Christianity in his philosophy; he also continued his religious activity, teaching Bible classes at the university and participating in the affairs of the First Congregational Church of Ann Arbor. But, as historian Lawrence Crunden has ably pointed out, Dewey increasingly used the language of Christianity to discuss his new concern—a concern for a moral universe; in fact, his interest in social problems increased as his religious activity declined.[54] In such essays as "The Obligation to Knowledge of God" (1884), "Christianity and Democracy" (1892), and "The Relationship of Philosophy to Theology" (1893) (all originally addresses to the University's Student Christian Association), Dewey argued that in man's social organizations were to be found the central ideas of Christianity. Democracy itself became a revelation of Christianity. In "Christianity and Democracy" he writes: "It is in democracy, the community of ideas and interest through community and action, that the incarnation of God in man . . . becomes a living, present thing, having its ordinary and natural sense."[55]

Everywhere Dewey sought unity; in looking at society as an organic whole he found it consistent with the unity offered him by his semireligious Hegelianism. Increasingly, however, he was able to value society's organicism as an ideal in and of itself, no longer dependent on a religious framework for its cohesion. Democracy itself provided the spiritual unity of men; in the social organism was the complete revelation of truth.

Dewey's excitement over the unity of society not only corresponded with but directly reflected the violent social and technological upheaval that characterized the newly industrialized country. He perceived society as an organic whole, and this perception was enormously dependent on his faith in the new science—a faith many of his contemporaries, who would become the Progressives of a later era, shared. Thus Dewey's gradual philosophical shift from neo-Hegelianism to instrumentalism did not reflect his disillusionment with unity. Instead, it meant that he now believed that new technology made total unity—perfect democracy—a possibility. As Dewey wrote,

> It is no accident that the growing organization of democracy coincides with the rise of science, including the machinery of telegraph and locomotive for distributing truth. There is but one fact—the more complete movement of man to his unity with his fellows through realizing the truth of life.[56]

Here we should pause to consider two aspects of considerable importance in Dewey's language in such key passages as the one just cited—not just because the Dewey image requires total disparagement of his writing, but because the two impulses that drove Dewey to this kind of language are essential to understanding his place in cultural history. In fact, Dewey's early writing is notable for its vigor and clarity. In a series of informal essays for the student publication the *Inlander*, under the caption "The Angle of Reflection," Dewey discussed literature and art and addressed such topical issues as the fad for Volapük, a precursor of Esperanto, in a spirit of lively inquiry and with some wit. Though his philosophical writing in these years is often highly technical, it yields to careful reading. Dewey's writing only takes on the irritating vagueness that characterizes his later work when he begins to address social issues. "The more complete movement of man to his unity," "the community of ideas and interest through community of action"—just what is he trying to say?

Part of Dewey's problem was a Victorian heritage. Commenting on the Victorian crisis of faith, one observer has remarked that late Victorians, confused by the obligation to doubt that was Darwin's legacy, tended to produce statements of belief that were "tenuously established, floridly expressed, elaborately vague."[57] Unwilling to sacrifice entirely the unity of a world that operated by design, they sought to rediscover it in suspiciously sentimental intellectualism. And here, too, was Dewey, caught between the age of faith and the age of science—using the language of one to discuss the other with results that were, indeed, elaborately vague.

But there is another aspect of Dewey's language that needs to be addressed. How are we to interpret phrases like "the one fact" and "the truth of life"? This is the language of a man with a vision. Had these words not been written by a man whom we recognize today as a "pragmatist," one of the sanest and most reasonable social thinkers, we might find them highly suspect— the words not of a visionary but of a deluded crank. And, in fact, in several key episodes in his life Dewey was exposed to and greatly influenced by highly eccentric individuals, some of whom were actually madmen. These episodes are instructive, for they point to the genial tolerance and genuine curiosity that made it possible for Dewey to respond to someone as iconoclastic as Anzia Yezierska.

What his biographer Neil Coughlan calls Dewey's "lifelong weakness for quacks" is central to an understanding of the man behind the official image. Coughlan understands this impulse in Dewey as an indication of his "democracy"; Dewey never wanted to see philosophy confined to the university but hoped rather that it could be a public activity, and this made him susceptible to "the amateurs, irregulars, or holy fools [who] approached him."[58] Indeed, Dewey's genial open-mindedness explains this weakness at least in part. But something in Dewey—a holdover, perhaps, from his evangelical upbringing, and evinced earlier in his enthusiastic embrace of a neo-Hegelian "system"—loved a revelation, a new way of ordering the world, a system that provided the "unity" a man tragically committed to dualisms so eagerly sought. In this light, Dewey's attraction to a figure like Anzia Yezierska, for instance, can be seen as a manifestation of this impulse toward revelation. Union with her was a unity of dualisms—a revelation indeed. And while Anzia Yezierska was not mad, of course, Dewey's relationship with her was marked by the deep intensity that characterizes a revelatory experience.

Dewey experienced one such revelatory moment in his Michigan years: his encounter with the eccentric Ford brothers, which led to the embarrassing *Thought News* venture, an ambitious attempt to create a new organ of communication to serve the new America. The Ford brothers claimed to have found a practical way of implementing the organicism of society; they proposed a new national newspaper, *Thought News*, as an "arterial system," a "social sensorium" to distribute knowledge and unify the "nervous system" of the state. Explaining his system in his 1893 "Draft of Action," Franklin Ford proposed an "Intelligence Triangle," a clearinghouse for information that consisted of a magazine called *Ford's*, in which one could "buy" facts; a Class News Company, which would put out a newspaper for each industry in the country; and the News Association, which would publish regional and advertising issues. The Fords saw the "Intelligence Trust," the men who would disseminate information, as helping to make socialism a reality. Dewey, transfixed by the Fords' vision, described the master plan as follows:

> That which finally touches everybody is the public thing—politics—the state of the social organism. The newspaper in giving publicity to public matters (not for reform, or for any other purpose excepting that it is its business to sell facts) becomes the representative of public interests. Thus Ford says the municipal question is essentially a publicity question. No paper can afford now to tell the truth about the actual conduct of the city's business. But have a newspaper whose *business*, i.e. whose livelihood, was to sell intelligence, and it couldn't afford to do anything else, any more than genuine business can afford to sell spurious goods.[59]

If "intelligence" was available to all members of society so that, for instance, buyers and sellers were acquainted with the actual state of supply and demand, the inevitable result would be an improved economy and an actively organic society. The idea had implicit appeal for Dewey.

Dewey was involved with the Fords not just in the season of *Thought News*, the spring of 1892; by then he had known them for five years. He was to write of them enthusiastically to William James and to introduce them to sociologist Robert Park. He publicly acknowledged his debt to Franklin Ford in the preface to his 1891 *Outline of a Critical Theory of Ethics*, citing Ford's clarification of "the treatment of the social bearings of science and art."[60] Dewey's experience with the Ford brothers has too often been treated as a momentary lapse, a brief indiscretion. But it was not a passing fancy. Nor were the Fords simple cranks, eccentrics with a vision that had enough practical reality to attract a tolerant man like Dewey, who could ground the vision in reality. One of them was, in fact, quite mad.

Franklin Ford was born in 1849 in Dundee, Michigan, and his brother Corydon about five years later. Franklin entered the news business as a reporter for the *Philadelphia Gazette* in 1875; he worked for the *Philadelphia Record* and the *New York Sun* before becoming editor of *Bradstreet's* in 1880. In 1883, when a railroad investor appeared at the paper's office asking for information about the agricultural future of the area in which he wanted to invest, Franklin's idea began to take shape: A news bureau should be created that gathered and disseminated data "scientifically." When the owners of *Bradstreet's* failed to implement Franklin's vision, Franklin left for the West, seeking interested journalists and editors. When that failed, he sought out university presidents (the university, after all, was but "the ganglion in the nervous system of the state"); at the University of Michigan he found "a man . . . who would give more than passive assent to the principle. . . . I got to John Dewey."[61]

Corydon had paved the way for his brother Franklin. A medical student at the University of Michigan when his brother arrived, Corydon had turned up there after a rocky youth that saw him thrown out of various normal schools and driven out by angry citizens from a succession of towns where he held teaching posts. (Indeed, Corydon's autobiographical *The Child of Democracy: Being the Adventures of the Embryo State* recounts the adventures of a cheerful lunatic. When still a youth, he too became interested in the idea that newspapers did not disseminate information as they were supposed to do; that they even, at times, printed lies. Ostensibly to prove this, but more in the nature of a sick joke, Corydon and a young friend contrived to get Franklin to publish a ghoulish account of their twin suicides, an account Corydon generously provides the reader in the appendix of his book.)

Although their earlier efforts to reach university president James Angell had failed, the Ford brothers took Dewey by storm. As Corydon recounts it, his brother appeared in Ann Arbor having discovered "the necessity of a closer organization of the reporter class in the way of news gathering, and looking more to the basic fact as in the physiology of life that should supplant the pathology of rumor, or accident, then and now so crowding the columns of our papers." When Angell met Franklin, he turned to Corydon and asked if "our friend was 'quite right?'"[62]

Corydon, it seems clear, was himself not "quite right." But most interesting is the propinquity of his ideas and his healthier brother's to those of the undeniably sane John Dewey. In his autobiography, Corydon describes the social organism, the state:

> Social Unity is not in the *precept* of interests, but in their *organization*. The reality is the degree of attained unity as of the adjusted divisions of labor. The meaning of America is the approximation of the organism. . . . Its way is the adjustment of the Part in light of the interests of the Whole. The brotherhood of man is the dependence of the varied interests, making the Unity.[63]

How different is this from John Dewey in his 1888 "The Ethics of Democracy"?

> The whole lives truly in every member, and there is no longer the appearance of physical aggregation, or continuity. The organism manifests itself as what it truly is, an ideal or spiritual life, a unity of *will*. If, then, society and the individual are really organic to each other, then the individual is society concentrated.[64]

(Corydon follows the above passage with further explanation: "We love a man because he grows celery for us; we eat him. We love him because he makes our shoes; we wear him."[65] But Corydon was insane, and Dewey was not.)

This propinquity of ideas suggests a cultural fact: It was difficult, in late Victorian America, to tell the holy man from the fool, the visionary from the lunatic, and the scientist from the crank. All kinds of panaceas and prophets presented themselves to the American people: single-taxers, homeopaths, socialists, syndicalists, and lunatics. In 1881, when the madman Charles Guiteau shot President James A. Garfield, the public watched the first trial to hinge on the question of insanity; Guiteau had lived as a normal citizen prior to his violent act, practicing law and lobbying for his own eccentric causes in Washington.[66] Insanity was nothing new to Americans, of course; what was new was the existence of a fine line that separated it from the idealism of, for instance, Edward Bellamy's *Looking Backward* (a book that Dewey cited as one of the most influential books in his lifetime).[67]

It is not difficult to understand how this came to be. To remain for a moment with Dewey's own field, psychology/philosophy, the new scientific method promised insights that today seem bizarre. G. Stanley Hall, for instance, spent considerable time exploring whether abnormal psychological behavior could be correlated with cosmic phenomena like the weather or planetary movements.[68] Consider, too, this strange letter that Dewey addressed to the editor of *Science*, in which Dewey asked for reader comment regarding a curious sensation he had experienced:

> On falling asleep with any weight in my arms I have noticed that on waking at a certain stage of drowsiness the feeling of solidity has entirely vanished. It is not only that the sensation of weight is very much dulled, but the sense of continuity in the held body is gone. Indeed, it often seems as if the hole between the parts whose contact is actually experienced could be felt. The contrast with early experience is so great that it serves to bring out very effectually the fact that ordinarily in holding an object we have not only a sense of contact and of weight, but also a sense of "filling in," of tactile solidity or continuous extension.

Dewey closes by noting, enigmatically, that the sensation had a "granular rather than a continuous character."[69]

In these same years, and more meaningfully, psychologist William James was attempting to document spiritual life and explain it scientifically in his 1902 *Varieties of Religious Experience*. It is not altogether surprising that the year 1906 would see John Dewey and William James sitting over a Ouija board.[70]

Moreover, in the realm of applied science, the sudden appearance of advanced technology, particularly in the form of the telegraph and the railroad, brought in its wake the exciting vision of the interconnectedness of all things. Herbert Spencer, in his

*Principles of Sociology* (1883–1897), described how these technolog-ical changes would affect the "nervous system" of society so that, as both ideas and goods moved more freely, society would become more unified.[71] Dewey considered the changes even more sweeping: in defending the rationale behind *Thought News*, he wrote:

> When it can be seen for example, that Walt Whitman's poetry, the great development of short stories at present, the centralizing tendency in the railroads and the introduction of business methods into charity organizations are all parts of one organic social move-ment, then the philosophic ideas about organism begin to look like something definite.[72]

Franklin Ford saw the telegraph and the railroads eliminating dis-tance, making room for "a flood of new ideas, making the new American literature for which the public has been waiting."[73]

Excitement over the drastic changes in society was matched by anxiety, which in turn developed into the "search for order" noted by historian Robert Wiebe. Progress was inevitable—but could it be managed, controlled, made less unpredictable?[74] The sociologist Robert Park, whom Dewey introduced to the Fords in 1887, saw in *Thought News* a possible check to the violence that often accompanied change. Looking back in his posthumously published *Race and Culture*, Park wrote of the Fords' brainchild that "with more accurate and adequate reporting of current events the historical process would be appreciably stepped up, and progress would go forward steadily, without the interruption and disorder of depression or violence, and at a rapid pace."[75]

The publication of *Thought News* was announced by Dewey and the Fords in March of 1892. There ensued a volley of mocking reportage and earnest defenses by Dewey in the Michigan pa-pers. As the *Detroit Tribune* reported, it was "generally under-stood that . . . Mr. Dewey proposes to get out an 'extra' every-time [sic] he has a new thought."[76] In April there appeared an announcement that publication was to be delayed, and that was the last the public heard of it. Dewey and the Fords seem to have parted on harsh terms; Franklin went on to New York where he opened a "News Office" and managed to interest no less than Supreme Court Justice Oliver Wendell Holmes, with whom he carried on a voluminous correspondence for over ten years

(Holmes called Ford a "half crank," conceding, "He seems to have ideas").[77] Dewey later said that Franklin Ford was "probably a scoundrel."[78]

Dewey's venture with the Fords represents not only his attempt to make philosophy practical—that was his most common defense of the plan in the press—but a new social conscience. He had tried to formulate his idea of society as an organic whole through journalism, but that attempt had failed. (One could argue, however, that he later realized the early goals of *Thought News* in his editorials for the *New Republic*, and he was to return to many of the same ideas in his 1927 *The Public and Its Problems*.) The episode with the Fords marks the beginning of Dewey's career as a radical social thinker, eager to put his ideas into action. His political thought was to be profoundly influenced in the coming years by his exposure to such phenomena as Jane Addams's Hull House, the seminally important settlement house founded in Chicago in 1889. Less committed now to perfecting a "system" than to putting his ideas into action, Dewey opened Chicago's famous Laboratory School, an experimental school where children "learned by doing," and thus began his career as a profoundly influential reformer. The *Thought News* episode is also instructive in that it marks Dewey's openness to new ideas; in the years to come, he would need to distinguish more carefully between social visions and mad fancies. He had come to believe in the inevitability of progress, and he now sought to manage it.

# 2

## *Yezierska: The Making of the* Teacherin

"I am a Russian Jewess, a flame—a longing"—so Anzia Yezierska's autobiographical heroine describes herself to her Dewey-esque suitor. "I am the ache of unvoiced dreams, the clamor of suppressed desires. I am the unlived lives of generations stifled in Siberian prisons."[1] Yezierska imagined herself as one who was expected to speak for those "generations" of immigrants within her. In his poetry, John Dewey echoes her words in addressing her: "Generations of stifled words reaching out/Through you."[2] With Anzia Yezierska, as with John Dewey, we must begin with the old question of origins. Both saw their origins as defining them in a central and inescapable way. In Dewey's case it was his Vermont upbringing; in Yezierska's it was her Russian birth and early poverty.

Though Anzia Yezierska made America the subject of her fiction—America as promised land, America as the land where promises are broken—she never saw herself as an American. She chose to remain a "Russian Jewess," defined by her past. And the past that defined her was, like John Dewey's, largely the creation of romantic reading of cultural history. Just as our cultural nostalgia demands that we "read" Dewey's Vermont beginnings in terms of stereotypes of Yankee simplicity and bucolic virtues, so too does a different cultural nostalgia dictate that we understand the Jewish immigrant's beginnings in the Old World in terms of mud huts and pogroms, warm Sabbath family meals broken up by cossack raids. Such romantic readings—however based on historical reality—are culturally constructed; writers like Yezierska create them in their fiction, and Hollywood reprocesses

33

them for national consumption (as it did in the film made from
Yezierska's evocation of Old World village life in her *Hungry
Hearts*). In Dewey's case, the Yankee myth was largely consructed
by those around him who sought to explain this enigmatic man.
In Yezierska's case, she herself very consciously constructed and
repeatedly refined the mythical scenario of the immigrant who
has exchanged an Old World ghetto for a New.

Of course, just as surely as clichés derive from eternal verities,
so too do our romantic readings of history have sure grounding
in historical realities. This is all the more true when the historical
record is largely oral and fragmentary, as it is with the conditions
and circumstances that surrounded the massive waves of Eastern
European immigration of the late nineteenth and early twentieth
centuries. An irony of history emerges: The more difficult it is to
recover the past, the more romantic readings take over, so that
the past slips still further from our grasp.

Yezierska's "history" provides a clear example. Her family's
life in Polish Russia and their immigration to this country were
not documented except in her fiction; her memories of these
years and those of her family were sketchy and conflicting. Cultural legend surrounding Jewish immigration took over, and the
Yezierska family story sounds like one we have heard before, like
the script of a movie we have already seen.

Of course, we cannot discount this story because it has been
obscured by legend. Like thousands of other immigrant families,
the Yezierskas fled a life of oppression and poverty for the
"promised land," where they encountered bitter disappointment—poverty, prejudice, and oppressive working and living
conditions. Denying the realities of their suffering makes it impossible to understand the person Anzia Yezierska became. And,
too, however "legendary" her past seems in her fiction, however
sketchy, however stereotypical, it is the only detailed history
available to us. And, in any event, she defined herself in its
terms.

Those early years in Russia and on New York's Lower East
Side—years of poverty, persecution, and hope—remained with
Yezierska throughout her ninety-odd years. Born in Ploch, a town
on the Vistula River in the Polish part of Russia, around 1880—
her mother had ten children and could not keep track of their
birthdates—Yezierska was the daughter of Pearl and Bernard Ye-

zierska.[3] Her father was "a Hebrew scholar and dreamer,"[4] a rabbi who depended on the largesse of the community to support his studies. All the elements of the immigrant legend were present: Yezierska recalled vividly Ploch's ghetto community, its mud huts and the warm, rich family life within them ("I closed my eyes and could almost see Mother spreading the red-checked Sabbath tablecloth. The steaming platter of *gefüllte* fish, the smell of fresh-baked *hallah*, Sabbath white bread. Mother blessing the lighted candles, ushering in the Sabbath"[5]). She recalled as well the constant threat under which her family lived.

Pogroms and extortion against the Jews penetrate her writings about this period. She wrote that the family was fined for such offenses as holding *cheder*, the delivery of religious lessons, under the same roof as their home (a practice forbidden under a regime that sought to eliminate religious Judaism), and that cossacks swept through the village with terrifying unpredictability. If the father happened to be out during one of these raids—at the synagogue, for instance—the family waited in terror to see if he had survived. Then, too, there was always the threat that Bernard might be drafted into the Czar's army—forced to "drink vodka with the drunken *mouzhiks*, eat pig, and shoot [his own] people."[6]

As it was for thousands of their time, the only promise of deliverance for the Yezierska family seemed to be America. The scenario again is a commonplace of immigrant history: Struggling families in the Old Country gather to hear letters from countrymen who have been successful in the "promised land"—letters describing gold-paved streets in a land of milk and honey—pack their belongings, sell the best featherbed, and make the long trip overland to some European port where they buy passage in steerage to the New World. "In America you can say what you feel—you can voice your thoughts in the open streets without fear of a Cossack." "Everybody is with everybody alike, in America. Christians and Jews are brothers together." "Plenty for all. Learning flows free like milk and honey."[7] So, according to Yezierska, went the murmurings and dreams of the Ploch villagers.

"Learning flows free like milk and honey": This promise had particular resonance for Anzia Yezierska. "The words painted pictures in my mind. I saw before me free schools, free colleges, free libraries, where I could learn and learn and keep on learning," she later wrote.[8] In Russia, only Christian children attended schools; among Jews, boys were sent to study Talmud, but girls were expected to learn little beyond how to maintain a household. In America, Yezierska was sure she would be freed from the daily grind of poverty—able, in her words, "To work [herself] up for a person."[9]

In 1893, when Yezierska was about thirteen, the family made the great journey to the "promised land."[10] The disappointment they met there was profound. Rather than green fields and open spaces, they found the choked and dirty streets of New York's Lower East Side. Their home—they had dreamed of "separate rooms like in a palace"—was an airless, dark tenement apartment. As often as not, the millionaire who had bragged to his Old World neighbors of his New World success turned out to be a pushcart peddler or a slave to a sweatshop boss.

Mayer Yezierska, the eldest son, came to America first, in 1886. His family—Bernard and Pearl and their children Isidore, Mascha, David, Gustave, Fania, Anzia, Henry, and Bill, the baby—came to America with high hopes indeed. Like many others, they willingly took American names. Mayer Yezierska had taken the name Max Mayer, and the family took their oldest son's first name, Mayer, as their surname. Mascha became Helena (called Annie), Fania became Felicia (called Fanny), and Anzia became Harriet (called Hattie).[11] Thus "Hattie Mayer," the American Anzia Yezierska, was born.

The family immediately met with poverty as absolute as that they had known in Russia. One of the first jobs they found consisted of making paper bags at home and selling them in the streets. Anzia, who later described an autobiographical heroine peddling herring with a great voice that transfixed the hordes thronging the ghetto streets, was particularly good at the job; she later recalled that she sold her wares "as if she were giving away emeralds."[12]

The poverty suffered by the Yezierska/Mayer family was bone crushing and spirit deadening. Pearl, the mother, seems to have had the life drained from her in her struggles to support her family. Of course, Bernard, the Hebrew scholar, did not work but spent his time with his holy books. If Anzia's autobiographical fictions are to be believed, the mother and children worked to feed him chicken while they lived off the broth in which it was cooked. Anzia's 1925 *Bread Givers* provides a chilling portrait of Reb Smolinsky, a man modeled on her own father. Reb Smolinsky is a tyrannical dreamer who fiercely defends his pious disdain of worldly cares. His wife, beaten down by hard work but still spellbound by her husband's spiritual fineness, sighs, ''If he was only so fit for this world, like he is fit for Heaven, then I wouldn't have to dry out the marrow from my head worrying for the rent.''[13] Inflated with his own importance, Reb marries off his daughters, one by one, to husbands they do not love. He deigns to enter the business world, buying a grocery store in Elizabeth, New Jersey (as Bernard Mayer did), but makes a dismal failure of the venture. He so tyrannizes his youngest daughter—based on Anzia herself—that she must leave home and make her way in the world alone.

The ambitious Anzia found the atmosphere in her parents' home stifling. For one thing, the patriarchal nature of her father's faith left her only one option—being a wife and mother, as beaten down by poverty as her sisters and her own mother. For Reb Smolinsky, Yezierska later wrote:

> The prayers of his daughters didn't count because God didn't listen to women. Heaven and the next world were only for men. Women could get into Heaven because they were wives and daughters of men. Women had no brains for the study of God's Torah, but they could be the servants of men who studied the Torah. Only if they cooked for the men, and washed for the men, and didn't nag or curse the men out of their homes; only if they let the men study the Torah in peace, then, maybe, they could push themselves into Heaven with the men, to wait on them there.[14]

Yezierska's rejection of this patriarchal ethos, however much it may have reflected an incipient feminism, at this point was motivated by her desire for a vocation of her own, a desire to be more than a wife and mother and to attain more than material wealth. What form this vocation would take was not clear. Yezierska tried a variety of occupations before settling into a writing career: cook, teacher, and social worker. She did not even attempt writing fiction until about 1913, when she was about thirty-three. In her fiction she describes her desire for self-expression, her desire to write—but in her early years in America she longed mostly to become an American, to sever herself from her immigrant past. An insistent theme in her work is her awe of "American" cleanliness, her desire to live in a clean, uncluttered, and sunlit "room of one's own."

Yezierska's vaguely understood but emotionally insistent desire for a vocation meant that she had to leave her family, to renounce her father and mother and their values. She saw her mother defeated by poverty and her sisters married off to men they did not love. Her sister Fanny married a clothing manufacturer and moved to Los Angeles, where she enjoyed material comfort but, Yezierska felt, spiritual death. The fate of her sister Helena touched Anzia deeply; Helena married Abraham Katz, who made a precarious living in the jewelry business, and had ten children. Yezierska's first story, "The Free Vacation House," borrowed an experience of Helena's, a vacation for overworked mothers provided by charity. Sending a copy of her 1925 *Bread Givers* to a friend of these years, Yezierska wrote, "Here you will also recognize Helena and her brute bread giver."[15] This sister appears in Yezierska's fiction as a broken and exhausted woman who has lost her beauty and her spirit in the daily round of poverty and raising too many children.

Yezierska was around eighteen, then, when she left her family and began her life alone, living in a succession of "hall bedrooms" that she tried to keep clean and uncluttered and simple. She worked where she could—as a servant, sometimes, or in the sweatshops—each job as dreary and demeaning as the last. What she lived for were the nights, when, exhausted and sweaty, she made her way to the night schools and settlement houses that were mushrooming all over New York's Lower East Side.

Yezierska's renunciation of her past caused her considerable guilt. "Can a tree hate the roots from which it sprang?" asks the autobiographical heroine of *Bread Givers*.[16] The language she used to describe her guilt betrays its intensity: She called her novel *Children of Loneliness* a "double-murder" story whose plot is the "expiation of guilt." Trying to clarify, she explained:

> I had to break away from my mother's cursing and my father's preaching to live my life; but without them I had no life. When you deny your parents, you deny the ground under your feet, the sky over your head. You become an outlaw, a pariah. . . . They mourned me as if I were dead. I am like Cain, forever bound to the brother he slew with his hate.[17]

Strong words, indeed—Yezierska never flinched in her intensity—but they convey how deeply felt and difficult was her decision to leave her family, how hard won was her independence.

Yezierska found a new "home" at the Educational Alliance. The Alliance was the most visible and typical of the night schools and settlements she frequented. Founded in 1889 by the Hebrew Free School Association, the Young Men's Hebrew Association, and the Aguilar Free Library Society, and renamed the Educational Alliance in 1891, this "curious mixture of . . . school, settlement house, day care center, gymnasium and public forum"[18] was located on the northeast corner of Jefferson Street and East Broadway, in the heart of the Lower East Side. The Alliance offered classes in English, American government and history, literature, stenography, typewriting, and a number of other subjects. But its function was only in part educational. It was also host to a number of clubs and activities, many geared to national holidays and "American" values. Its function was really to Americanize the immigrant, to remold the young immigrant as an American citizen. It filled a social need in the immigrant's life as well, drawing young men and women to its public lectures, roof garden entertainments, music and art exhibitions, plays, and pageants. An estimated 37,000 adults and children participated in some way in the activities of the Educational Alliance in any given week.[19]

The "uptown" reformers, many of them German Jews, had great hopes for the Americanization potential of the Alliance. There, it was hoped, the immigrants would shed their "Orientalism" for an American identity, which was generally presented as an Anglo-Saxon ideal. If the Lower East Side was, as the *New York Post* commented at the time, "the precipice over which the Niagara of immigration people had plunged into the stream of our national life,"[20] Americanizing agencies like the Alliance were thought to play the role of preparing the immigrant to enter this stream, shedding his Old World habits and loyalties. Indeed, the Educational Alliance was perceived as a model for such efforts, and some social visionaries considered it a cure for all social ills. One commentator wrote:

> And let us now, for a moment, indulge in a glance into the future, into the promised land itself. The Jewish quarter is gone. The Hebrew Institute, under the management of the Hebrew Educational

Alliance, fulfilled its mission. It becomes in time a national institute, supported by the Government, and served, in turn, to break
up also the Irish, the German, the Italian and Chinese quarters.
It becomes in foreign lands the American Institute for emigrants.
Whoever wants to go to America, in whatever country he is, has
first to undergo a course of study in that American Institute for
emigrants. . . . The Immigrant Question is solved. No more pau-
pers, idiots, or criminals, no more fools or adventurers, no more
deluded immigrants and self-seeking social reformers and anarchists, no more strikes and boycotts, no more strife between capital
and labor.[21]

Other reformers questioned the potential results of Americanization, recognizing what would be lost if immigrants were to shed
their old customs and habits entirely. It was this impulse, for instance, that prompted Jane Addams to open the Labor Museum
at Hull House, where immigrant women displayed their Old
World crafts and customs. Thus, too, the numerous plays and
pageants the settlement houses produced, in which immigrants
turned out in their native dress and performed folk dances.

By and large, however, the immigrant endorsed the agenda of
Americanization. Immigrant children adopted new American
ways so avidly that a great rift developed between first and second generations. Yezierska wished fervently to make herself over
as an American. In one of her stories, the heroine rejects her suit-
or's herring and onions, explaining, "There's something in me—
I can't help—that so quickly takes onto the American taste. It's as
if my outside skin only was Russian; the heart in me is for everything of the new world—even the eating."[22] Another heroine ex-
horts herself, "Make a person of yourself. . . . Begin to learn English. Make yourself for an American if you want to live in
America."[23]

It was not surprising, then, that Yezierska found a second
home at the Educational Alliance. It was there that she improved
her English, learned to read and love literature, met friends, and
searched for a way out of the daily round of manual labor, and
there that she found her escape. An interesting record exists of
both a representative year in Yezierska's life and the Alliance's
place among the immigrants: the *Alliance Review* of 1901–1902, a
short-lived journal established to document Alliance activities.

In the *Review's* pages one reads of such clubs as the Martha

Washington Literary Society, which in the fall of 1901 studied the lives of Martha's contemporaries but in the spring inexplicably switched its focus to the works of Washington Irving. Here, too, are recorded the clubs' fierce athletic rivalries, the teams vying weekly against each other in football and baseball. Of the "Normal College Cooking Class," the *Review* reported: "Twelve young ladies, students of Normal College, have organized a Cooking Class under the leadership of Miss Hattie Mayer, who is a member of the Clara de Hirsch Home. The club meets at 52 Henry St." In January 1902 the journal reported the progress of the "Sat. Evening Cooking Class":

> The members of this class, under the excellent leadership of Miss Hattie Mayer and Miss Schwartzman, are accomplishing wonderful progress in the mysteries of the kitchen and the stove. . . . On Saturday evening, December 26th, the class cooked a dinner for the household of the Nurses' Settlement, at which Miss Sommerfeld and Miss Lindner were present.[24]

"Miss Hattie Mayer," aka Anzia Yezierska, had, as the record makes clear, found a way out of the ghetto, a vocation. Her way out began with her discovery of cooking and charity.

The story of how this came to be shows just how difficult was Yezierska's struggle, just how precariously she escaped a future of poverty, and just how bitterly her escape was won. Cooking was to haunt her for the rest of her life; she earned her living by it for many years, and it is impossible to overstate her hatred of it. Charity, too, was to become her nemesis—a constant source of fresh humiliations, a constant source of hope.

In 1900, Yezierska became a resident—or "inmate," as the girls were revealingly called—of the Clara de Hirsch Home for Working Girls. Founded in 1889 with funds from the massive Baron and Clara de Hirsch fortune, the Home was designed both to house working girls and to prepare them for lives of domestic service, to rescue them from the moral backwaters of the sweatshop and factory. The Home's statement of purpose reveals motivations that to the modern reader might seem suspect, based as they seem to be on an assumption of the innate immorality of the working girl, but at the time probably were viewed as entirely well-meaning:

[T]he object of the founder was to benefit respectable girls and women, either residents or immigrants, who are dependent on their own exertions for a livelihood. The purpose of the home is to broaden the mental, moral, and physical condition of the girls by providing a good home, and also to train them for such occupations as may be practical, and for which they are best satisfied. Arrangements have been made to give the inmates a thorough training in domestic science, including cooking and sewing, so as to enable them to find positions in families instead of going into factories and sweatshops.[25]

The Home had two groups of "inmates"—"trainees," who were given courses in domestic science, and "residents," working girls who paid a small sum of board money. Yezierska read about the Home in the newspapers and applied for a place as a resident in February 1900; she was eager especially for a clean place to live. It was "the only chance I had for shelter," she later recalled: "All I wanted was a place to live and those white curtains were as far from me as the millionaires were."[26]

Yezierska fictionalized her experience at the de Hirsch Home in stories in her 1919 *Hungry Hearts* and at length in her 1927 novel *Arrogant Beggar*. Adele Lindner, the heroine of *Arrogant Beggar*, overhears the Home's director discussing the monthly report; the director is pleased to say that "the moral and religious talks on Friday evening are doing much to give the girls that come to us a new outlook on life, a higher vision of their obligation to be patriotic and useful women," but she has no such good news to report about the course in domestic service, for which the girls show little enthusiasm.[27] When Adele loses her job in a department store, the director convinces her to join the domestic science course. Adele is initially horrified ("Was I to be lost to myself as a servant? Come down from all I dreamed of being to washing dishes, peeling potatoes, taking orders from a mistress?"[28]) but then acquiesces, resolving, "If housework can't lift me, I'll lift housework. . . . I'll do for servants what Florence Nightingale did for nurses."[29] After she writes a letter of fulsome gratitude to the board of the Home, the Home sends her to a "Training School," where she takes the "Teacher's Course in Domestic Science." Gradually, however, Adele comes to resent this mean-spirited charity: She sees her benefactress, Mrs. Hellman, wipe with a handkerchief the cheek Adele has just impulsively kissed.

She learns that Mrs. Hellman has hired her as a servant at half
the wage the agency charges; and, in a brilliantly executed scene,
she overhears a philanthropic luncheon conversation in which
the ladies, gorging themselves on out-of-season strawberries, be-
moan their inability to keep thin while they discuss how to cut
back on menus at the institutions they run.

Yezierska's great bitterness about charity comes through in the
dubiously motivated "uptown" matrons of her fiction. To *Arrogant Beggar* she affixed an epigraph from Emerson: "We do not
quite forgive a giver. The hand that feeds us is in some danger of
being bitten."

All this did not stop Yezierska from turning to "givers," however, at several desperate junctures in her life. In 1916 she worked
for the Hebrew Charities in San Francisco, describing her job as
"the dirtiest most dehumanizing work a human being can do."[30]
In the depression years, she had to go on relief to qualify for a
job with the Works Progress Administration (WPA). Her early dependence on charity formed a fundamental pattern to her life:
she was always looking for a patron, always thinking she had
found the one person who really understood and could help her.
She was always disappointed. In 1953—at seventy-three—she
wrote to the poet Charles Olson at the Black Mountain School,
asking if "there wasn't some humble spot such as teaching English or helping in the kitchen where I might earn a roof over my
head."[31]

While she held a deep distrust for the "friendly visitor"—the
charity worker who unexpectedly appeared in immigrant homes,
often catching the family eating a rare treat that seemingly belied
their poverty—Yezierska was in fact deeply grateful to a trustee
of the Clara de Hirsch Home. Sarah Ollesheimer, the wife of a
wealthy German Jewish banker, to whom Yezierska dedicated her
first book, was instrumental in securing for Yezierska a college
scholarship. The Clara de Hirsch Home Report of Officers for the
year 1901 was able to report that "one [girl] received through the
Educational Alliance a scholarship to the Domestic Science Department of the Teachers College, which training will enable her
to become a teacher of cooking."[32] The charitable impulses she so
distrusted had opened for Yezierska a door out of the ghetto.

Teachers College, Yezierska's destination, was itself a child of
the reform movement and the philanthropic impulse; it was also

at the center of the educational reform movement, attracting such educators as Edward Thorndike and, later, John Dewey to its faculty. It grew out of Grace Hoadley Dodge's Association of Working Girls Society and the Kitchen Garden Association, which had joined to become the Industrial Educational Association in 1894. As these beginnings suggest, the college had always stressed manual and practical education. The IEA was mainly philanthropic in its activities, but it provided "normal classes"—classes for the training of teachers. In 1887, when future Columbia University president Nicholas Murray Butler took over the IEA, the New York College for the Training of Teachers was formed; in 1892 its name was changed to Teachers College, and in 1898 it became part of Columbia University. Under James Earl Russell, who became dean in 1897, Teachers College moved to the educational forefront; Russell, like John Dewey, saw education as a social force, an instrument of democracy.[33]

Yezierska was not supposed to be much affected by the grander scheme behind Teachers College; she was there to study domestic science. But, naively, she paid more attention to the "Teachers College" part of her scholarship than to the department to which she was assigned. She would be what her mother called, in Yiddish dialect, a *teacherin*, a calling that seemed holy to this girl who had so longed for learning and so idolized her own teachers. It was an occupation she hoped even her estranged family would understand; in *Bread Givers* she wistfully imagines the heroine's reunion with her mother, the mother crying "Praise be to God! I lived to see my daughter a *teacherin*."[34]

In fact, however, what she became was a teacher of cooking, an occupation none of her fictional heroines was cursed with. She was to study not literature but "home sanitation," not art but the domestic arts. She was an unwitting "test case" in the new "domestic science" movement, a movement designed to elevate the status of woman but tragically destined to chain her more solidly than ever to the home, thought to be her proper sphere. Because Yezierska's story is intertwined at every point with the debate about woman's proper place that raged so fiercely in these years, it is important to understand exactly how this came to be.

What was this new "science" that called itself "domestic"? Some saw it as the salvation of the modern woman, whose expectations had been raised by increased access to higher education.

Ellen Swallow Richards, the guiding light of the movement and the first president of the American Home Economics Association, founded in 1908, stated, "The educated woman longs for a career, for an opportunity to influence the world. Just now the greatest field offered to her is the elevation of the home into its place in American life."[35] The home economists met their fellow reformers—the settlement workers and the leaders of the "new education" movement—and saw the potential of reform in the home as great as the potential John Dewey and others saw of reform in the school. One home economist, speaking at one of a series of annual conferences on the subject held at Lake Placid from 1899 on, told her audience that "the home is the social workshop for the making of men."[36] Another stated categorically that "the fundamental way in which to improve society is through improvement of the home."[37] Others stressed the "scientific" nature of household work, seeing as Dewey did the enormous potential of science to transform every sphere of life. According to Ellen Richards, who held a position in "sanitary chemistry" at MIT until her death in 1911, the principal goal of the movement was "the utilization of all the resources of science to improve the home life."[38] At the Chicago World's Fair in 1893, Mrs. Richards set up a scientific kitchen in a small clapboard house, complete with scientific charts on the walls and the latest in technologically advanced equipment; thousands flocked to admire it.

In the context of the social changes that marked the years at the turn of the century, domestic science appeared to be a cure for everything from labor unrest to the problem of the un-Americanized immigrant. Sarah Tyson Rorer write in *Household News* in 1893, during a time of violent labor strikes, that the working man's diet was at fault: "I verily believe if the rigid instructions for food and feeding were implanted in the minds of our girls during their early school days, the labor element would not be such discontented individuals."[39] At another Lake Placid conference, in 1899, the domestic scientists conferred with Melvil Dewey—the inventor of the Dewey decimal system and himself a great believer in home economics—as to how the new subject should be classed in the decimal system. It was decided to catalog it with the books assigned the decimal number of "pauperism"— for was not poor housekeeping itself the cause of poverty?[40]

Products of the domestic science movement, Yezierska and thousands like her were turned loose on the public schools to teach little girls "food principles," which they would in turn impart to their recalcitrant Old World mothers. Irving Howe has pointed out how Jewish immigrants who ate few vegetables "except for horse-radish, carrots, cabbage, and beets" came to see lettuce and tomatoes as "'good for the children'—the cult of the vegetable being transmitted to the immigrant kitchen by . . . the American school."[41]

There were those who saw things differently. Many feminists, at first attracted to the movement because it appeared to elevate the role of woman, later came to see that it bound her even more tightly to the home. Reformers like Charlotte Perkins Gilman borrowed many of the genuine advances of the movement but applied them to communal living. Novelist Zona Gale, later a good friend of Yezierska, wrote extensively on this subject in the *Ladies Home Journal*, concluding, "The private kitchen must go the way of the spinning wheel, of which it is the contemporary."[42]

Yezierska too sensed that domestic science was little more than what a contemporary *New York Times* article called it: "a widespread movement . . . to raise the standard of menial domestic duties by honoring them with the title of science."[43] The autobiographical heroine of *Arrogant Beggar* knows full well what her patron is trying to pass off on her when she says, "It is almost a religion with me, this mission of teaching the masses that there is no such thing as drudgery. . . . In doing your cheerful, conscientious best, in your humble sphere, you are doing your part toward the harmony and perfection of the whole universe."[44] Yezierska had far bigger things in mind for herself.

She also heartily disagreed with some of the aims and techniques of the domestic science agenda. In her years at Teachers College (1901 to 1904), Yezierska took such classes as Foods; Food Production and Manufacture; Food Principles; Foods, Advanced Course; Physiology and Hygiene; and Home Sanitation and Economics.[45] At the de Hirsch Home she had been initiated in her Advanced Class in Cookery to such mysteries as "croquettes, soufflés, sandwiches, salads and salad dressings, entrées and sauces, [and] fancy desserts";[46] in short, she was given full exposure to the silliness of the "scientific cookery" school that Laura Shapiro has outlined so brilliantly in her book about women and cooking at the turn of the century, *Perfection Salad* (1986). As Shapiro writes, the goal of the domestic scientists

> was to transubstantiate food, and it didn't matter a great deal whether the preferred method was to reduce a dish to its simplest components or to blanket it with whipped cream and candied violets. Containing and controlling food, draining it of taste and texture, packaging it, tucking . . . raisins deep inside . . . marshmallows, decorating it—these were some of the major culinary themes of the domestic-science movement.[47]

This was the era best characterized by the "white sauce" that drenched all manner of food blandly and without texture, rendering it all "dainty," tasteless, and "American." One can imagine the disdain and unreality Yezierska felt when her college staged such events as a "pink dinner," at which every food was either naturally or artificially pink. One of her fictional heroines complains bitterly about her domestic science training, "I thought I'd die of dullness trying to be 'scientific'! A whole morning spent on different ways to make white sauce."[48] (Some of these lessons, however, seem to have taken—in a letter of later years Yezierska complained that her boardinghouse didn't serve enough of the "green fruits, green vegetables and salads that brain workers must have."[49])

Moreover, such courses as Physiology and Hygiene and Home Sanitation (the latter covered such subjects as "water supply, disposal of waste, heating and ventilation, lighting, healthful furnishing, and cleansing of the house"[50]) simply enraged her. A child of poverty whose first desire was for a clean and simply furnished room of her own, Yezierska knew well how difficult it was for the poor to keep clean. It is a theme she returns to over and over in her work. In "Soap and Water," in *Hungry Hearts*, the heroine puts herself through college by working mornings and evenings in a laundry. When she is chided for her appearance by the college dean, who tells her that "soap and water are cheap" and that "any one can be clean," she remembers all those nights at the laundry, when she was "so bathed in the sweat of exhaustion that [she] could not think of a bath of soap and water."[51] The heroine of *Salome of the Tenements*, bent on wooing her WASP millionaire lover, scrapes together hundreds of dollars merely to outfit herself in a simple and tasteful dress and to redo her tenement hall bedroom as a clean and simple studio. Her lover admires the simplicity of her appearance and environment, saying, "I maintain that beauty is *not* expensive. Pardon me for being so personal, but your charm lies in that you instinctively know how to choose the simple."[52] With this ironic scene Yezierska insists that simple cleanliness is a luxury the poor often cannot afford.

Yezierska had learned from bitter experience the luxury of cleanliness. She knew that naive remarks like "soap and water are cheap" could leave painful wounds. About her years at the de Hirsch Home, she later recalled the ladies' condescension to her because of her appearance; they thought "her shirt and her waist never [came] together and her eyes were always in the air. She'll never amount to anything."[53] There are indications too that she was singled out at Teachers College for her appearance. While Yezierska probably never appeared dirty, it is likely that, working her way through school, she may have arrived at classes sweaty and disheveled; on her strict budget she could hardly afford, for instance, enough waists so as not to be forced to wear an occasional soiled one or enough woolen stockings so that some did not have to be heavily darned. Certainly collegiate standards would have been hard for her to meet; in her senior year, for example, the seniors were expected to wear to a reception "white pique skirts, white shirtwaists, turn-over white collars, and a short black bow-tie."[54] In *Bread Givers*, Yezierska describes the autobiographical heroine's reaction to her college classmates:

> What a sight I was in my gray pushcart clothes against the beautiful gay colours and the fine things those young girls wore. . . . Never had I seen such plain beautifulness. . . . And the spick-and-span cleanliness of these people! It smelled from them, the soap and the bathing. Their finger-nails so white and pink. Their hands and necks white like milk. I wondered how did those girls get their hair so soft, so shiny, and so smooth about their heads. Even their black shoes had a clean look.[55]

There was some controversy in Yezierska's senior year at Teachers College over matters of appearance. The students learned that the dean was to forgo his usual talk on the "Ideals of Teaching" and would instead lecture the students on cleanliness and good taste. The students sensed that the talk would offend certain people in their midst, and they sent the class president to meet with the dean to try to change his mind. This student acknowledged to the dean that she saw the "absolute need of something of this kind . . . because of the failure of bright students to obtain positions because of personal untidiness or unattractiveness in dress or manner," but she pointed out "the resentment of students who are grown men and women at being talked to on such matters."[56]

The dean gave his talk anyway, but the class president noted that the issue would probably remain a problem: "There will always be individual cases of untidiness, lack of breeding, unfortunate [meanness?] and lack of knowledge of the best way of doing things."[57] Yezierska's classmates may have made a conscious or unconscious association of dirt with ethnicity—certainly the popular press was full of nativist expressions of fear about the "unwashed hordes" of immigrants filling the cities—an association Yezierska may well have internalized.

Yezierska must have resented bitterly being lectured on her appearance, and perhaps she bridled as well at the very mixed solicitude of her fellow students. In these years she was a beautiful young woman, with abundant red hair, blue eyes, and lovely white skin; it must have been painful for her to dwell among the clean and privileged and lack the means to keep herself clean and neat—not to mention being singled out for her "failure." And, as the heroine of "Soap and Water" discovers when she looks for a job and is not presentable enough to find one, poverty and its concomitant dirt are part of a vicious cycle.

Whether because of her appearance or not, Yezierska had difficulty finding a teaching position after her graduation from Teachers College in 1904. Over the next seven years she worked at a variety of posts in the New York City school system, most commonly as an itinerant teacher of cooking. Only in one year, 1911, do the Board of Education records list her as having a permanent job associated with a single school, P.S. 147 at Henry and Grosvenour Streets in lower Manhattan.[58] These years were difficult; she really did hate cooking and liked teaching it even less. Remembering her teaching in later years, she described her methods: Ask the class if anyone knew how to bake a ham, and direct whoever answered to teach the class.[59]

Materially, however, Yezierska's condition improved over the next decade. She left the Clara de Hirsch Home in 1902, after her first year of college, and lived at a succession of addresses, usually in the upper reaches of Manhattan or in Greenwich Village. Yezierska the *teacherin* had escaped the ghetto. She was still struggling, still frustrated in her search for a vocation, but free from material poverty. Only outside the ghetto, she felt, could she discover America. She now sought to find her place in the new land.

# 3

# Dewey, 1894–1904: The Chicago Years

John Dewey's early years were marked by an openness to ideas and a belief in progress. Beginning his intellectual journey by questioning the liberal evangelical Protestant tradition in which he had been raised, he moved through Hegelian idealism to pragmatism, which reflected a wider social shift toward a new secular social consciousness. Increasingly, he sought to translate ideas into social progress; as a pragmatic social thinker, he believed that ideas are nothing but hypotheses for social change. In this belief, he was no less than an exemplar for the burgeoning Progressive movement. With the Progressives, he believed that new gains in scientific knowledge would lead to the amelioration and eradication of most social ills. Ideas like Dewey's were sweeping the country; he was at once cause and effect of the new social consciousness.

Dewey's openness to ideas—a far more active quality than the phrase implies—was never to leave him. At his seventieth birthday celebration, Dewey described himself as

> a man who was somewhat sensitive to the movements of things about him. He had a certain appreciation of what things were passing away and dying and of what things were being born and growing. And on the strength of that response he foretold some of the things that were going to happen in the future. When he was seventy years old the people gave him a birthday party and they gave him credit for bringing to pass the things he had foreseen might come to pass.[1]

Self-deprecating, disingenuous, or humble—whatever the tone of this strange little statement, its accuracy is uncanny. John Dewey was a man with a finger on the pulse of the nation; he was always wherever change was in the air. At no point does this seem more true than in his move to Chicago in 1894.

Chicago was the new urban center, chosen as the natural site for the World's Columbian Exposition—the Chicago World's Fair—the year before Dewey's arrival. Founded in 1803 as Fort Dearborn, the city had grown to a population of almost 1.5 million by the 1890s. The novelist Theodore Dreiser commented on Chicago's sudden emergence: "All at once, and out of nothing in this dingy city . . . which but a few years before had been a wilderness of wet grass and mud flats . . . had now been reared this vast collection of perfectly harmonious and showy buildings."[2] The World's Fair of 1893 focused world attention on what was now called "the White City"; over 25.5 million people visited the fair. The exhibits and numerous "congresses" represented the currents of the day, and everyone of any importance appeared at the fair. John Dewey spoke before the Philosophy Congress on "The Reconciliation of Science and Philosophy"; Woodrow Wilson and G. Stanley Hall appeared before the Education Congress; single-taxer Henry George, whom Dewey praised as "one of the world's great social philosophers, certainly the greatest which this country has produced,"[3] before the Social and Economic Congresses. At the Congress of Social Settlements—arranged by Jane Addams—Florence Kelley, Ellen Starr, and Henry Demarest Lloyd read papers on urban reform. Frederick Jackson Turner delivered his enormously influential speech about the significance of the frontier in American life before the Historical Congress. The existence of the women's movement was attested to by the great Women's Building, where panels by Mary MacMonnies and Mary Cassatt depicted primitive woman and modern woman—modern woman engaged in picking (presumably symbolic) fruit, playing music, and reaching heavenward for ideals or fame. Feminists Lucy Stone, Elizabeth Cady Stanton, and Susan B. Anthony appeared before the Women's Congress. In a related sphere, home economist Ellen Richards displayed her "Rumsford Kitchen," where the principles of scientific management that she hoped would transform the home were displayed. For Henry Adams, who had recently beheld the dynamo, which he saw as marking the beginning of an awesome new era, the fair "was the first expression of American thought as a unity."[4] Chicago's "White City" held out to America and the world the promise of the century to come.[5]

The fair acknowledged the emergence of Chicago as a center of change and activity, a place of new ideas. Indeed, the city was emerging as a formidable intellectual center, due in part to the efforts of University of Chicago president William Rainey Harper, who in the four years of the university's existence assembled some of the most innovative—and most politically involved—minds in America: Albion Small and W. I. Thomas in sociology, Edward W. Bemis and Thorstein Veblen in political economy, Frederick Starr in anthropology, and James Tufts, George Herbert Mead, and James R. Angell in philosophy. But the atmosphere was not one of dry academic scholarship. The spirits of reform and experiment were in the air. As the new century approached, thinkers like Dewey sensed that social change was a mandate for a new intellectual elite.

Dewey himself, now thirty-five, had come into his own professionally and personally. No longer handicapped by painful shyness—though still mild-mannered and quiet—Dewey initially rejected President Harper's offer of a position at Chicago, stating that the salary offered, four thousand dollars a year, was not enough to support his growing family adequately. Having negotiated for an additional three-month vacation that would give him an uninterrupted nine months off before his appointment began, Dewey, his wife, and three small children—Frederick, Evelyn, and Morris—traveled through Europe before moving to Chicago in 1894. In Milan young Morris—named for Dewey's philosophical mentor—fell ill with diphtheria and died, after which the family drew still more closely together. Three more children—Gordon, Lucy, and Jane—were born during the Chicago years, during which Dewey and his wife also worked side by side; Alice helped set up the experimental Laboratory School and later taught there and administered it. Alice Dewey had turned her husband's contemplative mind toward the realm of action; now, together, they sought out new arenas for social change, enjoying the heady spirit of reform that characterized turn-of-the-century Chicago.

Chicago's Hull House, founded in 1889 by another social visionary, Jane Addams, who sought to promote a new democracy through social work among Chicago's poor immigrants, was representative of this spirit. John Dewey had visited Hull House in his Michigan years, and when he arrived in Chicago he became a trustee. Jane Addams became an extremely close personal friend; she was a profound influence on Dewey and he on her. The goals of progressive education and the settlement house movement, of Jane Addams and John Dewey, were intertwined at every point. Both sought to broaden the role of the institution—the school or the settlement house—to take in, learn from, and in turn shape the values of children and immigrants. Because they could shape the child and the immigrant—indeed, the family, the neighborhood, and ultimately the city—the school and the settlement house could transform society. Dewey never broke off his involvement with the settlement movement. He lectured at all kinds of neighborhood houses, supported their fund-raising efforts, and on visiting a new city always sought out the best-known settlement house as a place to stay.

John Dewey and Jane Addams shared a common temperament—a fervent belief in the potency of reform. Their movement toward the progressive frame of mind shared several reference points. Although Jane Addams suffered greatly in her search for a vocation—perhaps the more so because of her sex—like Dewey, she eventually found a career that was immensely fulfilling personally and perfectly in tune with the spirit of the times. For Dewey, the profession of "philosopher" provided a solid identity; Jane Addams, on the other hand, had to invent her profession.

Born in Cedarville, Illinois, in 1860, one year after Dewey, Jane Addams had conviction in her blood. She was greatly influenced by the moral integrity and commitment of her father, whom she idealized with what she remembered as a "doglike affection."[6] Her father was a well-to-do miller, a good friend of Lincoln's and a staunch abolitionist who served eight terms as an Illinois state senator. His favorite axiom was "mental integrity above all else."[7] The young Jane Addams so worshiped her father that as a child she spent hours trying to flatten her right thumb into his "miller's thumb"; remembering this adoration in her autobiography, she quoted Elizabeth Barrett Browning's lines about a daughter and her father: "He wrapt me in his large/Man's doublet, careless did it fit or no."[8]

Of course, her father's doublet, being a man's, did not fit, and Jane Addams had to find her own way in the world, a way that would satisfy her sense that she was to serve humanity in some as-yet-ill-defined fashion. She attended the Rockville Female Seminary, where she found other young women who shared her vague idealism; there, too, she discovered a female community that sustained her, one that she would reproduce in Hull House, which was very much a women's project. But when Jane Addams left the seminary in 1881, she was "at sea" as to how she should channel her conviction. She tried to study medicine, but she became severely ill and underwent an operation on her spine. She traveled to Europe twice, and she tried her hand at charity work among blacks in Baltimore. Her stepmother hoped that Jane could find happiness in the traditional woman's role and tried to promote a marriage between Jane and her son. A complete breakdown ensued.

Like Dewey, Jane Addams found no solace in traditional religion but felt a sense of mission that could not be ignored. In her autobiography, she described the confusion she felt in the years between leaving Rockville and the opening of Hull House in 1889. It took eight years, she said, "to formulate my convictions even in the least satisfactory manner, much less to reduce them to a plan for action. During most of that time I was absolutely at sea so far as any moral purpose was concerned, clinging only to the desire to live in a really living world and refusing to be content with a shadowy intellectual or aesthetic reflection of it."[9]

How to translate conviction into action, to live in a "really living" world as an actor and not as a spectator? This same question confronted Addams, Dewey, and a whole generation of reformers. The solution for Addams and many others like her—college-educated, intelligent, independent women who were not satisfied with remaining in the home—lay in the settlement movement. In city after city, young men and women of vision—but especially women—established settlement houses where they lived among the poor, working to effect social change. Many, like Addams, had been deeply influenced by John Ruskin's *Unto This Last*. In London in 1887, Addams sought out Toynbee Hall, where a group of Oxford men were living among the poor hoping to alleviate some of the human ills caused by the dramatic social changes of the time, putting into action the ideals of Ruskin and Tolstoy. In 1889 Addams and her close friend Ellen Gates Starr rented the Hull Mansion on Polk and Halstead Streets in the Nineteenth Ward of Chicago, a district swarming with the new immigrant poor. She found some peace, too, in accepting the fact that she preferred close female friendships to conventional marriage.

For Addams, as for Dewey, the choice of vocation was deeply satisfying personally and highly judicious in terms of the spirit of the times. It was a time when ideas were put into action, when reformers held great hopes for social change. "Enthusiasm" is the word Addams used to describe the spirit of these men and women, and it is perhaps as good a word as any: "A Settlement is above all a place for enthusiasms, a spot to which those who have a passion for the equalization of human joys and opportunities are early attracted."[10]

Jane Addams's contemporaries were, indeed, attracted to Hull House—so much so that Henry Demarest Lloyd, the journalist so instrumental in "busting" the Standard Oil trust, described it as "the best club in Chicago."[11] In residence were Julia Lathrop, active in child welfare and public institutional reform; Alice Hamilton, a physician and social reformer who opened a "well-baby" clinic at the settlement; Florence Kelley, who initiated sweatshop investigations; Edith and Grace Abbott, founders with fellow resident Sophonisba Breckinridge of the Immigrants' Protection League; and Ellen Starr, who oversaw the settlement's cultural activities. As this list suggests, Hull House was extremely influential in municipal reform; it was equally important as a neighborhood center, embracing some forty clubs as well as countless other activities and services, including a nursery, a dispensary, a boardinghouse for working girls, cooking and sewing classes, an art gallery, music school, and a repertory theatre. Moreover, it was a community of women, living together openly. Traditional social mores condoned close female friendships—so-called "Boston marriages"—and the Hull House women took advantage of this freedom.

For young Chicago intellectuals like John Dewey, Hull House was a hotbed of ideas, a center of activity with magnetic appeal.

Henry Demarest Lloyd and Lyman Gage met there to discuss reform, and Henry George, the famous single-taxer whose 1879 *Progress and Poverty* had galvanized the nation's liberal thinkers, led well-attended seminars. For radicals and revolutionists, like the Russian anarchist Kropotkin, as well as for celebrities of all casts of thought—among them Beatrice and Sidney Webb, W. E. B. Du Bois, and Frank Lloyd Wright—it was a home away from home. A typical evening saw Theodore Roosevelt rubbing elbows with a working-class audience after the American premiere of John Galsworthy's *Justice*.[12] Hull House's "open door" policy welcomed all doctrines within its doors, which often made it a target for misunderstanding as well. The shooting of President McKinley, for example, was linked by the press to an anarchist conspiracy said to have originated at Hull House.

In the years of Dewey's association with it, Hull House was also linked with the trade union movement, at that time still considered a radical phenomenon. Dewey participated enthusiastically in the settlement's labor activities; he lectured weekly before the Working-People's Social Science Club. Later he delivered a lecture series before the Plato Club on "Social Psychology." At Hull House, John Dewey was exposed to the most exciting political thought of his day; his exposure to reformers like Addams led him to participate in a wide range of reform activities and to support of whatever causes he found important, however unpopular. These years marked the birth of Dewey the political man, the person who could be counted on to join committees to free political prisoners, to award radicals Nobel prizes, to wage campaigns for academic freedom. His concerns shifted from the speculative to the active, just as he had moved philosophically from neo-Hegelian idealism to pragmatism.

Jane Addams and John Dewey, coming from similar backgrounds, shared common beliefs and goals; it is not surprising that they enjoyed a close friendship that was to endure over several decades, weathering such differences as their disagreement over America's entry into the First World War. Dewey's friendship with Addams was such that when one of Dewey's sons died while the family was abroad, a memorial service was held at Hull House, with Jane Addams giving the memorial address.[13] Dewey named his second daughter Jane Mary, after the iconoclastic Addams and her close friend Mary Smith.

But Jane Addams and Hull House were important to Dewey in ways that went beyond the development of his social and political thought or his personal life. The climate that produced Hull House was environmentally well suited to his own great educational effort. John Dewey saw Hull House as a kind of laboratory, and as such it made possible Dewey's great Laboratory School, which was profoundly to shape the future of American education and to thrust Dewey into the forefront of the country's most influential thinkers. As Dewey's daughter wrote, in the abstract sense, Addams's introduction of "democracy" to social work sparked his "faith in democracy as a guiding force in education."[14] On a material level, he watched the activities at Hull House with great interest—the classes in cooking and sewing, the folk pageants and festivals, and the Labor Museum, where Addams had immigrants recreate the manual skills used in their native art and industry. From Hull House Dewey learned both theory and technique.

The "University Elementary School"—such was its official title, though it was always to be known as the Laboratory School or, later, in tribute, the Dewey School—opened its doors in January 1896, under the guidance of the Department of Pedagogy, of which Dewey was chairman. There were sixteen pupils and two teachers; by 1902 there would be 140 pupils and 23 teachers, as well as numerous graduate student assistants. University of Chicago President William Rainey Harper claimed that he saw the school as serving the same function for the university that a hospital serves for a medical department. But in reality the school was very much an experiment. Dewey clashed continually with the Harper administration and finally saw his creation merged with another university progressive school. The eventual result was Dewey's departure from Chicago for Columbia University in 1904.[15]

The axioms we associate with "Deweyism" in education—that the child must learn by doing, that learning comes through social activity, that the teacher merely presents the child with tools to learn—were all put into practice at the Laboratory School. Books and reading were deemphasized, treated merely as tools that the child would turn to as needed. Study began with the home and occupations of the home—learning about the preparation of food, the making of clothing, and so forth. Typical activities included cooking, sewing, weaving, and carpentry. All these had some practical application—in carpentry, for instance, children made the tools they used in the gymnasium and the science lab. Numbers were to be learned through cooking and carpentry. As children progressed, study moved outside the home to primitive industries, and then to invention and modern industry. History was studied in terms of how it affected contemporary life.

The impression is one of constant activity; indeed, the account that best describes the school—by two teachers, Katherine Camp Mayhew and Anna Camp Edwards, called *The Dewey School*—abounds with photographs of children cooking, spinning wool, gardening, and building.[16] One commentator observed:

> The visitor is impressed, first of all, with the freedom and unconstraint everywhere manifest. He sees clusters of children here and there in the different rooms, gathered about an older person, all talking familiarly together about something which seems to be extremely interesting. He thinks at first that he must have stumbled into a very big family, where every one is having the happiest kind of a time.[17]

With his shift to pragmatism, Dewey was now convinced that ideas were useless unless given practical application. And he must have been immensely satisfied to see his ideas about education achieve such ready success. He had been interested in education since his early years at Michigan, when he served as investigator of Michigan high school standards; he was one of nineteen charter members of the Michigan Schoolmasters Club in 1886 and was its vice president in 1887 and 1888.[18] He had expressed faith in the study of the child and the study of education as early as 1884, when in his "The New Psychology" he predicted that "The cradle . . . [is] becoming the laboratory of the psychologist of the latter half of the nineteenth century."[19]

By 1897, Dewey the pragmatist was able to write his famous "My Pedagogic Creed," which consisted of litanylike statements beginning with the words "I believe":

> I believe that education . . . is a process of living and not a preparation for future living.
> I believe that the school must represent life. . . .
> I believe that every teacher should realize the dignity of his calling; that he is a social servant set apart for the maintenance of

> proper social order and . . . the right social growth. . . . In this
> way the teacher always is the prophet of the true God and the
> usherer in of the true kingdom of God.[20]

The language of "belief," the teacher as "the prophet of the true
God," in fact, the very idea of a pedagogic "creed" should alert
us to Dewey's fervor about what he was talking about. As always, he turned to the language of religious belief when he spoke
about ideas that had for him a strong emotional resonance.

Education was close to his heart, for in it Dewey saw again a
way to resolve the dualisms that so troubled him. Education, he
felt, could heal the split between the mind and body—the split
that we know he suffered and blamed for his own as-yet-vaguely-
felt discontent. Dewey seldom referred to education's potential
to heal this split, preferring to talk instead in vague terms of "democracy" and "education," as if he were aware that he was talking about a highly personal subject. In a speech titled "Body and
Mind," given before the New York Academy of Medicine, Dewey
made explicit his belief that education could heal the split between mind and body that extended itself to theory and practice,
thought and action. Condemning forms of education that are
"aloof from the concerns of life," he cites as the leading flaw in
these types of "divisive education"

> that separation of mind and body which is incarnated in religion,
> morals and business as well as in science and philosophy. The full
> realization of the integration of mind and body in action waits
> upon the reunion of philosophy and science in art—above all, in
> the supreme art—the art of education.[21]

With the last sentence Dewey joins the "integration" of mind
and body he so highly valued with the "reunion" of his own
interests and activities—science, philosophy, and art—in the
"art" of education. Dewey prized education so earnestly over so
many years because, both intellectually and emotionally, it allowed him to perceive himself and the world as a unified whole.

Perhaps it was because of his deep personal stake in it that the
"new" education came to be associated with Dewey and that he
became its chief spokesman. For much of the terrain that Dewey
was exploring was already well known by the time the Laboratory
School was opened. His 1899 *School and Society*, which set forth
most systematically and thoroughly his educational thought, im-

mediately sold a thousand copies; a second printing in February 1900 sold fifteen hundred, and a third printing that July sold five thousand copies.[22] And this was before Dewey was nationally known and had cultivated an audience for his writing. Clearly there was a public remarkably eager to hear about the latest in educational thought.

Again, given the context of the age, the avid public interest in education is not surprising. As the agrarian family was transformed into an industrial family and neighborhoods dissolved in the face of urbanization, the care of the child moved outside the home. The huge influx of immigrants in these years also contributed to the broadened role of the school and the public's increased interest in its role, as immigrant families necessarily relinquished their rearing of the children to the school and the school became an essential agent in Americanizing the foreign-born.[23]

As Dewey saw it, the industrial revolution had changed the very nature of knowledge itself. In *School and Society*, he noted that learning had previously been a "class matter." Now, however,

> as a direct result of the industrial revolution . . . this has been changed. Printing was invented; it was made commercial. Books, magazines, papers were multiplied and cheapened. As a result of the locomotive and telegraph, frequent, rapid, and cheap intercommunication by rails and electricity was called into being. Travel has been rendered easy; freedom of movement, with its accompanying exchange of ideas, indefinitely facilitated. The result has been an intellectual revolution. While there still is, and probably always will be, a particular class having the special business of inquiry in hand, a distinctively learned class is henceforth out of the question. It is an anachronism. Knowledge is no longer an immobile solid; it has been liquefied. It is actively moving in all the currents of society itself.[24]

Dewey's educational thought was not as innovative as it now seems. In fact, he was again very much in touch with the spirit of his time in turning to education as a crucial social concern. There was a widespread "cult of the child" in late Victorian America; European educational thinkers like Pestalozzi, Herbart, and Froebel followed Rousseau in romanticizing the child and the child's development. In America this found expression in the work of, for instance, G. Stanley Hall, who gave child study a scientific basis, arguing that the curriculum should be shaped by the child's needs. Hall's *Adolescence* (1904) influenced a whole generation of American educators, as did Edward L. Thorndike's *Educational Psychology* (1903). An opposing point of view regarding education, which called for the inculcation of moral values rather than the study of "science" in the school, was expounded by Dewey's old Hegelian friend W. T. Harris, who as U. S. Commissioner of Education from 1899 to 1906 often raised his voice in counterpoint to Dewey's.[25] By the turn of the century, education had become a certifiable intellectual fad.

Nowhere is this more apparent than in the figure of Colonel Francis Parker, a colorful precursor and later a colleague of Dewey's. In 1875, Parker achieved renown as superintendent of the public schools in Quincy, Massachusetts, where he rejected such traditional pedagogical methods as repetition, punishment, and ritual rewards in favor of a child-centered curriculum. He made popular the notion that there is no such thing as a "bad child." As principal of the Cook County Normal School in Illinois he continued his crusade. A rotund man with an enormous bald head and a walrus mustache, Parker commanded large and enthusiastic audiences. At the 1891 Teachers Retreat organized at Chatauqua, New York, Parker gave a talk on "democracy in education," insisting that every school be an "embryonic democracy."[26] His presence at the retreat prompted a Chatauqua reporter to remark that Chicago was now as famous for its teachers as it was for its beef and pork.[27]

Dewey's thinking found a close parallel in Parker's and, in fact, Parker was a great influence, which Dewey fully acknowledged. Dewey's children attended the school Parker ran in Chicago before Dewey's own school opened. And both schools were under the jurisdiction of the University of Chicago—a condition that led to considerable friction but never affected the deep affinity and friendship between the two men. Dewey was correct in crediting Parker as a pioneer in American education; Parker was an enormously affable and vivid man who paved the way for Dewey's more reticent and carefully thought out approach to reform. Dewey himself acknowledged that Parker appeared to many as "a faddist, a fanatic."[28] Parker appealed to the people; he toured extensively, bringing children onto the lecture platforms with him, delighting the public with his eccentric appearance and manner. A newspaper account of an appearance of Dewey and Parker together gives a detailed impression of the contrast between the two men, which the reporter notes is striking but misleading:

> Dr. Dewey is one of the quietest and most modest appearing men imaginable. He appears like a gentle young man who is studious and willing to learn. To see him on the platform in his gray sack coat, drooping moustache, hair parted in the middle and his "excuse me for intruding" air, as opposed to Col. Parker, with his massive bald head, his impressive and aggressive personality and his "you had better not get in my way" air one would never dream that the quiet man with his level eyebrows and pleasant gentle voice was the lion, and the great Colonel Parker was the lamb.

But that conclusion, in fact, was quite accurate, as the reporter points out:

> Col. Parker sits at one side of the platform, listening, often with closed eyes, as is his wont, to the agreeable voice of Dr. Dewey, as he quietly argues those radical ideas which simply remove the bottom from all existing forms of educational effort. . . . Col. Parker, in his aggressively earnest way, has been lustily pounding for years, on the same thing. Dr. Dewey does not pound. He quietly loosens the hoops, and the bottom insensibly vanishes.[29]

By virtue of his large popularity, the colorful Colonel Parker made it possible for the quiet voice of John Dewey to be heard. So, in his quiet way—but with real emotional conviction—this "gentle young man" with his "excuse me for intruding" air slipped into the foreground of the new education and, because in his focus on education he was responsive to the tenor of his time, into the foreground of social thought. The Chicago years marked Dewey's debut on the national stage.

In his interest in the social settlement and his passion for education John Dewey was alert to two of the most significant movements that were to shape early-twentieth-century American life. Indeed, he rightly saw the impulse behind the social settlement and the new school as one and the same. In an address before the National Education Association in 1902 on "The School as Social Center," Dewey explicitly brought together the two concepts. (He was later to return to the conceit in a chapter of his

1915 *Schools of To-Morrow*, "The School as a Social Settlement.")
Because the "new" school played such a large part in the growth
of the child—particularly the immigrant child—the work of the
school must, like that of Hull House, be "not that of conveying
intellectual instruction, but of being a social clearing-house." Describing what went on at Hull House, Dewey makes it clear that
he saw the settlement house and the school as sharing a common
function:

> It is a place where ideas and beliefs may be exchanged, not merely
> in the arena of formal instruction . . . but in ways where ideas are
> incarnated in human form and clothed with the winning grace of
> personal life. Classes for study may be numerous, but all are re-
> garded as modes of bringing people together, of doing away with
> barriers of caste, or class, or race, or type of experience that keep
> people from real communion with each other.[30]

Dewey argued that the social settlement and the school had
both a common function and a common purpose. The social settlement workers and Dewey shared an ongoing dialogue about
their mutual influence. Jane Addams wrote that Dewey's "insistence upon an atmosphere of freedom and confidence between
the teacher and the pupil, of a common interest in the life they
led together, profoundly affected all similar relationships, certainly those between the social worker and his client."[31] Lillian
Wald, the founder of the Henry Street Settlement on New York's
Lower East Side, wrote to Dewey that she had always thought the
settlement workers were "trying to live up to" his philosophy.[32]

Though Hull House was particularly close to Dewey's heart,
the settlement houses of America's cities were his homes away
from home. After his move to Columbia University in 1904,
Dewey, like many of his colleagues, gave over numerous evenings to lecturing and leading seminars "downtown"—in the
clubs, night schools, and settlement houses of New York's Greenwich Village and Lower East Side. He was closely associated with
both the Henry Street Settlement and Mary Simkhovitch's
Greenwich House, serving at the latter as chairman of the educational committee.

Dewey's close involvement with progressive movements like
the social settlement is illustrated by his relationship with an
equally important influence on his thought: the philosopher

Thomas Davidson. Dewey and Davidson first met at a summer school run by Davidson in Farmington, Connecticut, where Dewey and W. T. Harris lectured on philosophy. Davidson's intellectual interests were broad and eclectic, ranging from Thomas Aquinas, Greek sculpture, Tennyson, and Aristotle to Dante Giordano Bruno. He was one of the last of the "pure" philosophers, not associated with any university. Quite in contrast to Dewey, Davidson profoundly mistrusted American education and was skeptical about social change.

Yet Dewey and Davidson also had a good deal in common. The Deweys had a summer home in Hurricane, New York, in the Adirondacks, close to Davidson's home, and in the summers of the 1890s they attended his Glenmore School for Culture Sciences there. It is not clear whether Dewey pointed his skeptical friend to the social realm, but the fact is that the dubious Davidson gradually came to place his trust in education and the work of the social settlement, to the extent that he became one of the most influential figures in the lives of many New York immigrant intellectuals. In her *Twenty Years at Hull-House*, Jane Addams noted Davidson's distrust of the social settlement impulse; Davidson suggested that it was really a narcissistic yearning for collective living.[33] But he became a convert; in 1898 he was somehow induced to give four lectures at New York City's Educational Alliance, which was not strictly speaking a settlement house but rather a broad network of homes, agencies, clubs, and classes that served as an important social and cultural center for New York's immigrants. Davidson spoke on "The Problems Which the Nineteenth Century Hands On to the Twentieth." After the third lecture, one young man raised his hand and protested, "It is all very well to talk about education for the breadwinners; but how can people like us, who work nine or ten, and sometimes more, hours a day, who come home tired, with no convenience there for study, few books, and no one to guide or instruct us, obtain any liberal education?"[34]

Davidson, who had heretofore rather disliked students, was a little taken aback, but he recovered himself quickly and offered to come to New York himself and teach twice a week. Thus was born the famous "Breadwinners' College," a group of young immigrants eager to learn, who became officially "Branch B" of the Educational Alliance and informally Davidson's pupils and devotees, visiting him at his Adirondack retreat and eagerly reading his letters to the group during his absences from the "school." Davidson's most notable pupil was Morris Cohen, whom Dewey met in the Adirondacks before the turn of the century. Though Dewey and Cohen differed intellectually a great deal, they shared a devotion to Davidson. And Dewey was a frequent visitor at the Educational Alliance and a speaker at the "Breadwinners' College." When Davidson died in 1900, Cohen wrote a tribute that to the modern reader sounds suspiciously Deweyan. Davidson's letters to the "class," Cohen wrote,

> pointed out the great defect in the ordinary college and university education, viz., "that it stops with knowing and does not go on with loving and doing. It therefore, really never is appropriated, for knowing does not pass into act and habit, is never ours, but remains an eternal thing, a mere useless accomplishment, to be vain about."[35]

Even an old philosopher-war horse like Thomas Davidson, then, could be "converted" to the new social ethic of the social settlement, the new education, and the ideals of John Dewey. Moreover, the contiguity between Davidson, Dewey, and a figure like Morris Cohen suggests how closely Dewey was to be associated with a variety of social and reform movements that in turn brought him into contact with individuals far beyond the realm of the university—individuals like Anzia Yezierska, who, in 1900, the year Davidson died and the year before Dewey was to call for recognition of the social influence of the school on immigrants, was taking night courses at the very same Educational Alliance that had drawn Davidson from the realm of "pure" philosophy to social action.

# 4

## *Yezierska, 1904–1917: Hattie Mayer, New Woman*

With her graduation from Teachers College in 1904, Anzia Yezierska left behind the social settlements, the Lower East Side, and the Educational Alliance, where Thomas Davidson and, later, John Dewey lectured to packed audiences. As Hattie Mayer, *teacherin*, she sought now to make her way in the American world.

Who was this Hattie Mayer, this new woman? However traumatized she may have been by being treated as a literally unclean outsider at Teachers College, she remained warmly gregarious and open-hearted. Alone in the big city, she no doubt felt adrift and alone but also alive to life's possibilities. She was healthy and young—about twenty-four—and must have felt elated to be out of the immigrant underclass. She had lost her family, to be sure, but she found a circle of friends with whom she would maintain intimate friendships over many years.

Minnie Shomer was one such friend. Born Manya Shaikevitsch in Odessa in 1882, Minnie (her Anglicized name was Miriam, but she was often called Minnie, a nickname she hated) was the daughter of the novelist and playwright known as Shomer, who was hugely popular in the Old Country. When the family immigrated in 1890 they adopted Shomer as their name. The father's literary fortune fell off in the New World, but he remained a prolific playwright. When the seventeen-year-old Minnie met Charles Zunser and the two fell in love and married, the match represented the merging of two Jewish literary dynasties. Charles was the son of Eliakum Zunser, a Jewish bard whose reputation Abraham Cahan, the American spokesman for Jewish art at the turn of the century, described in 1929 as ''a popularity that would have been considered stupendous in our own day.''[1] Zunser was a *badkhon*, a wedding jester who performed a rhymed mono- logue, supposedly spontaneously, witty but also serious; many have suggested that the *badkhon* was the precursor of the stand- up comic.[2] Zunser's songs, like ''The Golden Land,'' ''The Greenhorn,'' and ''Columbus and Washington,'' were widely recognized and loved on the Jewish Lower East Side.

Minnie Shomer too had literary aspirations. And, like Yezier- ska, she fought fiercely for an education, although her mother staunchly and successfully opposed her going to college. Minnie became a librarian and club leader at the Hebrew Educational So- ciety, studied art at the Educational Alliance, and eventually came to teach art at the Alliance and for the New York City Board of Education.[3] It was at the Educational Alliance, where Anzia was still teaching cooking, that she and Minnie met and became fast friends.

Seeking an outlet for her literary efforts, Minnie began writing columns for the English section of the Yiddish newspaper *Ta- geblatt*. There she met the vibrant, red-haired Rose Pastor, a Rus- sian immigrant who had come to America and settled in Cleve- land, where she worked for twelve years in a cigar factory. Around 1901 Rose—herself self-educated—began writing letters to the *Tageblatt* under the pen name Zelda. These became so pop- ular that the editor promised her a column at fifteen dollars a week; following the promise of Rose's success, the Pastor family moved to New York City in 1903. Shortly thereafter Rose was sent to interview the millionaire James Graham Phelps Stokes, who had left his Madison Avenue mansion to live and work among the poor at the University Settlement on the Lower East Side. Rose went reluctantly—she had developed socialist leanings and was impatient with the idea of meeting a millionaire capitalist. But she turned in an impassioned write-up of Stokes, calling him a second Abraham Lincoln. Writing about Rose Pastor years later, Minnie Zunser recalled, ''She came back shining. She was madly in love.''

Minnie and Anzia—Anzia had met Rose through Minnie— shared in Rose's dramatic love affair. One day Rose appeared breathlessly in Minnie's classroom at the Alliance and announced that she had something to tell her—''but wait let us call Hattie.

Let her hear it too." They found Anzia, and Rose made her announcement: "Children, listen to me. I am going to be married to the millionaire Stokes. Riches and poverty, Jew and Christian will be united. Here is an indication of the new era."[4] Minnie, "Hattie," and Rose—three shirtwaisted "Gibson girls"—must have felt that America had fulfilled its promise.

The American public was as transfixed by the romance as were Rose's girlfriends. Sunday supplements, the voice of middlebrow values at the turn of the century, heralded the ghetto romance, declaring the "Israelitish maiden" "the luckiest girl in America." Anzia and Minnie attended the formal wedding at Stokes's Connecticut family estate, Caritas Island. The Stokes family watched with contempt the entrance of an aunt of Rose's, "attired in silk and spangles," as Minnie recalled. The girls themselves were humiliated when they asked a Stokes butler to identify the sparkling drinks they were served. "Beer," he informed them, covering the label on the champagne bottle.

Minnie remembered that she and Anzia were skeptical about the future of the union—Rose wore a cross, and a Christian minister performed the ceremony. But Anzia was actually deeply affected by the promise her friend's marriage seemed to represent. Rose and her husband united two worlds; they proved that America and the immigrant could be wed. In Yezierska's *Salome of the Tenements*, whose plot is modeled on the Stokes romance, the heroine describes her marriage in terms of the melting pot: "Races and classes and creeds, the religion of your people and my people melt like mist in our togetherness."[5] Union with a native-born American became a dream fraught with promise for Anzia. She saw Rose's marriage as confirming the self-made American individuality she herself sought, an individuality won through what must have seemed to Anzia a reassuringly traditional means.

So the lives of the girlhood friends were touched by romance. But, as the years went by, the friendship of Rose Pastor Stokes came to mean more to Anzia than the stuff of a young woman's fantasy.

A socialist and feminist, Rose introduced Anzia to a variety of radical personalities and causes. Rose headed the Intercollegiate Socialist Society from 1907 to 1917 and was a key figure in the 1912 New York restaurant and hotel workers' strike. In 1917 she split from the Socialist Party over its antiwar stand, but in 1918 she was convicted under the wartime Espionage Act, a conviction that was later reversed. After this she moved farther to the left, becoming an active member of the Communist party.[6]

Among Rose's activities was her membership in Heterodoxy, a remarkable club whose members included some of the most original and radical women of the twentieth century. Heterodoxy met every other week in Greenwich Village from 1912 until World War II. Mabel Dodge Luhan called it a club "for unorthodox women, women who did things and did them openly."[7] Political activist Elizabeth Gurley Flynn said of Heterodoxy, "It has been a glimpse of the women of the future, big-spirited, intellectually alert, devoid of the old 'femininity' which has been replaced by a wonderful free masonry of women."[8] Other members included social activist Crystal Eastman, anthropologist Elsie Clews Parson, journalist Mary Heaton Vorse, and feminist Charlotte Perkins Gilman. No political doctrine prevailed as far as party loyalties were concerned, but the members, all "women who did things," were ardent supporters of women's "new freedom." Anzia's involvement with Heterodoxy is not documented, but at least five of her closest friends were members—Rose, novelists Zona Gale, Mary Austin, and Fannie Hurst, and teacher and activist Henrietta Rodman—and she was inevitably exposed to its views. Heterodoxy's members were what in the early years of the century known as "new women," and Rose Pastor Stokes introduced "Hattie Mayer," soon to become Anzia Yezierska, into the "new woman's" world.

Though the "new woman" remained "new" until the end of the 1920s, and though she came to be confused with the flapper, the real new women were the feminist pioneers of the first decade of the century, the passionate idealists who sought to change traditional notions of woman's place, of love and marriage, of the organization of the home. Historian Carroll Smith-Rosenberg identifies the new women as

> women associated with the settlement-house movements, women educational reformers, physicians and public-health experts, women writers and artists. . . . The term should incorporate, as well, a host of less visible women who worked as teachers, social workers, physicians, nurses, businesswomen—provided these women lived economically and socially autonomous lives.[9]

The emergence of the new woman coincided with revolutionary social changes on the American scene. Women were entering
the workplace in growing numbers; between 1880 and 1890 the
number of women in the workplace doubled; between 1900 and
1919 it doubled again.[10] The new generation of educated women
who looked for fulfillment outside the home—the generation
of social workers Jane Addams and Lillian Wald, educators
M. Carey Thomas and Helen Thompson Woolley, writers Sarah
Orne Jewett and Willa Cather—provided models for many working-class and middle-class women who previously would not
have considered a future outside the home. And, as Freudian
thinking reached America, sex and sexuality became socially acceptable topics of discussion and even of debate.

For it was in the arena of sex—particularly of relations between
the sexes—that the new woman was most outspoken. As early
as 1901, an article in the popular *Atlantic Monthly*, "The Steel-
Engraving Lady and the Gibson Girl," had the "Gibson Girl"
announce to her outdated counterpart that things had changed
between men and women:

> It very likely seems odd to you who are so far behind the times;
> but we are so imbued with modern thought that we have done
> away with all the oversensitiveness and overwhelming modesty in
> which you are enveloped. We have progressed in every way.
> When a man approaches, we do not tremble and droop our eye-
> lids, or gaze adoringly while he lays down the law. We meet him
> on a ground of perfect fellowship, and converse freely on every
> topic.[11]

Many observers watched in horror as women married and kept
their own names, married and openly held adulterous affairs,
bore children out of wedlock, or lived with men without marriage. "The home is in grave danger" was a clarion call sounded
repeatedly in the early years of the century. Sexual freedom was
in the air. Emma Goldman, finding marriage inimical to love,
preached and practiced free love; well-known Village couples like
Ida Rauh and Max Eastman, John Reed and Louise Bryant, Hutchins Hapgood and Neith Boyce, Susan Glaspell and George
Cram Cook all sought to redefine traditional marriage. Mabel
Dodge took lovers freely; Elizabeth Gurley Flynn lived openly
with anarchist Carlo Tresca. Rose Pastor Stokes authored a play,

*The Woman Who Wouldn't*, whose heroine, Mary Lacey, chooses to bear her child out of wedlock over the father's protests. The message of the play, and a recurring theme of the time, was that no woman should marry without love.

In these years, Yezierska formed one of her closest and most lasting friendships—with Henrietta Rodman, schoolteacher, activist, and one of the archetypal new women. Floyd Dell, in *Love in Greenwich Village*, credits Egeria, a character based directly on Rodman, with "starting" Greenwich Village—in other words, sparking a new radical community that brought together new women, artists, writers, and reformers of all stripes—idealists who shared a new vision of society and others who simply enjoyed the freedom of this new world.

In a sense, Rodman did "start" Greenwich Village. At least, she was responsible for a turning point in its history, when she moved the Liberal Club, "an organization of genteel reformers, philanthropists, and middle-class reformers"[12] to a new location "downtown"—to its famous headquarters over Polly's Restaurant on MacDougal Street, where it attracted such speakers as Margaret Sanger and Emma Goldman and became a social and political center for new radicals like Lincoln Steffens and left-leaning "uptown" folks like John Dewey. The move was precipitated in part because the "uptown" faction of the Liberal Club disapproved of Rodman's marriage to Herman de Fremery, a naturalist at the Museum of Natural History, who had been living out of wedlock with Village poet Grace Norton for eight years. Rodman not only married de Fremery but welcomed his mistress as a member of the household, which was the gesture that particularly offended the Liberal Club's "old guard."[13]

Rodman campaigned for a variety of radical and feminist causes, the best-known of which was her fight for "teacher mothers." In 1914 she challenged the Board of Education's rules regarding married women holding teaching jobs by announcing her marriage to de Fremery—about which she had not formally petitioned the board—and then challenged their rule against mothers continuing to teach, accusing the Board of "mother-baiting." She was suspended but eventually reinstated, and in early 1915 the *Times* was able to report "Teacher Mothers Win Final Verdict."[14]

Yezierska's friend was the epitome of the new woman in attitude, dress, and life-style. Gorham Munson could have been describing Rodman when he wrote

> The bachelor girl wore batiks and sandals, she bobbed her hair and smoked cigarettes when few women smoked; she earned her livelihood, and at Bertalotti's on West 3rd St. she stood at the bar with the men. She read Ellen Key and Freud; she made speeches at the Liberal Club and got herself arrested for birth control propaganda; she acted in little theaters and painted cubist pictures and wrote *vers libre.*[15]

Henrietta Rodman wore, according to one commentator, "a loose-flowing gown that looked like a meal sack, and did not conceal the trim lines of her body. She wore sandals on her small, shapely feet, making the queer, brown socks visible."[16] Yezierska remembered Rodman's advocacy of Chinese dress for women, which Yezierska saw as "timeless, not subject to the whim of fashion, and yet elegant."[17]

Rodman had a large and enthusiastic following; on the roof of her apartment house she gave impromptu suppers of spaghetti and beer that were famous among the writers, artists, and radicals of the day. To her followers, known as "Henrietta's girls," she was charismatic and vital. Floyd Dell's Egeria

> had the rare gift of being able to start things. Some people, it is true, said that what she inevitably started was trouble; but that was scarcely just to her. Incredibly naïve, preposterously reckless, believing wistfully in beauty and goodness, a *Candide* in petticoats and sandals, she did always manage to involve herself in complicated difficulties; but she faced these difficulties serenely, and fought her way out of them—into some new thorn-patch. People laughed at her a good deal, and followed at her beck into the beautiful and absurd schemes she was forever inventing.[18]

As Janice Godman in Village novelist Harry Kemp's *More Miles,* Rodman is described as "the strange Socratic-looking woman in the meal-sack gown, sandals, bobbed hair . . . the radical schoolteacher and dress reformer" who was "interested in helping out girls . . . in teaching them to become economically independent."[19]

Yezierska, of course, was not only one of Rodman's followers but a close friend. Another friend, Dorothy Canfield Fisher, remembered Yezierska as being "totally at sea" for ten years after Rodman's death in 1923. Yezierska said about Rodman in a 1969 interview, "To me she was a very great person because she conquered the thing that was an obstacle to her. . . . There were meetings in her house that tied in with the women's rights struggle. . . . She wanted to live and be married and help people." If Yezierska learned from Rodman the courage of her convictions, she learned too the rights of the new woman. Yezierska said, quite simply, that Rodman taught her how to be a woman, "instead of a woman with a big belly being such a glorious thing."[20]

The "bibles" of new women like Henrietta Rodman included Charlotte Perkins Gilman's *Women and Economics* (1898), which Jane Addams hailed as a "masterpiece" and which went through seven printings over the next twenty-five years and was translated into six languages.[21] Gilman's book asserted women's right to economic independence and marriage for love. The heroine of another feminist favorite, Olive Schreiner's *The Story of an African Farm* (1883), proposes a "companionate marriage" to her besotted suitor, claiming that she is speaking "plain, matter-of-fact business."[22] Schreiner's *Women and Labor* (1911) presented a view of marriage that was "one more largely psychic and intellectual than crudely and purely physical."[23] Also hugely influential was Swedish feminist Ellen Key's *Love and Marriage* (1911), which asserted that "the ideal form of marriage is considered to be the perfectly free union of a man and a woman, who through mutual love desire to promote the happiness of each other and of the race" and which advocated free (extralegal) divorce.[24] Floyd Dell—himself a supporter of sexual freedom if not of the new woman—called Key's *Love and Marriage* "the Talmud of sexual morality."[25]

How directly did the new sexual freedom, epitomized by Henrietta Rodman, affect Anzia Yezierska? We know that she had read and enjoyed Olive Schreiner. In fact, one of Yezierska's fictional characters says that among the first books she read in English was Schreiner's *Dreams*, while in a 1969 interview Yezierska herself cited Schreiner's *The Story of an African Farm* as a major influence in her life.[26] She listened to Rose Pastor Stokes read drafts of *The Woman Who Wouldn't* and wrote her friend in 1916 of her eagerness to see the play staged.[27] In 1911 Yezierska sent

an inscribed copy of Ellen Key's *Love and Marriage* to a friend—
the same year Yezierska was pregnant and married to her second
husband, whom she was soon to desert.

The years 1909 to 1912—the period of Yezierska's two marriages—were years in which public concern over divorce was at
its most intense; a third of all the books published on marriage
and divorce in the years between 1889 and 1919, writes historian
of divorce William O'Neill, appeared in this four-year span.[28] Yezierska, if not a new woman in the strictest sense of the term,
was certainly a woman of the times.

By the year of her first marriage, Yezierska was no longer content with holding a safe job as a *teacherin;* she was beginning to
live a less conventional life and was developing the iconoclastic
personality of her mature years. She took a leave of absence from
teaching in 1909 to study for a year at the American Academy of
Dramatic Arts, hoping to become an actress. The students at the
academy had established something very close to communal living; they attended classes for six hours a day and in the evenings
attended plays together, using leftover tickets sent to the school
by theater managers. Yezierska's niece, a very young child at the
time, vividly remembered years later her aunt's "screaming,
feigning faints, body control and floor contortions in line with
her dramatic disciplines."[29] Yezierska didn't pursue an acting career, but the lessons she learned in her study may well have contributed to her dramatic mannerisms and her penchant for (and
skill at) invention.

During these years, Yezierska lived in the quarters of the Rand
School at 112 East 19th Street. Founded in 1906 by Carrie Rand,
the Rand School was a socialist institution—the *Forward* called it
the socialist yeshiva—that offered classes in the history of trade
unionism and the organization of industry as well as more traditional courses in literature and history. The faculty included John
Dewey, Charlotte Perkins Gilman, and Charles Beard; the students who attended their classes were mainly young immigrants
who had turned to the school after suffering disillusionment with
the atmosphere of the night schools and the settlement houses.
As one historian writes:

> The young immigrants often felt, correctly or not, that the teachers
> in other schools looked down on their foreign ways. But socialists
> believed in the brotherhood of man, they were internationalist in

their attitudes, and so the immigrant who happened to be a socialist was at home in the School whatever his origins.[30]

The Rand School was a breeding ground for new thought; in its
basement was a cafeteria run by the eccentric Piet Vlag, the original founder of *The Masses*. Poet Louis Untermeyer remembers
this cafeteria as "a gathering place of all the utopians, muckrakers, young intellectuals, and elderly malcontents south of
Forty-Second Street."[31] Radical ideas circulated freely, and Yezierska no doubt heard much talk about the new freedom of the new
woman.

Yezierska put some of these new ideas into practice. Within a
few months in 1910 and 1911 she experienced her first marriage
and her first brush with publicity. On November 9, 1910, she
married a young lawyer named Jacob Gordon. The following May
a flurry of articles appeared in the *New York American*, the first of
which was titled "Asks Separation from Spirit Wife." There it
was reported that Yezierska's new husband sought an annulment. His wife, who described herself as "simply a lonely, quiet
school teacher," had waited until her wedding night to inform
her husband that she believed "a man and woman should just
maintain a spiritual relation," that "people could live happily in
the way she proposed, and that otherwise the relation would be
'degrading.'" The next day she elaborated further for the *American:* "I did not realize that my views on marriage were unusual
until after we were married. . . . I wanted a chum, a friend, a
mental companion. Mr. Gordon wanted a mate."[32]

Surely Yezierska was being disingenuous when she stated that
before her wedding night she might have known "the standard
viewpoint of matrimony, but only vaguely." She had been raised
among the poor, in conditions in which the facts of life are all too
obvious to children at an early age. Certainly her exposure to radical views of sexual freedom belies her naïveté. On the other
hand, Yezierska's daughter believes that Yezierska was sexually
conflicted by the residue of her strict religious upbringing and
that Jacob Gordon was particularly aggressive sexually and may
have scared her mother away.[33]

For whatever reason, Yezierska immediately realized her marriage was a mistake and sought—whether to gain publicity for

herself or for her feminist beliefs—to turn her husband's suit for an annulment into a political cause. A romantic young woman, entranced by the fiction of Olive Schreiner and the dramatic couplings and uncouplings of her peers, might easily have been seduced by the lure of becoming a cause célèbre. The facts are that within a matter of months after the annulment she married a friend of Jacob Gordon's, a schoolteacher named Arnold Levitas, and almost immediately became pregnant with her daughter Louise.

Yezierska's second marriage was not a success either. She may have expected the worst from the start, when she refused to marry Levitas in a civil ceremony and only allowed a religious one, with the result that he had to adopt his daughter upon her birth in 1912. Certainly Yezierska was already showing signs of independence and a desire to create a new life. She signed her letters to Levitas with the name Anzia, and in September 1911 she had her name changed in the Board of Education's records to Anzia Levitas. With her second marriage, "Hattie Mayer" was at last laid to rest.

In the early months of her pregnancy Yezierska "fled"—in her words—to her sister Fanny, who was living in Long Beach, California. She returned to New York City with Louise in 1913 and attempted to live with Levitas for the next two or three years, then returned to California with Louise. This time, she sent Louise back and found work with a Jewish charitable organization in San Francisco. Yezierska returned to her husband a third time, in 1917, but by this time Levitas had given up. Yezierska left Louise in his care and never again attempted a conventional relationship with a man.[34]

By all accounts, Arnold Levitas was a traditional husband with traditional expectations of home life. Yezierska had no patience with cooking and housekeeping; she often served her family their meals on paper plates. Her husband's favorite saying was "A place for everything and everything in its place"; remembering this years later, Yezierska commented that this was all well and good—"but what if there aren't enough places?"[35] When she became pregnant, Levitas pushed her to marry him legally in order to "legitimize" the child. The result, Yezierska wrote to Rose Pastor Stokes at the time, was that Levitas hated her with "a hatred of black pitch,'' seeing her refusal as ''a subtle insult to [his] respectability.''[36]

For her part, Yezierska found the dilemma of leaving her husband and caring for her child terribly painful. In letters written at the time she presented it as a material problem: She did not have the money to provide the child with a secure home and enough food, but Levitas did. To Rose Pastor Stokes, she wrote that she envied anarchist Warren Billings his jail sentence:

> In one blow he is freed from the dragging down wear and tear of making a living—and in the solitude of the prison, he can think out his thoughts and dream out his dreams as he never could while chained to stomach needs.

''If I did not have Tynkabel [Louise] to care for,'' she continued, ''I would be in prison writing.''[37]

Yezierska adored her child, and giving up Louise was a huge wrench. She likened it to ''tearing the heart out of her body''[38] and continually implored Rose Pastor Stokes to visit the child, to sing for Louise some favorite Yiddish lullabies, and to help establish the fact that she had not abandoned the child but merely surrendered her to the father's care for a few years.[39]

Evidence, too, shows that before giving up her daughter Yezierska labored to find practical solutions to what she saw as a practical problem: how to support the child and still find time to write. In 1913 she sent a letter to a New York City charity journal, the *Survey*, describing the plight of the middle-class working mother. The rich, she argued, could leave their children in the care of servants, and the poor were helped by settlement nurseries. But, she wrote, ''the intelligent self-supporting mothers, such as school-teachers and journalists, are utterly helpless, each groping blindly with her own individual problem that can no longer be solved individually. These women, while compelled to do a man's work, never can have that singleness of mind that a man has while attending to his business.''[40]

Yezierska's answer was a system of ''baby gardens,'' cooperative centers staffed by ''specialists'' in child care, which would eventually become either self-supporting or public institutions. Her letter stated that she had found financial backing for such a venture, and invited interested mothers to write to her.[41]

Yezierska's baby garden proposal gained an enthusiastic response from Henrietta Rodman and other feminist reformers. Rodman's latest cause, in fact, was the feminist apartment house, based on the theories of Charlotte Perkins Gilman and supported by just such "ordinary" women as Yezierska, teetering between the identities of housewives and new women. In 1914, Rodman's Feminist Alliance—a group of men and women who met at Rodman's home, probably one of the many women's rights meetings Yezierska remembered[42]—proposed plans for a home that would put cooperative living into practice. Built to hold 380 rooms and 170 apartments, the twelve-story house would have a communal kitchen and dining room, a staffed laundry in the basement, a Montessori school on the roof, and a communal nursery with cribs for the children to sleep in "while their parents go out together at night to places of entertainment and public instruction," reported the *New York Times*.[43] The design of the home would be conducive to modern housekeeping: there would be built-in bath tubs, hardware of a dull finish, and "beds of the disappearing type in use on the Pacific Coast," but no wallpaper or difficult-to-clean moldings. The house would be run by "trained experts," graduates of high school domestic programs. The plan was no pipe dream; an architect had been hired, a site chosen, and $480,000 had been raised.[44]

The rationale for the apartment house was explicitly feminist. Arguing that "the care of the baby is the weak point of feminism," Rodman and her supporters explained that "a man doesn't love a woman any more because she does his washing, nor does its mother love her child any better to have to wash its face a dozen times a day." Their goal was simple: "We want to see a condition where both men and women work in chosen professional life as equals."[45]

"The care of the baby" may well have been "the weak point of feminism"; certainly it became a dividing issue in the feminist ranks, and one to which Yezierska must have given much thought. Opponents of the feminist apartment house—which never did get built—found most offensive its challenge to traditional motherhood. The debate over women's proper place increasingly became a debate over the proper place of motherhood. Just as feminists stumbled when they embraced the goals of the domestic science movement, so too did they stumble when they began to address such issues as "instinctive versus intelligent mothering."

Yezierska's old favorite Ellen Key leaped right into this fray. Arguing that "the very worst suggestion" about the question of motherhood was the idea of a "family colony" like that proposed by the Feminist Alliance, Key wrote that "each young soul needs to be enveloped in its own mother's tenderness."[46] Against Charlotte Perkins Gilman, who wrote that motherhood is a social and not an individual role and that the child needs experts in child culture, Key argued that there is an "insoluable conflict" between motherhood and a vocation and broadened her argument further to insist that there were "ineradicable differences" between the sexes.[47] Arguments like these came inevitably to an impasse; they led no less inevitably to the eclipse of feminism by the end of the 1920s, and they remain to plague the feminist movement today.

They were arguments that must profoundly have upset Yezierska. Whatever her convictions, and however strong the necessity of giving up her child, it was not emotionally easy. In an essay she wrote at the time, "The Rebellion of a Supported Wife," she described the child as "the ball and chain of the prisoner that keep him chained to his cell."[48] We have seen evidence of the real pain she felt in giving up her child. The mother and daughter were to become very close; Yezierska saw Louise every weekend, and the two enjoyed a playful conspiracy to upset the straitlaced Levitas. As Louise grew up, mother and daughter became friends, Louise often helping her mother with her writing. But as late as 1932 Yezierska could write to a friend, expressing her gratitude for a holiday present from her daughter, "Anything my daughter does for me is always such a joyous surprise [sic] to me—because I haven't been a conscientious parent and my daughter's friendship is an undreamed of gift."[49]

However painful were the choices Yezierska had to make in these years, she made them with a sure knowledge, at last, of her vocation. She was determined to write. In the coming years, in story after story she described the burning desire she felt as she entered her thirties to become a writer, a desire she expressed as a need to build a bridge between her world and native-born America. In "America and I" Yezierska's autobiographical heroine describes how she reads about the Pilgrims and understands that the Pilgrim and the immigrant share a common heritage: "I, the last comer, had her share to give, small or great, to the making of America, like those Pilgrims who came in the Mayflower." She explains:

> Fired up by this revealing light, I began to build a bridge of understanding between the American-born and myself. Since their life was shut out from such as me, I began to open up my life and the lives of my people to them. And life draws life. In only writing about the Ghetto I found America.[50]

If America misunderstood and disappointed Yezierska, she felt, it was only due to a failure in communication. She had appointed herself to fulfill a mission.

Yezierska's desire to write was born out of an equation of self-expression with the formation of identity itself. Only by writing could she "make herself for a person." And, accordingly, she found writing extremely difficult; the language she uses to describe the process includes expressions like "torn from my heart," or "wrested from my soul." In *Hungry Hearts* she writes, "The beat from my heart—the blood from my veins—must flow out into my words."[51] Later in life she often told a story that one hopes was an invention, probably fabricated to convince her listeners of how desperate was her wrestling with writing: Enraged at her inability to get the words right, she took the pencil with which she was writing and plunged its point into her eye.[52]

Yezierska's stories of ghetto life may seem simply told, but she worked on them tirelessly, writing and rewriting every word. In her autobiographical *Red Ribbon on a White Horse*, she describes her conversation with another writer, expressing her amazement that anyone could write with no revisions:

> I only want to take the hurt out of my heart when I write. But the minute my pencil touches paper, I begin to worry how to write instead of going ahead and writing. And I become stiff and self-conscious. Is it the fear of being a foreigner that makes me want to explain myself so much?[53]

Yezierska struggled to become a writer under almost impossible circumstances. Simply finding the time and support she needed to write was difficult, as she juggled her vocation with teaching, charity work, and her brief stint at homemaking. It was against great odds that she wrote anything at all in these years. But by 1915 she saw her first story, "The Free Vacation House," appear in print, receiving twenty-five dollars for it. Her letters in this period are filled with her frustration at not having the time and money she needed to write. Upon her return to New York City in 1917, having given up her daughter and being even more determined to support herself as a writer, she examined her circumstances and saw that she again had to turn to teaching to support herself. This time, however, she hoped to secure a permanent teaching position in the New York City school system, so as not to have to endure the uncertainties of substitute or temporary positions. Her application for a permanent place was, for whatever reason, turned down by the Board of Education—perhaps because she had left her post so abruptly to flee to California in 1916. Frustrated and disbelieving, she wondered where to turn. She remembered that her mother had told her that when you are disappointed—with a purchase, for instance—you should go to the top to complain—to the head of the department store, said her mother. Yezierska set out for the office of the dean of Teachers College. The dean was John Dewey, and Anzia Yezierska's life was about to change.

# 5

## Dewey, 1904–1917: "His mind was eager, ardent for the fray"

He was hurried by the restless throng
Of feverish desires to seek
The promised land of honeyed streams
Of smooth success. . . .
. . . . . . . . . . . .
　　　　　　　　His mind
Was eager, ardent for the fray. Dim
Was his closeby vision made blind
Through searchings for a bright remote
Paradise of joys.
　　　　　　　　　　　—John Dewey

What of John Dewey in these years, when Anzia Yezierska was making her way out of the ghetto, becoming first a teacher and then a fledgling writer? Intellectually, as he grew still more involved in the settlement house movement, immigrant education, the professionalization of teachers, and women's suffrage, his concerns overlapped with Yezierska's. While he prospered professionally, he maintained his affinity for new ideas, however eccentric; he was equally at home uptown on Columbia University's campus and in radical circles downtown. But as 1917 approached, he was for the first time forced to examine carefully his more radical beliefs and to reassess his relationships with some radical or eccentric figures. He had become a public man, a celebrity, and his actions and beliefs were scrutinized by the nation if not the world.

In these years, too, John Dewey achieved fame. His first decade in New York saw the publication of his *Ethics* (with James Tufts, 1908), *The Influence of Darwin on Philosophy* (1910), *How We Think* (1910), *Schools of To-Morrow* (with his daughter Evelyn, 1915), *German Philosophy and Politics* (1915), and numerous articles for the *Cyclopedia of Education*, scholarly journals, and the *New Republic*. His 1916 *Democracy and Education* was welcomed by a large general audience and became in professional educational circles an immediate classic. One reviewer said that, with Plato's *Republic* and Rousseau's *Émile*, *Democracy and Education* completed a triad of epochal works in the philosophy of education.[1]

These were the years of John Dewey's middle age, and, like many men and women at that time of life, he was undergoing a kind of rebirth, a painful but often exhilarating reevaluation of his values, goals, and beliefs. Moreover, though his family remained important to him, he grew apart from the "companion of his youth," his wife Alice. Like her husband, Alice had been stunned by the death of a second Dewey son when Gordon died of typhoid fever in Europe in 1904. Daughter Jane wrote that her mother "never fully recovered her former energy."[2] Others marked the change more frankly. Max Eastman remembers her as querulous and demanding, "nervous," preoccupied with her own troubles, and increasingly distant from Dewey. She was "caustic where she had been keen, captious where she had been critical"; her perfectionism "turned into a vice of ironical nagging."[3] A friend to hundreds, Dewey underwent the journey through middle age in emotional near isolation. He did, however, form new friendships with some remarkable men and women, friendships that were to culminate in his relationship with Anzia Yezierska. Some of these friends rivaled the Ford brothers in eccentricity; Dewey seems to have sought in them solutions, however radical, to his loneliness.

Professionally, Dewey flourished. At Columbia he found a richly satisfying community of scholars, many of whom shared his political beliefs as well as his philosophical concerns. Under the leadership of Nicholas Murray Butler—himself a philosopher by training—Columbia was transformed from a small provincial college into a large cosmopolitan university. In philosophy, Dewey's colleagues included Felix Adler, F. J. E. Woodbridge, James Cattell, and, later, Herbert Schneider, Irwin Edman, and

Archibald and Lucina Dewey were of old Yankee stock, and their son is commonly remembered as a New England philosopher. But when John Dewey got out of Vermont, he "got out of there for good," as he later said, and made his way to the new educational centers of the Midwest. The young philosopher (above right) during his University of Chicago years (1894–1904). In Chicago Dewey flourished in the heady atmosphere of social change, perhaps best symbolized by Jane Addams' Hull House. Addams (below left) and Chicago educator Ella Flagg Young (below right) were two women cited by John Dewey as the most important influences in his life, directing his attention away from "pure" philosophy to social thought and action.

The immigrant matriarch (above left) of the family Anzia Yezierska believed she had to leave behind in order to free herself from the ghetto of New York's Lower East Side. Renamed Hattie Mayer, Yezierska found her place in the promised land as a teacher of cooking, a trade she learned at the Clara de Hirsch Home for Working Girls (below) and, later, on scholarship at Teachers College, Columbia University. An early photograph she arranged to have taken of herself (above right) shows a young woman who appears to have left the ghetto far behind her.

Henrietta Rodman, Zona Gale, and Rose Pastor Stokes (above, from left to right), three of Greenwich Village's "new women," helped the struggling schoolteacher "Hattie Mayer" reach for a greater destiny for herself than that of cooking instructor or housewife. Already she had married and borne a daughter, Louise Levitas, in 1913 (below right). But Yezierska found that marriage and motherhood were incompatible with the writing career she sought, and she had regretfully relinquished the care of "Tynkabel" to the child's father in 1917. By then, Yezierska (below left) had one story published; determined to find a teaching position that would allow her to write, she made her way to the office of the Dean of Teachers College—John Dewey.

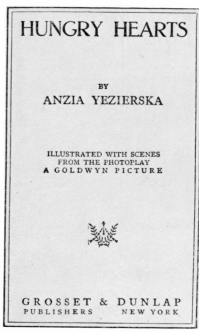

# HUNGRY HEARTS

BY

ANZIA YEZIERSKA

ILLUSTRATED WITH SCENES
FROM THE PHOTOPLAY
A GOLDWYN PICTURE

GROSSET & DUNLAP
PUBLISHERS       NEW YORK

During the period of their intense involvement, in 1917 and 1918, Dewey materially aided Yezierska's writing career by giving her a typewriter and by bringing one of her stories to *The New Republic.* That story was included in Yezierska's 1920 *Hungry Hearts,* a volume that caught the eye of Hollywood producer Sam Goldwyn. The frontispiece and title page (above) of a film tie-in edition of the overnight success. For a public eager to hear an immigrant voice, Yezierska told and retold the story of her relationship with Dewey: that of a cold-blooded, emotionally repressed American man in intimate confrontation with an emotional, passionate immigrant woman. In the film version of *Hungry Hearts,* the hero courts his immigrant love on the steps of her tenement (below).

Yezierska's fellow immigrant Rose Pastor, a reporter for a Yiddish daily, interviewed, met, and won millionaire WASP James Graham Phelps Stokes. To Yezierska, her friend's Cinderella marriage had its parallel in her own relationship with Dewey. In a scene from the film of Yezierska's 1923 *Salome of the Tenements* (above), the Rose Pastor figure returns to her paper's newsroom to write up her interview with the WASP millionaire. From a *Literary Digest* of 1923 (below), a typical rendering of the image of herself Yezierska helped to create after her first book was sold to Hollywood, when she was celebrated as "the historian of Hester Street." For her charmed public, she willingly presented herself as a "sweatshop Cinderella," fresh from the ghetto and miraculously discovered as a writer—though in fact she had been out of the ghetto for about twenty years and was a long-time apprentice at writing and being published.

ANZIA YEZIERSKA'S WAY OUT

"By writing out my protests and disillusions," says this immigrant girl, who has become a successful author, "I aired and clarified them. Slowly I began to understand what America had to offer."

Art collector Albert Coombs Barnes shows Dewey a valued piece (above left). The eccentric Barnes, whom Sidney Hook called Dewey's "most serious shortcoming," began his lifelong friendship with Dewey in 1917, when Dewey enrolled both Barnes and Yezierska in his Columbia seminar in social and political philosophy. Barnes bankrolled a study of Polish Jews in Philadelphia undertaken by a group of Columbia students including Yezierska—under Dewey's direction. During these months Dewey was secretly writing the love poems that would later reveal the relationship he sought to conceal. In 1918, in the wake of his involvement with Yezierska, Dewey undertook a two-year trip to the Far East with his family (below). Dewey and his wife Alice (second from right) with daughters Lucy and Evelyn (far right) in China, August 11, 1920. Dewey drew great comfort in his later years from family life. Dewey, with grandson John Dewey II in 1921 (above right).

Called by Waldo Frank "the man who made us what we are," Dewey the public man was always an active member of various liberal and radical committees and social movements. As chairman of the Unemployment Conference in 1931 (above), with Norman Thomas, Ethel Klyde, and Sidney Goldman. Awarding birth control activist Margaret Sanger (below left) the American Women's Association Medal, April 20, 1932. At the age of 87, over the objections of his children, Dewey married 42-year-old Roberta Grant, a widow who was an old family friend. The pair posed for a news photo (below right) on December 11, 1946, the eve of their wedding.

Yezierska at her typewriter (above left). Yezierska lived out her old age in a rented room in the shadow of Columbia University, writing—and then dictating—right up until her death in 1970. John Dewey, the nation's educator, surrounded by children on his ninetieth birthday (above right). In later years, his birthdays were virtually national holidays. A rotogravure (below left) shows a popular image of the spectacled, gentle professor. A romantic portrait from the 1920s presents a determined and independent Yezierska (below right); this drawing appeared on the cover of an enthusiastically received 1970 reprint of *Hungry Hearts*, which had initially won her fame in 1920.

Ernest Nagel. Also influential were Charles Beard in political science, E. R. A. Seligman and Vladimir Simkhovitch in economics, James Harvey Robinson in history, and Franz Boas in anthropology. These men constituted an intellectual elite; the first professional "academics," they were based institutionally but enjoyed broad cultural influence. Working out of such known disciplinary frameworks as philosophy, political science, and history, they felt free to express their social concerns in any number of popular forums, from the pages of the *New Republic* to the public lecture hall. They were the intellectual precursors and in some cases mentors of such men as Herbert Croly, Walter Lippmann, Van Wyck Brooks, Walter Weyl, and Randolph Bourne—Bourne being first a disciple and later a harsh critic of his teacher John Dewey.[4]

While the immigrant Anzia Yezierska was struggling to leave the profession of education, one contemporary debate to which Dewey added his voice concerned the education of immigrants. In recently industrialized America there was a lack of trained industrial workers; children who left school at twelve or fourteen joined the work force without skills, with predictably unfortunate consequences—they moved from job to job, seldom advancing in position or pay rate. Educators, reformers, employers, and philanthropic organizations had long advocated some form of vocational training in the schools, and they now sought legislation to ensure that it was provided.

Dewey, who felt that all education was vocational, and who advocated "manual training" for all children as an integral part of their schooling, was a powerful force in the industrial education movement. As usual, however, his views did not reflect those of the entire movement. In an article written in 1913 for the *Survey*, a journal that covered philanthropic activity and reform, Dewey called for an integrated system in which all children would be taught some skill in the normal course of their time at school. This set him apart from the faction that supported the formation of a dual system that would distinguish between the students who would receive vocational training and those who would not, with each group following different courses of study. Most industrialist employers favored a dual system on the grounds of efficiency, while their opponents—mostly educators—opposed a dual system on the grounds that such a system would require unnecessary expense. Moreover, educators like Dewey immediately saw the potential for discrimination in a dual system, which would in effect transform working-class students—usually immigrants—into trainees for industry.[5] (It was just such discrimination that had confronted ''Hattie Mayer'' when she sought to go to college but was allowed to only in order to learn a trade.) For the New York City Board of Education's *Directory of the Trades and Occupations*, which listed the printing and typesetting classes taught by Yezierska's new husband Arnold Levitas, Dewey wrote an enthusiastic introduction.[6]

Other educational issues concerning the immigrant drew Dewey's attention. The years preceding the First World War saw increasing public apprehension about the loyalties of the new immigrant Americans. Nativist overtones colored public demands for an educational system that would effectively ''Americanize'' or ''nationalize'' the immigrant. Ellwood Cubberly, a distinctive voice in the Americanization movement, saw the school's proper function as the transformation of the immigrant according to Anglo-Saxon ideals, believing that the goal of the schools must be

> to assimilate and amalgamate these people as part of our American race, and to implant in their children as far as can be done, the Anglo-Saxon conception of righteousness, law and order, and popular government, and to awaken in them a reverence for our democratic institutions and for those things in our national life which we as a people hold to be of abiding worth.[7]

John Dewey, who had worked with Jane Addams at Hull House to develop programs that would encourage the gifts immigrants brought with them to American culture, was naturally suspicious of the Americanizers' agenda. ''Nationalization'' was dangerously akin to homogenization, Dewey felt, and was predicated on values implicitly antithetical to democracy.

Dewey articulated his views on the role of the school in immigrant life in a 1916 address to the National Education Association. In it he revealed his perception of a society enriched by its newest members, vital in its diversity:

> the American nation is itself complex and compound. Strictly speaking, it is inter-racial and international in its make-up. It is composed of a multitude of peoples speaking different tongues,

inheriting diverse traditions, cherishing varying ideals of life. . . .
Our national motto, "One from Many," cuts deep and extends far.

Thus, somewhat cryptically, Dewey concludes that the true American is "not American plus Pole or German. But the American is himself Pole-German-English-French-Spanish-Italian-Greek-Irish-Scandinavian-Bohemian-Jew- and so on."[8]

For at least one immigrant who was well acquainted with the educational system, Dewey's words on the Americanization of the immigrant had particular resonance. In Yezierska's 1921 story "To The Stars," the student heroine approaches "President Irvine" to thank him for his encouragement and hears him expound on his views about immigrant education. He says, writes Yezierska:

> Teachers, above all others, have occasion to be distressed when the earlier idealism of welcome to the oppressed is treated as a weak sentimentalism; when sympathy to the unfortunate and those who have not had a fair chance is regarded as a weak indulgence fatal to efficiency. The new school must aim to make up to the disinherited masses by conscious instruction. . . . [9]

President Irvine's words are themselves resonant; in fact, they are taken verbatim from John Dewey's 1916 address, which had conveniently been published in the NEA's *Journal of Addresses and Proceedings* and was thus readily available to any earnest young schoolteacher.

Dewey gave numerous public lectures on educational principles, to which many schoolteachers—including, very possibly, Anzia Yezierska—flocked. In 1913, for instance, he addressed the alumnae of Teachers College on "The Training of Thinking in Children" and the Association of Women High School Teachers on "Social Education."

Dewey was also active in another educational arena that greatly interested Yezierska, an arena in which the concern was not the "rights" of students but the rights of teachers. The professional organization of teachers was under way, and John Dewey joined the activist Henrietta Rodman and other fellow teachers in the fight for better working conditions, higher wages, and increased job security. On October 17, 1912, under the leadership of Henry R. Linville, the Teachers League of New York was established at a meeting at Columbia University. The meeting had been advertised on some 15,000 handbills distributed to city teachers. The auditorium was filled to the rafters. At a February 1913 meeting Dewey delivered a talk on "Professional Spirit among Teachers." In 1915, the league became the New York Teachers Union and joined the American Federation of Teachers as one of eight charter locals. The union's slogan rather obviously reflected Dewey's influence: "Democracy in Education: Education in Democracy." Three years later, Dewey worked to bring the union into the American Federation of Labor.[10] For a young schoolteacher with a grievance—like Anzia Yezierska in 1917—John Dewey was an obvious person to turn to.

In fact, Dewey had intensified his involvement with the downtowners who were working to ease the immigrant's acculturation to American life. His colleagues at Columbia supported the settlement house movement with enthusiasm. Columbia president Nicholas Murray Butler was himself on the board of the University Settlement House and wrote that such neighborhood programs are "engaged, and beautifully engaged, not only in making men and women out of the children, but in the still more difficult task of making American men and women out of the children of another birth, heredity, and another environment."[11] The wife of Columbia professor Vladimir Simkhovitch ran Greenwich House, whose educational committee was headed by John Dewey. In Mary Simkhovitch's memoir about the settlement, she describes a memorable educational evening devoted to the reading of *Songs of Labor* by Morris Rosenfeld—the same songs that were translated by Yezierska's friend Rose Pastor Stokes and that Yezierska cited as one of the most important influences on her writing.[12]

Lillian Wald's Henry Street Settlement was among the best known of the settlements and one of Dewey's favorites. Wald fondly recalled the visit in 1910 of "two stalwart men in Russian blouses and high boots" to the house: "They said they came to this country in the interests of free education, meaning, as they defined it, freedom from uninteresting, rigid, traditional instruction." She wanted to help them in their "pilgrimage," and asked what she could do. "Without hesitation they answered, 'We want to meet John Dewey.'"[13]

In other downtown circles, among the Bohemians of Greenwich Village, progressive education and Deweyan ideas were becoming an intellectual fad along with imagism and anarchism. In 1919 Villager Floyd Dell wrote a popular account of progressive education called *Were You Ever a Child*. Two years earlier a New York schoolteacher named Jess Perlman had founded an experimental magazine called *Slate*, which followed both education and the new art and literature. It carried the work of Louis Untermeyer, Kenneth Burke, and Malcolm Cowley; Floyd Dell wrote articles on education and two *Masses* artists contributed illustrations. John Dewey's name was sprinkled liberally throughout its pages. At the same time Margaret Naumburg, wife of Waldo Frank, founded the progressive Greenwich Village Children's School, which later became the well-known Walden School. Another Villager, novelist Mary Heaton Vorse, migrated with the theater group to Provincetown, Massachusetts, and founded an experimental school there. Even the anarchists Emma Goldman and her lover Alexander Berkman saw education as a key factor in social revolution; in 1910 they founded the Modern School of the Ferrer Center, which later moved from the Village to the Columbia neighborhood, Morningside Heights.[14] As the influence of Dewey and his progressive education began to be felt across the country, it was felt in radical circles as well, where it was perceived as revolutionary, signaling as much as did the new modern art and poetry a dramatic change in the existing order of things. For the downtowners, John Dewey was a radical new messiah.

Randolph Bourne, one of the most radical and influential thinkers of his day, brought Dewey's ideas to the attention of the nation with his study of the schools of Gary, Indiana. In this small city in America's heartland, under the guidance of a Dewey disciple, superintendent William Wirt, Dewey's educational principles were put into practice in a spirit of enthusiastic experimentalism. Schools across the country began to adopt the "Gary system." Sent by the *New Republic* to investigate this new phenomenon, Bourne liked what he saw. And it was not only the liberal readers of the *New Republic* who wanted to hear about these new schools. When Bourne's account was published in 1916 as *The Gary Schools*, the book's popularity indicated that Dewey's radical experimentalism had caught the attention of mainstream America as well.[15] John Dewey was becoming a familiar name in almost every American household.

However much Dewey was emerging as a figure of national stature, his ideas did not become any less radical. Nor did Dewey mind being associated with the radical movement and its most extreme activists. Constitutionally avid for social change, Dewey showed little caution in those heady years when social revolution seemed a near reality. It was only with the First World War, which divided the ranks of the radical movement and clarified the magnitude of the issues at stake, that Dewey retreated, and then only slightly. He came to realize that, for all his advanced views and love of change, he was temperamentally unable to dwell on anything remotely resembling a radical fringe.

One cause that Dewey embraced with no reservations was woman suffrage, a movement most of his academic colleagues watched from the sidelines with some nervousness. In the era of the "new woman" Dewey was an old feminist. Indeed, he showed none of the prurience or ambivalence that characterized the responses of many radical men to feminism. Few Dewey scholars dwell on the fact, but feminism was one of Dewey's most deeply held beliefs. Feminists of the 1980s would find Dewey's views on women's issues remarkably familiar.

The term *feminism* implies more than an acceptance of women's equality; it requires a political commitment to realizing that equality as an inviolable principle. This was exactly where Dewey stood. Perhaps because he was raised by a strong-minded and independent mother, Dewey was never threatened by strong women; he had no difficulty accepting his wife Alice as an equal and freely admitted her great influence on him. In fact, as we have seen, he credited women—most notably his wife, Jane Addams, and educator Ella Flagg Young—as the most important figures in his development. Not W. T. Harris, G. Stanley Hall, Francis Parker, George Morris—not George Herbert Mead or William James—but three women. This is remarkable in itself. But Dewey went further. He experienced the political awakening that is essential to feminism. Writing to longtime correspondent Scudder Klyce in 1915, Dewey explained how he had come to see that he had long been what he described as—in language that would be strikingly familiar to modern feminists—a "hog" when it came to taking women seriously. His description is worth quoting at length:

If you ever have the fortune to hear some clear headed and honest women . . . express their opinions about men as a "class" you will find that they agree that men are essentially hogs—and that the worst of it is [men] haven't the slightest idea of the fact, since what they hog are intangible things—in other words they assume that *their* work is the really important thing in the world. Till my attention was called to it I am bound to say that I had always assumed that, and I don't think I have ever met a man who didn't practically say to himself, "Why of course it is. How funny that anybody should question it." If that isn't being a hog I don't know what it is.[16]

In writing to Klyce, Dewey realized that his correspondent was unlikely to have such an awakening and stated, "Now all this sex treatment is mostly a matter of experience and you won't see it till you do happen to see it."[17] So Dewey understood that a real commitment to feminism entails almost a conversion experience, which he himself underwent. He felt free to admit that he had met several women superior in intelligence to "almost any man" he knew. He expressed particular admiration for the way women think:

I have never met a man, no matter how much more he knew of something than I did, that I couldn't see how he did it intellectually. . . . In other words, his mind was essentially of the same order of my own. Only women have ever given [me] really intellectual surprises; I'll be damned if I can see how they do it— but they do. Their observations . . . are more honest than men's— they are much less easily imposed upon; and they are more willing to face the unpleasant side of facts.[18]

If this passage suggests a slightly starry-eyed admiration for women, it is balanced by Dewey's fierce advocacy of women's right to enter professions often closed to them. He wrote to Klyce that he found the current division of labor "historic, conventional" and that "the only way to find the real balance of division of labor is by experimenting":

Take law for example. . . . If you can give a fair quantitative estimate of how the prevailing type of law and lawyers is due to the absence of women, you can do more than I can, but I should put it well above 50 percent. In other words, you can't tell how women would humanize the profession. . . . Do you regard business as

balanced now, or is desire for pecuniary profit much greater than
the element of service? How about politics? Now since these ex-
balances coincide with an enforced occupational position of
women there is a fair bet that there is a connection—anyway, we
shan't know and get a free equilibrium until there has been a lot
of experimenting.[19]

In writing of the influence of feminist Charlotte Perkins Gilman
on his thinking, Dewey noted that Gilman was not as widely accepted as she should have been because avenues open to men
had been closed to her: "If she were a man, she would have had
a better technical training and become a specialist and won great
reputation and praise."[20]

Dewey's expressions of his feminist beliefs in his letters to
Klyce were of course made in personal correspondence. But in
public forums he was no less outspoken. In supporting the establishment of an Equal Franchise Society at Columbia, Dewey suc-
cinctly told the *New York Times:*

> The chief argument for woman suffrage is that it is necessary to
> make an argument at all. If it were not for a false mental standard,
> woman suffrage would be so axiomatic that, except that it meant
> justice, social unity, and co-operation, nothing would be said about
> it at all.[21]

In a 1911 symposium on woman suffrage Dewey was asked
whether a woman's moral standing should affect her right to
vote. Of course not, responded Dewey. "There is enough of a
double standard of morality now. When a man's 'moral standing'
affects his right to vote, it should also affect a woman's—not till
then."[22]

Dewey scholars have tended to minimize Dewey's feminism or
write it off as another mild eccentricity—a favorite anecdote among
Deweyans is his marching in a Fifth Avenue suffrage parade
carrying a placard that asked "Men can vote! Why can't I?" and
his bewilderment at the amused smiles of the spectators. In fact,
however, Dewey brought to the feminist movement the courage,
conviction, and high seriousness he brought to most social causes
in these years.

The courage of Dewey's convictions during this period was
remarkable; for as his position as a public figure grew, he laid
himself more open to criticism for his involvement in often-

unpopular causes. One representative incident occurred when Maxim Gorky visited the United States in 1906. The arrival of the Russian revolutionary author was eagerly anticipated in literary and political circles, with Mark Twain and William Dean Howells planning receptions and the White House arranging a meeting with Theodore Roosevelt. (The visit, it should be added, was eagerly awaited in downtown circles as well, as Jewish intellectuals and the Yiddish press excitedly passed along news of the arrival of this countryman and political visionary.) But others were more cautious in extending welcome to this political radical. They found their fears confirmed when in the days following Gorky's arrival rumors began to circulate that the woman with whom he was traveling, Madame Andreeva, was not his wife. Clarification of the matter—divorce was almost impossible to obtain in Russia, and Gorky's alliance with Andreeva was long-standing and stable—was to no avail. The literary receptions and White House meeting were canceled. Gorky was denounced in the press as an advocate of free love, with disastrous practical consequences: The couple were thrown out of their hotel, and then, when they moved to another and still another, out of all three on the same day.

Radical sympathizers swept the couple off to a residence on Staten Island, but publicity continued to hound them; they retreated to a cabin in the Adirondacks. It may well have been the Dewey summer home in Hurricane, New York. For Dewey—always tolerant of those whose behavior was at odds with conventional social mores—had immediately extended an invitation to Gorky and Andreeva, a move that excited equally prompt censure. Max Eastman wrote, "Dewey in turn was violently attacked for this magnanimity, so violently that he seemed for a time in danger of losing his job." Indeed, Dewey had held his Columbia job for less than a year, and his invitation to Gorky must have seemed an inauspicious beginning to university observers. Throughout the attacks on the Deweys, wrote Eastman, "Mrs. Dewey stood behind him like a rock. 'I would rather starve and see my children starve,' she said between clenched teeth, 'than have John sacrifice his principles.'"[23]

The same year, 1906, saw Dewey again fighting for principles, involved in a social experiment that sought to put into practice some of his more unconventional ideas. The incident until now has remained little known, perhaps because it brought Dewey a little too close to the radical fringe.

In its November issue, the staid organ of philanthropy *Charities and the Commons* announced the opening of the Helicon Hall Colony, an experiment in cooperative living set up on the grounds of Helicon Hall, a stately mansion, once a boys' school, located between the town of Englewood, New Jersey, and the Hudson River. The mastermind of the venture was Upton Sinclair, the socialist author of the muckraking best-seller *The Jungle.* The colony's opening announcement detailed plans to build a number of cottages around the main hall, which would be used for community purposes and the cooking and eating of both vegetarian and meat meals. The names and credentials of the cooks and child care workers were announced, along with those of the manager—Anna Noyes, the wife of a professor at Teachers College (and the woman with whom Sinclair was having an affair[24])—and the directors—Edwin S. Potter, "of the Universal News Analysis," and "Prof. John Dewey, of Columbia."[25]

How Upton Sinclair approached Dewey and gained his ear is not known. But that he did so successfully is not surprising. Sinclair's venture attracted many prominent radical thinkers: Charlotte Perkins Gilman, William James, and George Bernard Shaw were early visitors. Among the residents were the novelist Grace MacGowan Cooke, Columbia professor William Pepperell Montague, drama critic Edwin Bjorkman, as well as two Yale students attracted by the publicity—future novelists Allan Updegraff and Sinclair Lewis.

Publicity the venture received—and along with it censure and, ultimately, derision. The Helicon Hall Colony was launched as an earnest social experiment, and for a time the atmosphere was exhilarating. One resident remembered the "Talk, talk, talk!" that went on among the "socialists, intellectual anarchists, single taxers, vegetarians, spiritualists, mental scientists, Free Lovers, suffragists, and other varieties of Ism-ites" who populated the place. "Lecturers and writers on Sex, on Sociology, on Anarchism, on Dress Reform, Child Training, Vegetarianism, Fletcherism, Socialism, and all the other modes and manifestations of the restless mind of the age" passed through Helicon Hall.[26]

The press found the colony, like Gorky's American visit, a natural target and began hinting broadly at Sinclair's "love-nest."

This kind of publicity attracted less-than-purely motivated radicals; one cloudy incident involving a drunken middle-of-the-night visit by the Japanese-German poet-painter Sadakichi Hartmann, the sculptor Jo Davidson, and an unidentified female companion created a considerable scandal. Headlines like "Helicon Hall Has Taken to Bloomers" began to appear; when the hall was nearly destroyed by a fire that took one resident's life the press in effect closed down the venture.[27]

The extent of John Dewey's involvement in the Helicon Hall Colony is difficult to calculate. He doesn't seem to have remained as a "director" for very long. But Upton Sinclair writes that he visited "frequently," and he describes a wonderful incident involving Dewey, William James, an unnamed woman, and a Ouija board. As the three sat over the board, the woman's hand moved and spelled out the sentence "Providence child has been carried to bed." The group puzzled over how to interpret the message; but a colony member who had a business in Providence, Rhode Island, took it to mean that he should call home. When he did so and learned one of his children had pneumonia, Dewey and James were exultant.[28]

Although it would be wrong to claim the Helicon Hall Colony experience as a central one in John Dewey's life, it was in many ways a typical one. At first formally associated with the colony, Dewey is on record only as a visitor, and he never spoke about the project afterward. The same pattern marked his involvement in other ventures whose potential eccentricity was realized, as well as his involvement with Anzia Yezierska.

Some of Dewey's friendships with young radicals were not so publicized as his association with the Helicon Hall Colony. His friendship with Carlo Tresca—a well-known "swarthy, bearded foreigner" and anarchist with scant knowledge of English, who was the lover of Elizabeth Gurley Flynn—was remembered by his contemporaries but nowhere documented.[29] About others, however, he often spoke publicly. He called Emma Goldman "a romantically idealistic personality and a highly attractive personality," defending her by saying "her reputation as a dangerous woman was built up entirely by a conjunction of yellow journalism and police raids."[30]

On the other hand, Dewey formed three deep and lasting friendships with men who were genuine eccentrics, friendships that bewildered and disturbed his colleagues and continue to trouble Dewey scholars today. F. Matthias Alexander, Albert Coombs Barnes, and Scudder Klyce—all three so addled that they could not be said to be politically either this or that—were as important to Dewey as his family, his professional colleagues, and such well-respected disciples as Randolph Bourne, Waldo Frank, and Max Eastman.

Dewey met the Australian F. Matthias Alexander in 1916, probably through the Columbia historian James Harvey Robinson. Dewey was plagued by eye and neck problems, and Robinson convinced him that Alexander had a unique new method for treating such troubles. Alexander seems to have been an early chiropractor, and, like many of his modern-day copractitioners, his practice borrowed from popular psychology and philosophy. He set forth his singular ideas on human well-being in his *Man's Supreme Inheritance: Conscious Guidance and Control in Relation to Human Evolution in Civilization* (1910), in whose preface he predicted that the work would grow from one volume to twelve, like Frazer's *Golden Bough*.

Alexander's approach demanded a complete "re-education of the individual" in the processes of breathing and posture, so that the "whole organism" would be used in such a way that the mental and physical realms were not distinct. What appealed to Dewey may have been the system's promise to heal over the old dualisms that so troubled him, especially the old dualism between mind and body. In an introduction to the 1918 reprint of Alexander's book, Dewey describes the method as solving "the crisis in the physical and mental health of the individual produced by the conflict between the functions of the brain and the nervous system on one side and the functions of digestion, circulation, respiration and the muscular system on the other."[31] Later Dewey described his early sessions with Alexander; each one was "a laboratory experimental education"—which must have appealed to him—at which he was "an inept, awkward, and slow pupil." In fact, Dewey found it

the most humiliating experience of my life, intellectually speaking. For to find that one is unable to execute directions . . . in doing such a seemingly simple act as to sit down, when one is using all the mental capacity which one prides oneself upon possessing, is not an experience congenial to one's vanity.[32]

In a typical session, held in Dewey's office or home, Alexander ran his patient through a series of hand-eye coordination, breathing, and posture exercises. The picture is slightly poignant: the aging Dewey submitting to a "humiliating" sequence of activities designed to make him unlearn old habits of posture and breathing and learn new ones in their place. He probably sought more than relief from eyestrain or neck pain—rather, he must have hoped he could gain from his friend and healer a second chance at life, a whole new way of being. At any rate, Alexander's "treatments" brought Dewey immediate relief and, he felt, permanent improvement. "I used to shuffle and sag," he said. "Now, I hold myself up." He told Max Eastman that this was why he never looked old, for which he gave 10 percent credit to "a regular physician who taught him how to keep things moving through the alimentary canal" and 90 percent to Alexander.[33] For his daughter's "official" biography, Dewey provided the following statement:

> My theories of mind-body, of the coördination of the active elements of the self and of the place of ideas in inhibition and control of overt action required contact with the work of F. M. Alexander and in later years his brother, A. R., to transform them into realities.[34]

What is remarkable is not that Dewey turned to an alternative "healer" in seeking to cure his physical woes—though his doing so does suggest that he might have been in the throes of a so-called midlife crisis—but that he credited Alexander as a philosopher whose ideas contributed to his own intellectual development. He took Alexander very seriously, often to the discomfiture of his friends; once, for example, he refused to write any further for the *New Republic* unless something was done about Randolph Bourne, who had recently published a negative review of an Alexander book in the magazine.[35]

Dewey's friendship with millionaire art collector Albert Coombs Barnes was of an entirely different order, though Barnes too was decidedly eccentric. Barnes introduced himself to Dewey in 1917 and became a member of his seminar on "Ethics and Educational Problems." A colleague later remembered that

Barnes would sit in the front row and promptly fall asleep, often remaining asleep through the closing bell, in which case Dewey would turn and smile at him and go out the door, leaving Barnes sleeping soundly.[36] This seminar marked the beginning of a life-long friendship. The closeness between the two men is not easy to explain—they were almost absurdly mismatched—and the light shed on Dewey by the length and depth of their friendship is not altogether flattering.

Albert Barnes made his fortune at the turn of the century by inventing Argyrol, a replacement for the silver nitrate that was routinely used on the eyes of newborn babies to prevent conjunctivitis, after which he turned to collecting art. In 1924 he established the Barnes Foundation to administer his almost unsurpassed collection of modern French art, located near his home in Merion, Pennsylvania; he named his friend John Dewey the foundation's educational director. The public was avid to see the collection, and Barnes thoroughly enjoyed dictating who could or could not get in; novelist James Michener described how he tried three times to storm the doors, succeeding only when he posed as an "illiterate young steelworker." Inexplicably, in the space of a month Barnes granted Greta Garbo admission and then denied it to a rajah. His letters to those seeking admission were often signed with his dog's name; he denied admission with fanciful excuses, telling one applicant that the foundation was occupied in selecting the shapeliest debutante and could not receive visitors at that time. He particularly delighted in denying admission to Jewish applicants, writing them nasty replies filled with anti-Semitic jibes. Bertrand Russell once claimed that Barnes set up the foundation in order to keep people from seeing the pictures in it.[37]

Barnes was by all accounts a strange man. A contemporary magazine profile described his common mode of dress: "At home and about the grounds his favorite garb is a pair of bright-red Breton fisherman's pants, a blue-and-red plaid shirt and a blouse."[38] But Barnes was more than a harmless eccentric who dressed in funny clothes. He was vitriolic, ribald, obnoxious, and racist. Few could understand Dewey's relation to the man. Dewey once tried to persuade Barnes to leave the art collection to Sarah Lawrence College; to that end, he introduced Barnes to the college president, Harold Taylor. Taylor later remembered that "about a day and a half of abuse" from Barnes convinced him that the deal could not be made. But Dewey continued to make extraordinary efforts: "[Dewey] could not understand that the man himself was so difficult that it would be impossible for anyone but Barnes himself to take that Collection into immortality."[39] (Taylor was right; at this writing, the collection is legally public, but one must apply in writing to visit on specified days and under strict conditions, including dress codes.)

Fellow philosopher Sidney Hook recalled vividly how Dewey used to apologize for Barnes; Dewey explained to his friends that Barnes was so obnoxious because he had an inferiority complex. As Hook wrote, "Every time Barnes got into a scrape as a result of browbeating, insulting, or cheating someone, he dragged Dewey into it." According to Hook, Albert Coombs Barnes was John Dewey's most "serious shortcoming."[40]

What could Dewey possibly have seen in the man? He seems to have listened to Barnes first because Barnes flattered him; Barnes had read *Democracy and Education* with enthusiasm and had tried to apply its principles in his Argyrol factories (a touch that would particularly have appealed to Dewey). And, too, Barnes had much to offer the educator from rural Vermont. Barnes was a self-taught connoisseur of art; Dewey, who knew little about the subject but who had a decided aesthetic impulse, must have seen in Barnes an appealingly unintimidating guide. Barnes introduced Dewey to a whole new world, escorting him to the Village to see Ida Rauh act with the Provincetown Players and, in 1926, taking him to the museums of Madrid, Vienna, and Paris, Dewey taking avid notes the whole time (though he fell asleep when Barnes was talking about Raphael at the Prado).[41] Few doubt Barnes's influence on Dewey's developing philosophy of aesthetics, which he was to articulate in his *Art As Experience* (1934). In the book's introduction he acknowledged Barnes as a "chief factor" in shaping his thinking.

Some light is shed on their friendship by the fact that they met in 1917, a year that marked an emotional watershed in Dewey's life. And, too, their relationship was cemented by Barnes's certain knowledge of Dewey's relationship with Anzia Yezierska that year. It was a time when Dewey was especially vulnerable. Barnes biographer Henry Hart claims a simple explanation for the friendship between the two men: At the time of their meeting,

Dewey needed friends. "[Dewey's] children were grown," Hart wrote, "and his wife was no longer much of a companion. Dewey needed the sort of friend Barnes became as much as Barnes needed him."[42]

Indeed, Dewey's susceptibility to eccentrics was particularly apparent in the years preceding the First World War. Always ready to listen to new ideas, Dewey tried to ease his growing isolation by entertaining all kinds of eccentrics and visionaries. Of course, the war in and of itself was immensely troubling. Dewey's decision to support U.S. entry was a painful one, and it caused him the disapproval and sometimes cost him the friendship of many friends and colleagues. And, in these years, the private life of this public man was very troubled.

In 1915 Dewey had made the acquaintance of one of the oddest figures of the century, self-proclaimed "logician and mathematician" Scudder Klyce. Klyce struck up what was to be a voluminous and stormy fifteen-year correspondence with Dewey, introducing himself thus:

> For several years I have been searching for *definitely* competent living philosophers. James was all right; but he died before I got ready to say anything. . . . I have just discovered, by reading your "Influence of Darwin on Philosophy and Other Essays," that you are, in a curiously novel way, probably the most competent living philosopher I have found, out of the number I have read.[43]

What Klyce really wanted was help in finding a publisher. But in the same letter he engaged in a long, highly technical discussion of the "One and the Many." That Dewey should have responded to Klyce's lengthy (often twenty-odd pages long), highly technical, and closely typewritten letters can be explained not only by Dewey's receptivity to almost all ideas, however eccentric, but also by his susceptibility to his correspondent's personal attention. For Klyce constantly analyzed the quality of Dewey's mind, often critically and very aptly, as when he wrote that he saw Dewey as a "humorist," not unlike Mark Twain, "who keeps the whole gamut of feeling, from tragedy to comedy, in your grasp."[44] Also, Klyce often sent out signals that could be construed as "dares"; when he announced, early on, that he would no longer presume on Dewey's time as the two disagreed so fundamentally on philosophy, Dewey responded with three highly technical letters, Klyce-like in length, and the correspondence resumed.

Klyce's first book, which he typeset himself (a process he describes to the reader in his introduction, along with a description of some typographical symbols he felt it necessary to create to explain his more complex ideas) was called simply *Universe*; it explained, quite simply, everything. Klyce probably knew he was crazy; in one passage to Dewey regarding *Universe*, he explained,

> The tone of the book is, like myself, pathological,—at least from the point of view of the average man: not from mine. Personally, I can stand experience without perceptible damage that would almost kill the average man: I have always been called "crazy": I dislike the term, as I heartily dislike being perceptibly different from the average, but the term simply means that I am rather energetic nervously or mentally, and I suppose I have to admit that it is a fact.[45]

Dewey willingly provided an introduction for Klyce's book, but his letters to Klyce often included cautionary notes like the following:

> But when you say the things you do . . . about the human race being a disturbance in the difference surface &c, and about moving the position of the earth by getting electric reaction &c, it sounds just plumb crazy to me.[46]

There is no doubt Dewey took Klyce very seriously for a time, and their discussions touched on matters very close to Dewey. We have already seen that Dewey discussed his views on women with Klyce at length. At times Klyce complained about such matters as Dewey's lack of emotion, and Dewey responded freely. In 1915, for instance, he wrote, "I have been educated in social rather than physical terms (a onesidedness I regret but am too old to rectify)."[47] At another point he acknowledged that he often found himself obscure.[48] Indeed, at one point Dewey confessed, "I have written myself out to you, even if briefly and too carelessly, more than I have put myself on record anywhere."[49]

Probably it was just such candor that led to their falling out. As early as 1927, Dewey wrote, "I am regretfully forced to the conclusion that there is nothing worth while in substance to be gained for either of us in continuing our correspondence along past and present lines.''[50] But Dewey was not to get off quite so easily.

Klyce began to entertain the notion of publishing their correspondence, and, when Dewey flatly refused, Klyce sought legal advice. Dewey was forced to reply at length, and his reply is illuminating as to what he sought and found in his eccentric friendships:

> The real reason I refuse to have my letters published is that aside from the fact that they were written with no idea of publication I bore so impatiently with your extravagances that I have laid myself open to a charge of supineness that would seem cowardly. It would appear to many that I should at an early date have cut the correspondence short in self-respect. I kept on because of genuine feelings of respect for qualities in you other than those manifested in your personal remarks, unconsidered though those were. I had and have no desire to have friendliness misconstrued into lack of self-respect.[51]

Klyce continued to hound Dewey until as late as 1932, insisting that Dewey had agreed to collaborate with him on a book on logic. In 1928 he felt the need to publish *Dewey's Suppressed Psychology,* again printed by his own hand. He reminded Dewey more than once that the Columbia Library had copies of it and, in 1929, when Milton Halsey Thomas published an author's query in the *New York Times* as part of his effort to assemble a definitive bibliography of Dewey's writings, Klyce wrote to him of the existence of the volume; Thomas thanked him kindly and made note of it.[52]

Dewey was slowly becoming aware of the consequences of his responsiveness to others, and eccentrics in particular, and his correspondence with Klyce reveals this quite starkly. It was a sad coming to consciousness on Dewey's part, and a painful one. A man who considered himself ''pretty sensitive to ideas,'' who acknowledged that ''the quality of my mind is sensitivity, responsiveness, rather than creativeness,''[53] Dewey relinquished his responsiveness with regret. But as a public figure of enormous influence, he could no longer expose himself to the radicals and eccentrics with whom he felt a natural affinity. He had been badly burned in the years of his correspondence with Klyce, not least by the equally intense Anzia Yezierska.

The year 1917 marked a watershed in Dewey's life. He was headed for a crisis. This man who had spent a good part of his career thinking about America and about immigrants now came into intimate contact with an immigrant woman. And 1918 saw him undertake his most sustained professional response to the immigrant, his study of a Polish-American community in Philadelphia. In both his public and private lives, his confrontation with America's immigrants was far more violent than the Dewey image—that of a temperate and cautious man—can accommodate.

It was Albert Coombs Barnes, peculiarly enough, who bankrolled Dewey's 1918 study of Polish Americans in Philadelphia, a study that represents the culmination of Dewey's official interest in immigrants and radical causes. Dewey claimed that he saw the project as a vehicle to study certain divisive forces in the Polish-American community. In the United States, Jewish and Catholic Poles were divided on certain political issues. The events of World War I appeared to leave the formation of an independent Poland wide open, and Jewish Polish Americans were avidly following the work of the Paris Committee, a group of conservative, anti-Semitic, and imperialistic Catholic Poles who sought to establish a new monarchy in Poland and set up close ties with a non-Bolshevik Russia. Many observers felt the Paris Committee did not represent the interests of Jewish Poles, who, for the most part, favored a more democratic, mildly socialistic organization of their homeland. In America, the Paris Committee was represented by the celebrated pianist Ignace Jan Paderewski and his wife. The Paderewski faction had been empowered to issue certificates to Poles they deemed loyal to the American war effort, which gave them considerable power in the immigrant community. Moreover, this faction favored the formation of a Polish army that all "non-assimilated"—by which they seem to have meant Jewish—Poles would be forced to join. And, finally, the conservative Paderewski faction controlled the Polish Press Bureau in Washington, thus effectively controlling what news about Polish affairs was available to non-Polish Americans. As the conservatives sought to consolidate their control, they called for a Polish congress to be held in Detroit, a convention that many observers, Dewey included, felt would not properly represent the views of all Poles in the United States. Dewey saw the Paderewski faction as extremely dangerous—"monarchical, representative of conservative economic interests and largely anti-Semitic."[54]

The study that Dewey conducted in Philadelphia was largely of Jewish Poles, and he addressed directly the conservative view that these Poles were "non-assimilated." His study of the conditions he saw among this group led him to respond in two ways: First, he published an article in the *New Republic,* seeking to correct the conservatively slanted view of Polish affairs that he felt the magazine's liberal readers received. Second, he published *Conditions Among the Poles in the United States,* which he later made available to U.S. Military Intelligence and the Wilson administration largely for the same reason—because he felt they were receiving biased information about the "loyalty" of Jewish Polish Americans. Dewey's purpose was to make public the views of the more radical faction of Polish Americans, a group—largely Jewish—he rightly saw as more representative of the majority.

The average Polish American's loyalty was, for Dewey, not at issue: "There is not the slightest doubt that the great mass of Poles in this country, including those who are nominally following the Paderewski-Smulski leadership, are firmly convinced of the importance of American leadership in the war and peace policies regarding Poland."[55] Polish-American loyalty was not even the subject of the study, as Dewey explained in describing what his report would cover:

> The *Report* begins with European conditions and then takes up American conditions as influenced thereby, and finally takes local, specific and immediate conditions among the Poles in America which have a bearing upon the disposition and morale of the Poles with respect to the war, in that they breed dissension and disturb the unity which is desirable for efficient prosecution of the war.[56]

Dewey was a firm supporter of the war effort and naturally saw that unity in any American immigrant group helped that effort. But his fundamental interest was the lack of unity among Polish Americans, brought about by the dominance of Paderewski's overly powerful conservative clique.

Considered in the context of Dewey's long career, the Polish study appears as a detour into rather arcane issues; because of his interest in the immigrant and his elemental concern for democracy, Dewey seems to have been sidetracked into a bit of nasty infighting. But because the *New Republic* article and the *Report on Conditions Among the Poles* are two of the most sustained and direct documents of Dewey's response to the immigrant (the third is Dewey's poetry to the young Jewish Pole with whom he fell in love), they deserve considerable attention.

In fact, Dewey's involvement in the Polish-American trouble has been subject to a prolonged and passionate attack by revisionist historians in recent years. His attackers have claimed that Dewey initiated the study with the express intent of testing the loyalty of Polish Americans, that the study was "undercover," that Dewey sought to "manipulate" the Poles, that his study was designed to ensure the maintenance of a cheap labor supply after the war, and that the study was conducted "for the War Department."[57] It seems unnecessary to enter into this debate in detail. But it is important to explain the argument of which this debate is a larger part—an argument about the motives of social reformers like Jane Addams and John Dewey, motives that their critics find questionable. Dewey's critics see him as committed to social control, and they take his response to the immigrant as typical of that commitment. As one historian writes:

> Dewey viewed ethnic and religious differences as a threat to the survival of society, to be overcome through assimilation. Dewey, as well as other reformers, was committed to flexible, experimentally managed, orderly social change that included a high degree of manipulation.[58]

One critic expanded the accusations, suggesting that Dewey, though a member of the NAACP, would probably have supported de facto segregation.[59]

The broad accusation of an aim of social control belongs to a debate that is not, properly speaking, historical. Any attempt at reform can be construed as an effort at social control; indeed, much reform often requires a degree of social control. The debate seems rather of a highly theoretical nature, requiring examination of what the implications of "study" and "reform" entail. Historically speaking, Dewey's response to the immigrant and his approach to reform took all his critics' concerns into serious consideration. Dewey found explicitly ideological Americanization efforts highly problematic, for instance, and he was deeply disturbed by such blatant attempts at "social control" as efforts to establish vocational education programs for students from working-class families.

Dewey's response to the immigrant was, of course, highly complicated, and the Polish study was in fact curiously motivated. But if we want to understand Dewey's response, then instead of turning to contemporary standards of judgment, we must examine it in the context of his personal crisis in these years. The Polish study appears in an entirely new light when we understand that Dewey undertook it when he was in love with a Polish Jewish immigrant. In fact, the members of the group that took up residence at 2007 Richmond Street, a small house on the edge of Philadelphia's "Little Poland," were the members of John Dewey's 1917–1918 seminar on "Ethics and Educational Problems." In his *Report on Conditions Among the Poles* Dewey describes the group and their assignments:

> Brand Blanshard, religious convictions and the activity of the church; Miss Frances Bradshaw, educational conditions, including both public and parochial schools; Mrs. A. Levitas, conditions affecting family life and women; Mr. Irwin Edman . . . general intellectual, esthetic and neighborhood activities . . . [and later] conditions as affected by international politics.[60]

"Mrs. A. Levitas" was, of course, Anzia Yezierska, whose impetuous appeal to Dewey six months earlier had led to an intimate relationship between them. By the time "Mrs. A. Levitas" was appointed to study family and women's issues among Dewey's group of Jewish Poles in Philadelphia, John Dewey and Anzia Yezierska were in love.

# 6

## *John Dewey in Love*

By 1917, Anzia Yezierska had set higher goals for herself than a teaching career; a fledgling writer, she had become a tireless self-promoter, well-used to storming the offices of powerful men. But she approached John Dewey's door in November 1917 on a rather mundane mission; she sought his help in securing a better teaching position, one that would give her the security she needed in order to write. She immediately sensed, however, the implicit drama of the scene; she was a working girl in search of a savior, and she believed she would find one in the man inside the great office. The immigrant had come knocking at—or rather, was prepared to burst through—the office door of the man who she felt represented America itself.

She later described how she found beyond the door a man who was quite ordinary in appearance but who awakened in her a dream of what America and the immigrant could offer each other:

> His noble head and fine grey eyes contrasted strangely with a slip-shod appearance—clothes worn anyhow, pockets bulging with papers, tie crooked, often as not a boot-lace hanging. He looked like a small-town lawyer or tradesman, but [my] fanatic idealism made him the symbol of all [I] could never be. He was free of [our] sordid bondage for bread. He was culture, leisure, the freedom and glamor of the "Higher Life."[1]

All she could never be, Yezierska felt. From their first moment together she invested John Dewey with all the qualities she felt she lacked, all the avenues that were closed to her, all the possibilities of the promised land.

For Yezierska this was not a new pattern. She tended to look to any new acquaintance as a personal messiah, particularly if the friend was American-born. The fairy-tale marriage of her friend Rose Pastor had kindled her imagination about such encounters and, as she grew increasingly pragmatic in her struggle to get ahead in America, she saw in whose hands the reins of power lay. This was reflected in the language she used in addressing such new friends, which was dramatically intense, almost religious. To novelist Dorothy Canfield Fisher, Yezierska wrote that "God must have sent me to you to show me the way out of the prison of self."[2] To writer Mary Austin, she described the effect of their first meeting: "I walked away from you weeping. It was the first time an American woman spread for me a table in the wilderness and filled my cup with all she was and had."[3] To novelist Zona Gale she gushed, "I know why I sought you out— you are Vision—Revelation."[4] Her fiction too is filled with her discovery of such figures, teachers who finally understand her, women who spread out for her "bread and wine in the wilderness" (one of her favorite expressions), and, especially, native-born American men.

"The Miracle," a story written while Yezierska was involved with Dewey, suggests the desperate intensity that colored their encounter in his office in 1917; it is one of many stories with a Deweyan hero, but, as its title suggests, it ends in ecstatic union rather than disappointment. Sara Reisel, the heroine, comes to America from Poland, lured by the promise of love. "America is a lover's land," writes a recent immigrant to Sara's Polish villagers.[5] In America, however, she finds a life of hard toil and loneliness. Then she goes to her first night-school class. Looking at her teacher, she says to herself (echoing the language Yezierska used in addressing her native-born friends): "Here is a person! Here is America!"[6] And later, "My teacher was so much above me that he wasn't a man to me at all. He was a God."[7]

Sara is moved by her teacher's composure, his "high thoughts," and begs him to "teach [her] how to get cold in the heart and clear in the head like you are." The teacher—and here we can surely recognize Dewey—responds, "I am not so cold in the heart and clear in the head as I make-believe. I am bound. I am a prisoner of convention. . . . You are not repressed as I am by the fear and shame of feeling."[8] Sara hardly dares to hope that he might love her, but when the school term is over she writes a despairing letter to him. The miracle happens. The Deweyan hero professes his love:

> He put his cool, strong hand into mine. ''You can save me,'' he said. ''You can free me from the bondage of age-long repressions. You can lift me out of the dead grooves of sterile intellectuality. Without you I am the dry dust of hopes unrealized. You are fire and sunshine and desire. You make life changeable and beautiful and full of daily wonder.''[9]

These words Yezierska uses later in quoting a letter from the Dewey figure in her *Red Ribbon on a White Horse;* they seemed to her to represent the gist of his message to her accurately enough that she used them twice, just as she lifted a passage from Dewey's ''Nationalizing Education'' to put into the mouth of one of her Deweyan heroes in another story, and just as, too, she reproduced lines from his poetry in several of her books.

Dewey probably did, then, tell the striking young immigrant that to him she represented liberation from ''the bondage of age-old repressions'' and that she stood for not only ''fire and sunshine''—warmth and light—but desire itself. In fact, something profound was taking place in Dewey's emotional life, something quite difficult to characterize but unquestionably of extraordinary intensity. The sequence is this: What seems to have happened is that he responded to Yezierska's outrage over her treatment at the hands of the Board of Education by accompanying her downtown, where he watched her teach. He agreed that she was qualified. But by then she had shown him one of her stories—her best, as it happens, ''The Fat of the Land''—and he convinced her to put her energy into writing instead. Yezierska remembered that he said, ''I wish you well, but I don't wish you to be a teacher. Something creative, yes, but a teacher, no.''[10] He helped her materially, giving her the first typewriter she owned and later sending one of her stories to the *New Republic.* And, somewhere along the line, they began an intense and intimate relationship, a relationship that would entail for both great excitement, turmoil, and, finally, pain.

What drew the eminent philosopher and public figure to the struggling young immigrant? The question must be asked, though the mutual attraction does not seem surprising in light of their strong and complementary personalities. In 1917, Dewey was, as we have seen, a lonely man. He and his wife were no longer on affectionate terms—indeed, some of his friends compared Alice to Socrates' wife Xanthippe, that model of the nagging and unsympathetic mate. He was in the throes of a personal crisis as well, undone by the events of World War I, uncomfortable with his growing fame, wondering why his life had turned out as it had. At fifty-eight, it seemed that love was behind him, and he must have felt a deep sense of emptiness and regret. The evidence for this is in his love poetry to Yezierska.

A representative poem that speaks to the intensity of Dewey's feelings is his "Autumn," inspired not only by Yezierska's selection of October as the month in which she would celebrate her birthday, since she was ignorant of the actual date, but by the fact that, because of their ages, theirs would be a relationship of the "autumn" of their lives. Dewey describes her as "not spring's perilous daughter she/But child of fall, dear time of year."[11] In the last of three stanzas, he laments what he might have missed had Yezierska not come into his life:

> Had not rich fall her ripe fruit brought
> As proof of time's fulfillèd good
> Life's inner speech I had not caught.
> For how should I have understood
> Its final meaning missed?
>                                           (11–15)*

Dewey was not unaware that to others he seemed emotionally barren. Note, for example, his statement to Scudder Klyce in 1915: "I have been educated in social rather than physical terms (a onesidedness I regret but am too old to rectify.)"[12] Dewey's terms require translation; he was again speaking of the "separation of mind from body" that he had lamented so often in speaking of his life.

Dewey saw in Yezierska enormous potential, and not only to free him from the bondage of "age-old repressions." He saw union with her as healing over this split between mind and body, this most hated of dualisms. Intellectually, Dewey despised dualisms. His evolving pragmatism, which stemmed from his dissatisfaction with Hegel—who had once held out to Dewey the promise of a unified philosophy—led the philosopher in him to reject du-

---

*Line references given in this book refer to poems appearing in *The Poems of John Dewey*, Jo Ann Boydston, ed.

alisms on formalist grounds. The social critic in him saw dualisms as predemocratic and prescientific, archaic in every way. In Dewey's view, ancient Greek life, for instance, was based on dualisms: the differences between master and slave, knowledge as contemplation and knowledge as practical activity. The dualism between thought and action was Dewey's intellectual bugbear. Dewey scholar Morton White directs us to look up "dualism" in the index to Dewey's *Democracy and Education*, where we will find "a garden of *versuses*."[13]

But Dewey's hatred of dualisms was emotional as well. Here we must refer again to a key passage in his autobiographical essay "From Absolutism to Experimentalism," in which he spoke of the consequences of his New England upbringing:

> . . . the sense of divisions and separations that were, I suppose, borne in upon me as a consequence of a heritage of New England culture, divisions by way of isolation of self from the world, of soul from body, of nature from God, brought a painful oppression—or rather, they were an inward laceration.[14]

Dewey resolved for himself such issues as the isolation of nature from God, and perhaps even of self from world, but the isolation of soul from body always held for him a special poignancy. His view of this isolation clearly referred, ultimately, to sexuality. He viewed himself as one who led the life of the mind and who was denied healthy physicality. Passion, he felt, was beyond him, behind him, inaccessible to him. And passion was exactly what Anzia Yezierska represented and offered.

Time after time in her fiction Yezierska creates Deweyan lovers who "think with the head rather than the heart." The phrase was almost a code between them. Dewey alluded to it in "Two Weeks," his most sustained treatment of their relationship:

> *I am overcome as by thunder*
> *Of my blood that surges*
> *From my cold heart to my clear head—*
> *So at least she said—*

(43–46)

In 1920, when all was over between them, Yezierska persuaded *The Bookman* to let her review Dewey's four-year-old *Democracy and Education*. She took revenge on her former lover by using the head/heart code against him, asking rhetorically, "Can it be that

Professor Dewey, for all his large, social vision, has so choked the feelings in his own heart that he has killed in himself the power to reach the masses of people who think with the heart rather than with the head?"[15] Dewey to her was the cold "head," she the warm "body."

Both Dewey and Yezierska were aware that sexuality and sexual repression were at issue. Dewey had heard of Sigmund Freud's work, then enjoying considerable vogue among American intellectuals. He must have recognized certain clear parallels between his dilemma and Freud's monumental work on human drives, the psychic structure of the mind, and such psychoanalytic principles as that of repression. Dewey's thinking was in many ways antithetical to Freud's. Always looking toward the future rather than the past, he believed in the fundamental changeability of human nature.[16] But both men were tolerant and open-minded; though Dewey never commented on Freud's work, Freud stated that he considered Dewey one of the few great men of his time.[17] The author of a poem called "My Body and My Soul," who could write of "One love that high is and other that is low" (2), Dewey understood full well the notion of repressed desires, of the determinism of early experience. One remarkable poem, "Across the white of my mind's map," expresses his vividly conceived obsession with his own repressed emotional frigidity. He describes the equator as a belt across his mind's map, a belt drawn by the sun

> Around the bulging girth
> Of my hot swollen earth
> Where desert sand waves vainly lap
> To quench a heat they but swallow
> As fire after fire doth ceaseless follow.
> Thy mists benign, expelled my soul,
> Fly to the frozen pole
> Where rains that should have healed,
> In ice are soon congealed.
>
> . . . . . . . . . . . . . . . . . . . . . . . . . .
> So let it be till judgment day shall roll
> The spread out heavens as a scroll,
> And fervent heat dissolve away
> The loins of fire and head of grey.
> (4–12, 17–20)

Dewey describes himself as the earth, swollen and hot, split by an equator, feverish below and icy above—warm in the heart, or sexual body, and cold in the head. And the "fervent heat" from below—the passion that he feels—will dissolve away even his "head of grey," his relative old age.

Dewey saw in Yezierska a warm and vibrant source that could potentially transform even his cold, tightly drawn, and inhibited world. The philosopher Sidney Hook, who of Dewey's colleagues perhaps understood him best, once commented on Dewey's nature:

> His speech and judgments were so deliberate and qualified that they suggested a mass of inhibitions and repressions. Yet he himself was always impressed—and sometimes too much so—by the spontaneous, colorful, unguarded expressions of emotion.[18]

Yezierska was nothing if not a spontaneous, colorful, unguarded expression of emotion, and Dewey as surely responded.

Another, untitled, poem of Dewey's suggests that he felt that he had within him the stirrings of desire, or passion, and that Yezierska could awaken them. The poem begins,

> *There stirred within me*
> *The ghosts of many a love*
> *Some that had passed in birth,*
> *Some that I had murdered,*
> *And some that had feebly spent themselves*
> *In vain yearning for the light of day.*
>
> (1–9)

As the poem progresses, the "ghosts" of his buried love speak, and tell him not to let their "sister" into "this sepulcher." They give as their reason the beloved's potential to bring them alive: "For all we might have been/Eternally is she" (36–37).

Yezierska's fiction takes a parallel tack. She is not always reliable, of course, but when she produces documents—poems, for example—by the Dewey figure we have some assurance that they represent paraphrases if not transcriptions. (She kept Dewey's letters for a time, relinquishing them only after his repeated pleas.) The autobiographical *Red Ribbon on a White Horse* is perhaps most reliable on the subject, as Yezierska originally identified Dewey by name in it, changing it only reluctantly at her friend Miriam Zunser's insistence.[19] In *Red Ribbon*, John Morrow, the Dewey figure, not only sends the heroine an excerpt from his poem "Generations" but includes with it a passionate letter:

> My life has been an evasion of life. I substituted reason for emotion, hiding behind a shell of safe abstractions. I've been so repressed. . . . I never knew how starved I was until I met you. I was sunk inside my little world of business and family front, petrified by the inertia of substance. You saved me from the barren existence of eat, sleep, and multiply. I must begin humbly, like a child, to learn the meaning of life from you. Without you I'm the dry dust of hopes unrealized. You are fire, water, sunshine and desire.[20]

Dewey saw in Yezierska a potential savior, as she did in him. In a passage in her 1932 novel *All I Could Never Be*, the Dewey figure uses many of the same turns of phrase in confessing his stifled feelings. To the heroine, he confides:

> You make me realize that I have never really lived. My life is an evasion from life. It is not only that I have the habits of generations of repression to overcome, but I have the paths beaten out in my brain by the many years of intellectualizing.[21]

This glorified version of Yezierska was especially attractive to Dewey in her promise of articulateness; he was genuinely moved by her ability to write. "Generations," one of the two poems we know he showed her, begins with admiration for her voice: "Generations of stifled words reaching out/Through you,/Aching for utt'rance (1–3). For Dewey, who had such trouble expressing himself, was moved by this muse to write poetry.

Dewey's poetry is not great verse; it is often sentimental and curiously Victorian in form. Though Dewey had much in common philosophically with his contemporaries, the literary modernists, he turned to traditional models in his poetic efforts. Many of his poems are marred by the strange abstractness that characterized his prose, and by his recourse to metaphors or tropes that can be described as knotty, at best, in their expression. When he addresses philosophical questions he is at his poetic worst. But the poems written in the flush of his love for Yezierska are often remarkable; his images are vivid, if not always easy to follow, and the intensity of his voice is so marked that it stylistically buoys even his more sentimental efforts. These poems are not abstract, not philosophical, but vital and often sensuous, the outpourings of a man wracked by emotions that were new to him and that he could not fully understand.

Dewey had been trying, off and on since 1910, to scribble bits of poetry about his children, his farm, and philosophical issues, and most of these efforts were negligible.[22] But he had been thinking about poetry as early as 1890, when, in an essay on Arnold and Browning, he took issue with Arnold's statement that poetry would replace philosophy. The spheres are not as distinct as Arnold's statement implied, Dewey wrote. The "present separation of science and art, this division of life into prose and poetry, is an unnatural divorce of the spirit." Revealingly, he lapsed into the language of dualisms, wounds, as he often did when the subject was one close to his heart:

> We must bridge this gap of poetry from science. We must heal this unnatural wound. . . . The same movement of the spirit, bringing man and man, man and nature, into wider and closer unity, which has found expression by anticipation in poetry, must find expression by retrospection in philosophy. Thus will be hastened the day in which our sons and our daughters shall prophesy, our young men shall see visions, and our old men dream dreams.[23]

Dewey had an impulse to the poetic, as the last sentence above should indicate. Yet he was reticent about it, shy, as if he felt it was inappropriate for a man of intellect. Waldo Frank, in a recent memoir, remembered: "He confided; yes, he wrote poetry of a sort. Oh no! it was not to be seen."[24] And, in the year that Dewey fell in love with Yezierska, he disingenuously disavowed his poetry in an article for *Seven Arts*; writing about the necessity of American intervention in the war, he wrote, "Were I a poet, this should be, even at the dangerous risk of comparisons invited, an ode. But, alas, the passion as well as the art is lacking."[25]

Nevertheless, in 1917, Dewey was full of the passion as well as the art, and poems poured forth from his pen. In "Two Weeks," the most sustained declaration of his love for Yezierska, Dewey reckons his poetic talents thus: "I told you my diet should be prose" (87). Yezierska apparently had praised Dewey's language: "You said my logic you could never grasp,/While my poetic words—thus you blessed them—/Would fall like manna on a hung'ring soul." But, the poet concludes, "These words of mine make no poesy. They rasp/Like the harsh divisions of my mind. . ." (96–100).

The poet returns, then, to the "divisions" in his mind, divisions that brought him to Yezierska but made him unable to remain with her. For a time, he allowed himself to give in, as the last stanza of "Two Weeks" indicates. The poet presents himself to his beloved in an honest light, taking critical inventory of himself:

> *Then take me as I am,*
> *Partly true and partly sham*
> *Not from wilful choice*
> *But by too ready acceptance*
> *Of the constraining work of chance,*
> *Here a blow to shape, there a luring voice*
> *To call. If I have not wholly stood*
> *Neither have I wholly bent.*
> *Just th'usual mixed up mess of bad and good*
> *I bring to you as it was sent.*
>
> (105–115)

When the relationship began, then, Dewey was doubtful and skittish. His poems document his worries and fears and his ultimate withdrawal. But for a time they record too his passionate involvement. In "Two Weeks" he thinks of his beloved and wonders, "Does she now think or write or rest?/What happens at this minute—it's just eight—" (25–26). He pictures her in his intimate mind's eye:

> *Whate'er, howe'er you move or rest*
> *I see your body's breathing*
> *The curving of your breast*
> *And hear the warm thoughts seething.*
>
> (30–33)

"Even in the tortured tangles of the tenement" (35), he writes, she has visions "Of a life that's free and bold" (36).

In *All I Could Never Be,* the heroine receives a letter from her lover that contains "Generations"—Yezierska reproduces the poem in her text—and that expresses the Dewey figure's great feeling for his beloved. The letter—which Yezierska also reproduces in full, and which sounds like Dewey's voice throughout—

expresses the lover's solicitude for Yezierska's health and for her worries about writing. The letter concludes:

> You are beautifully communicative in simply being. You *are,* but you don't yet fully know that you are. You feel as if you wanted to be. You suffer from striving, but it is unnecessary. *You are already.* And perhaps I can have the great happiness of helping you to a realization that *you are,* and *what you are.* You do not have to reach, or strive, or try to achieve or accomplish. You already are. I repeat it a million times to you, my dear spirit. It only remains for you to do, and in order to do what you need most is material, earthly food, comfortable surroundings. All things of the spirit are yours, now.[26]

Dewey and Yezierska both brought a mystical intensity to the relationship. For her part, Yezierska saw their potential union as her chance to lay claim to the New World. The dissolving of ethnic differences this love represented is a recurrent motif in her work. Over and over she created cold, rational, successful men— all clearly modeled on Dewey—who are initially attracted to the immigrant for her warmth and intensity. In each case, the heroine sees in this possible union the chance to "open up her world" to America, and to find a place for herself in America. "Are we not the mingling of two races? The oriental mystery and the Anglo-Saxon clarity that will pioneer a new race of men?" a Yezierska heroine wistfully hopes.[27] In *All I Could Never Be,* the heroine believes the Dewey figure is "the promise of the century. The ancient discord between Gentile and Jew crashing through into rarest harmony."[28] In *Red Ribbon on a White Horse* Yezierska writes, "Our need for each other burned away the differences between Gentile and Jew, native and immigrant—the barriers of race, class, education."[29]

To Dewey, Yezierska offered not only passion and a second chance at life but a personal introduction to the immigrant world that had commanded his interest for so long. Yezierska literally guided him through the immigrant Lower East Side. She took him to the Yiddish theater and to Yonah Schimmel's neighborhood kosher restaurant. Together, they ate baked sweet potatoes from a pushcart.[30] For a man who believed that knowledge came from doing, from experience, the notion that with Yezierska he could eat, drink, and feel the immigrant experience—and thus truly know it—was compelling indeed.

In one of his poems Dewey addresses Yezierska as "[that] frail ship I load with limitless freight/Of hopes and loves" (1-2). Yezierska and Dewey loaded each other with limitless freight. Their love *represented* so much—so much, in fact, that it was doomed from the start. No romance could sustain such idealism, such high hopes. Inevitably one partner used the other in some way, and terrible disillusionment was inevitable. What forced Yezierska and Dewey apart is as complex as what brought them together.

Numerous problems confronted Yezierska and Dewey in the course of their relationship. For a time, material obstacles loomed large. Dewey was, after all, a married man and a father—what single women often ruefully term "very married." It is unlikely that he ever contemplated leaving his wife (though Yezierska apparently liked to tell her friends that he might; her friend Miriam Zunser was alarmed at the imminence of this possibility[31]), but there is no question that his being married did not stop him from becoming deeply involved with Yezierska. In *Red Ribbon*, Yezierska meets the Dewey figure's wife and is briefly aware of how "unpossessable" her lover is:

> But I consoled myself. I knew him as neither his wife nor children could know him. They had his name, his money, his reputation, but I had something that fed his spirit. He could never share with his family the thoughts he shared with me. . . . In my dreams I felt myself more married to him than his wife, closer to him than his children.[32]

Dewey's poetry indicates that his marriage—the "silken web in which I'm bound,(7)" as he wrote in "I wake from the long, long night"—was a continued topic of discussion between them. "Two Weeks" opens with Dewey's declaration that Yezierska has not "rightly guessed" the ties that hold him. It is not riches and possessions that keep him from leaving his family, he says, but the fact that he does not own himself, that he belongs to those who have made him what he is, his wife and children. "Who makes, has. Such the old old law," he writes ruefully:

> *Owned then am I by what I felt and saw*
> *But most by them with whom I've loved, and fought,*
> *Till within me has been wrought*

*My power to reach, to see and understand.*
*Such is the tie, such the iron band.*
*What I am to any one is but a loan*
*From those who made, and own.*

(7–14)

Using similar language, *All I Could Never Be*'s Henry Scott says, "I am an old-fashioned Yankee puritan. I do not belong to myself—".[33]

Dewey's poetry is filled with imagery of imprisonment, ties, chains, and shackles that keep him from renouncing all for his new love. Tragically, most of the ties that held him were not material but emotional.

"Then there's that matter of youth and age," as Dewey wrote in "Two Weeks" (49). Dewey was fifty-eight to Yezierska's thirty-seven. "You say you have lived longer and most," Dewey addresses her in the same poem. True enough, acknowledges the poet, if one measures age by the depth of one's passions. But age brings "unnumbered diversity" that is a truer measure. Again, Dewey concluded that the age difference was an emotional barrier rather than a material one. He *felt* old—far older than his lover, and too old for passion.

Finally, as Dewey begins an untitled poem, "He failed/He was not strong enough" (1–2). Though numerous factors contributed to the romance's end, finally it was Dewey's failure. What his poetry documents is tragic emotional cowardice. For a time, he writes in the same poem, "his mind was eager, ardent for the fray" of involvement:

*Then sudden walls*
*closed in. The thorns were hands which smote*
*Him. Rocks melted. Paths were pitfalls;*
*The promised land swallowed in cloud.*

(11, 14–16)

In "The Round of Passion" Dewey describes how the sun itself— a metaphor for his soul—had been turned to cold barren wood by the "slow dull years." Suddenly, though, the sun's mystery flames again: "Consumed in flame/The old was young" (8–9). After the sun's flame soars, somehow, inexplicably,

*Sun moves remote—*
*All as before.*
*The weary way is trod.*

(14–17)

At times the poems move the reader to compassion, for Dewey's failure of nerve is almost heartbreaking. At other times they reveal his cowardice for what it is, and the result is contempt and, finally, pity. Sometimes he steps back from himself, and what he sees is pitiful even to him. In one remarkable poem, "Romance," Dewey presents himself as slightly ridiculous, an old man teetering on the precipice of passion. The poem evokes the whole gamut of emotional responses. The poet "tiptoed springily, standing still":

> Then he jumped.
> Not jumped but started, darted,
> Like a bird,
> Clean, sharply, upward.
>
> (7–10)

Hanging in the air, he comes to rest on a platform—his own shadow. Sailing on his shadow, he enters the world of romance, and it is wonderful:

> He sailed afield, abroad
> And saw new lands with
> Flames of flowers, where gay-plumaged birds
> Flashed fire in the sun.
> Below incense bearing trees
> Fair women loved
> And brave men endured.
>
> (27–33)

Then, suddenly, the platform breaks, and the poet falls down, down to where he was before. The last stanza presents a poignant picture of a man who has tried at romance and failed, and now is doomed to a prosaic and homely existence:

> Down
> Into his wonted room; some eight by twelve
> It was, with carpet, yes and wall paper too.
> His muscles ached. Dull and sore,
> Sullen he dressed and as he dressed
> He kicked his bed and chair,
> And swore.
> Swore stupid oaths, and squirmed to try

> *Each muscle, dull, aching, sore.*
> *At self and shoes and shirt,*
> *Composing one void but full of*
> *Pain and emptiness, he swore.*
> *About him miles of dull blur*
> *Stretched out into the rut worn*
> *Roads of Day.*
>
> (40–55)

The image is a vivid one, and the tone is elegiac. The body of Dewey's poetry to Yezierska is marked by nostalgia and regret. For Dewey knew his own failure, and the tragedy of it. In "Two Weeks" he writes ruefully,

> *Renounce, renounce;*
> *The horizon is too far to reach.*
> *All things must be given up.*
> *Driest the lips, when most full the cup.*
>
> (64–66)

The image is of a Tantalus doomed to the hell of the everyday, an eight-by-twelve carpeted and wallpapered room, his hunger and thirst eternally unsated.

However lyrical and romantic the relationship may have been, it went along its prosaic way. Appropriately enough, the best record we have of the quotidian relationship is Yezierska's prose, and specifically her *All I Could Never Be* (1932), whose plot borrows from her participation in Dewey's study of a community of Jewish Poles in Philadelphia. Using this text with discretion—recognizing Yezierska's idiosyncratic use of fact in fiction—in conjunction with the factual evidence and passages from Dewey's poetry, it is possible to reconstruct their encounter in some detail.

Dewey's poetry leaves the impression of a valiant struggle and subsequent failure. It does not document his real failure, his ultimate refusal to take responsibility for his actions toward a woman whose deepest feelings he had engaged. Dewey failed to live up to his own precepts and principles in the course of the romance by refusing to accept the consequences of his actions. The facts of the relationship present a necessary counterweight to his poetry; for, in fact, Dewey treated Yezierska very shabbily, a failing to which he makes no allusion in his poems.

The relationship began before Dewey enrolled her in his seminar at Columbia University in the fall of 1917, the same seminar Albert Coombs Barnes often used to sleep through. Other members were Dewey's top graduate students, all of whom went on to illustrious careers. Irwin Edman became the head of the Philosophy Department at Columbia and Brand Blanshard the head of that at Yale. Blanshard's brother Paul published influential works on Catholicism, and Margaret Frances Bradshaw (who later married Brand Blanshard) contributed to the philosophy of aesthetics and became dean of women at Swarthmore College. Among this group, writes Barnes's biographer Schack, Yezierska felt extremely out of place because of her lack of formal education and her usual feeling of alienation among native-born Americans; "agonizingly self-conscious in the presence of all the members of the seminar as beings of a higher order, of which their formal education was only one sign."[34]

At the same time, Yezierska drank deeply of the heady atmosphere of ideas and Dewey's enthusiasm for what she as an immigrant could contribute to American society. Henry Scott, the Deweyan professor in *All I Could Never Be*, waxes rhapsodic about America as a "symphony of nations."[35] He cites Michael Pupin, Edward Bok, and Charles Steinmetz as immigrant success stories. But already conflicts were developing between professor and pupil, as each tried to educate each other about America and the immigrant. Fanya, the heroine, scoffs at Scott's "symphony of nations," and to Scott's list of notable immigrant successes she cites "the millions who remain hands for the machines."[36]

The contrast between Yezierska and his other students must have emerged starkly to Dewey. Perhaps he was charmed by it for a time. But he was becoming close to another student, Albert Barnes, who was anti-Semitic and who, according to Yezierska's later recollection, "did not even regard me as a human being."[37] Their romance was at its height in December and January, when Dewey began to be beset by doubts.

In *All I Could Never Be*, Scott/Dewey goes on a business trip to Chicago, in part to sort out his feelings for Fanya, he confides to her. Records show that Dewey made two trips to Chicago, in December and January.[38] When Dewey returned, he resumed the affair with more caution. At this point in the novel, Scott/Dewey returns to her the letters she had written to him.[39]

But when Barnes proposed the Philadelphia study of Polish Americans, Dewey asked that "Mrs. Levitas"—with all the distance this decorous title allowed him—be included. So, when school let out in May, Yezierska was among the group who rented a small house at 2007 Richmond Street in Philadelphia, on the border of the city's "Little Poland." Like the others, she received what to her must have seemed the princely stipend of $100 a month. The group, for the time being under Barnes's supervision, set up housekeeping with enthusiasm and began mapping out their research. Their reading included—along with their "bible," Dewey's *Democracy and Education*—F. Matthias Alexander's *Man's Supreme Inheritance* (Dewey evidently felt good posture was important for research) and Wilfred Trotter's *Instincts of the Herd in Peace and War*, a study of psychology in everyday life.[40]

Dewey could not join the group until June. In his absence his students gossiped about "the chief," speculating, for instance, that Dewey's adopted son Sabino was actually his own child by an Italian peasant woman. In Yezierska's novel, one follower confides that she feels sorry for "the chief's" wife. They discussed the story of one professor's visit to the Scott/Dewey home, where he observed the father at play with his children: "He found the four of them sitting on top of him, playing he was their donkey. The kids never called him father, just plain 'Henry' and treated him as though he were a mat under their feet."[41]

For Yezierska the Philadelphia study began badly. From the first, her status was unclear; she was hired both to translate and, as Dewey's *Confidential Report on Conditions among the Poles* indicates, to study "conditions affecting family life and women."[42] Barnes's biographer Hart describes Yezierska and Frances Bradshaw as approaching women in their homes and in stores and getting responses of "uninterested tolerance."[43] There were quarrels about methods; Paul Blanshard seems to have been fired for distributing a questionnaire without the group's approval.

In *All I Could Never Be*, Yezierska orders events with a precision only possible in hindsight. She represents herself as resenting the group's "cold research methods" from the start, and presents the group as jaded intellectuals who make fun of the Polish Jews they are studying. The heroine defends the immigrants passionately to the group, urging them—incoherently, she realizes—to try to understand "her people." Then she finds a carbon of a letter from "the chairman"—who would be Barnes—to "the chief," complaining of her "overemotionalism" and her "persecution mania." Fanya's colleagues complain that she has not read the most basic works in the field—John Dewey, Emily Balch, and W. I. Thomas—and that her research is not "scientific." When Scott/Dewey arrives on the scene he comes to her defense, but the end is in sight. By the time the study is over, the Dewey figure is accusing the heroine of overemotionalism. He asks her repeatedly to return the letters he has written her, saying at one point, "Understand, this is a very delicate matter to me. Supposing this were found out." The heroine, heartbroken and bitter, agrees.[44]

What really happened? Yezierska's fictional version is persuasive, though it is colored by a certain cynical regret. What happened with the study and what happened with Dewey are two different questions. About the relationship we must finally rely on the artistic treatment Yezierska and Dewey give it, she in her fiction, he in his poems. But the study is fully documented, and the evidence helps set the episode in its proper context.

In retrospect, it is easy to dismiss the study of Jewish Poles as a paternalistic effort at social control, as revisionist historians have done. Yezierska would have been sympathetic to such a view. Certainly, as a Jewish emigrant from Polish Russia, she must have felt a divided loyalty in her work on the project. She was both of the people she studied and at the same time, by virtue of her education and, not least, her involvement with the great man himself, a member of a socioeconomic and educated elite. This kind of divided loyalty was to haunt her throughout her life. Ultimately, in considering the Polish study, she identified with the immigrants. But this was less because her deepest loyalties rested there than because she grew disillusioned with the study's methodology and, finally, with Dewey himself.

There exists an interesting document, a letter to the popular critic William Lyons Phelps, in which Yezierska explained why she felt she had to write her own version of the study in *All I Could Never Be.* She confided that when the study was over, the participants were all required to file a report. She had been unable to write one, and this failure "preyed upon [her] and tormented" her. The novel, she wrote, is that report, written fourteen years later. She explained to Phelps how she had "come in contact with a group of educators who were making a research study of the Poles," and how she, though "uneducated," was chosen as the interpreter for the "Ph.D. professors in sociology and education." She tried to articulate her sense of what was wrong with the study:

> The "scientific approach" of these sociology professors seemed to me so unreal, so lacking in heart and feeling. . . . At the end of the study, it seemed to me they knew less about the Poles than when they began. When they started out, they knew they didn't know, but after a few months investigation they had cut the Poles into little sections, which they pigeon-holed and tabulated into [sic] sociological terms. They began turning out reports that seemed to bring out to me the deep, unutterable gulf between the professors who were analyzing the Poles and the Poles who were being analyzed.[45]

Yezierska's complaint about the "scientific" is familiar; she hated scientific cookery, scientific charity, and scientific reform. But what she clearly hated most was being the subject of scientific study. For to be a subject in this way is precisely not to be a subject: One becomes an object, losing a speaking voice. It is no wonder that Yezierska's failure to file a report, to become a speaking subject, so preyed upon her.

In a Yezierska story written around the time of the study, "Wings," the immigrant heroine falls in love with a sociology professor. Yezierska names him John Barnes, taking the first name of her lover and the last name of the man who funded the Polish study. She writes, describing "Barnes's" reaction to the immigrant girl, with considerable irony,

> John Barnes, the youngest instructor of sociology in his university, congratulated himself at his good fortune in encountering such a splendid type for his research. He was preparing his thesis on the "Educational Problems of the Russian Jews," and in order to get into closer touch with his subject, he had determined to live on the East Side during his spring and summer vacation.[46]

The heroine senses that she herself is seen as "a splendid type" to be studied. Yezierska hated being a "specimen" under a sociological microscope.

In fact, it was worse than Yezierska thought. For Dewey and Barnes, observing the tensions in the little household on the edge

of Little Poland, saw a wonderful opportunity for further research. They decided to study the study. As the participants in
the study muddled through their problems in communicating
with the Polish community and drawing conclusions from what
they saw, Dewey and Barnes recognized a wealth of sociological
material. As Barnes's biographer Hart writes:

> [Dewey] and Barnes decided *they* would do some research on the
> researchers, tacitly observe what [the researchers] did, how they
> did it, what they didn't do (and their rationalizations therefor), and
> what effect, if any, they had on the Poles they were investigating.[47]

The results of their "research" are nowhere recorded, so we
can't know their real motivations. But the impression is one of
voyeurism in the name of research, of gross violation of the principles of research and, finally, of privacy.

The subject of a study—by definition an object—becomes somehow less than human. Yezierska became a specimen. John Barnes
in Yezierska's "Wings" is delighted by his good fortune in finding the immigrant heroine Shenah Pessah; but his was "the enthusiasm of the scientist for the specimen of his experimenta-
tion."[48] Again, Yezierska forced herself to confront the Deweyan
hero's interest for what it was: the scientist's enthusiasm for a
specimen.

Dewey's was also the enthusiasm of a collector. For specimens
are to be collected as well as studied. And Albert Coombs Barnes
taught his friend a great deal about collecting. Yezierska herself
was a "picturesque" immigrant who knew how to appeal to reformers and settlement house workers by presenting herself as
such. She clearly resented being a collectible (though she was not
adverse to using it to her advantage). As early as Hutchins Hapgood's 1902 *The Spirit of the Ghetto,* it was clear to many that capital could be made of the immigrants' novel charm, their eminent
collectibility. Randolph Bourne attacked Jane Addams for
"collecting" immigrants out of admiration for their "quaint customs."[49] The reformers inevitably left themselves open to such
charges. Though these objections overlook the real motivations
of the reformers, they are not entirely inaccurate, and Dewey was
as guilty as Hapgood or Addams on this score.

Yezierska's fiction repeatedly expresses her resentment at being "collected." In "Children of Loneliness" the heroine's lover

works at an East Side settlement house; his comment about his surroundings is, "It's so picturesque!" He tells the heroine, "I've found wonderful material for my book in all this. I think I've found a new angle on the social types of your East Side."[50] The heroine of *Arrogant Beggar* is attracted by Arthur Hellman, a wealthy WASP who views Adele as a refreshing change from his sterile existence. Adele complains, "I'm to you a slumming tour. A sensation."[51] Explaining why he has sought her out in the ghetto after she ran from him, he says, "You were romance. Personality. A personality so rich and colourful it would be joy to help in the making." The heroine recognizes his passion for what it is; Yezierska writes, "His eyes travelled over me with a glow of possession that stiffened me against him."[52] Adele knows better than to encourage him further.

Perhaps because she knew from Dewey himself how valuable a specimen she was, Yezierska often attributes to her Deweyan characters remarks that reveal the Dewey figure's attempt to "use" her as material or as a vehicle toward understanding. College president Irvine in "To the Stars" thinks upon meeting Sophie that "Here was a personality . . . who might reveal to him those intangible qualities of the immigrant—qualities he did not grasp, which baffled, fascinated him."[53]

The Deweyan hero's remarks about his collectible specimen all share a certain quality. They attribute to their immigrant lovers romance, warmth, emotion—indeed, passion. Just as Yezierska herself did for Dewey, her immigrant heroines offer to their lovers the chance to bring emotion and warmth into their barren existences. The heroine of "The Miracle" asks her American-born lover how she can learn to be as composed and calm as native-born Americans. The Dewey figure replies,

> But I don't want you to get down on earth like the Americans. That is just the beauty and the wonder of you. We Americans are too much on earth; we need more of your power to fly. If you would only know how much you can teach us Americans. You are the promise of centuries to come. You are the heart, the creative pulse of America to be.[54]

Emotion, or passion, implies sensuality and sexuality, and, indeed, Yezierska's heroes often endow their lovers with heightened sensuality, a rare exoticism, and eroticism. The immigrant heroine, in all her "oriental mystery," knows in her very nature secrets of the Orient, sexual mysteries. Yezierska was speaking to a long tradition of the male equation of the female ethnic with the erotic. America's first ethnic heroine, Pocahontas, has been endowed by all male purveyors of her legend—beginning with John Smith—with an otherworldly and heightened sexuality. From Pocahontas to Hawthorne's "dark ladies," from William Wells Brown's Clotel to Tina Turner, American ethnic women in cultural representation appear exotic and—especially—erotic.[55]

While this tradition allows the ethnic heroine a certain power, it also makes her dangerous. Yezierska's heroines are ultimately rejected by their WASP lovers for the very reason they were initially attractive. Their promised sexuality becomes too threatening. In *Salome of the Tenements*, which presents a portrait of a sexually unsatisfied immigrant wife, the heroine's sexuality finally repulses her husband, and he rejects her as vigorously as he would shake dirt from his clothes.

Whether Yezierska represented a threat to Dewey in this way is not clear, for she was too ambivalent about her sexuality to identify herself with raw eroticism. Like Dewey, Yezierska suffered from repressions and inhibitions of her own, but they were of a different order. Dewey reopened old childhood wounds—related, probably, to her rejection of her father and mother, which still caused her considerable pain and guilt. Loving men was complicated by her feelings for her own father. We can see this in a work like *Bread Givers*, in which Sara, the heroine, marries a man who accepts her father in a way she cannot. The father will live with the married couple, and Sara is relieved to have fulfilled her obligation to him. The book closes, however, on a bleak note. Sara's husband's grip tightens on her arm as they walk along. She feels a shadow still over her: "It wasn't just my father, but the generations who made my father whose weight was still upon me."[56]

Yezierska admitted that she associated Dewey with her father and remembered that she had shown him a copy of "The Lord Giveth," the story she felt best represented Bernard Mayer.[57] In *All I Could Never Be*, Henry Scott's Biblical phrasings remind the heroine of her own father. Like Scott's, her father's language was always colored with words from the Bible. For an instant, Henry Scott had a strange resemblance to him. Her feeling of familiarity shocked and amazed her. Absurd! Her father had lived . . . in the ghetto of Poland. This man a Gentile—an American. And yet, for all their differences, there was that unworldly look about Henry Scott's eyes that made her feel her father. Her father as he might have been in a new world.[58]

The association she made between her father and Dewey was strong enough to complicate her sexual response to Dewey. In her fiction Yezierska always clouds the physical details of their affair. There are vague indications of a scene on a pier in the shadow of the Williamsburg Bridge in which Dewey made some advance to which she could not respond. In remembering the relationship's physical aspect, it was this ambivalent moment that remained with her. Describing in *Red Ribbon* her heroine's walk home after such an advance, she writes that the heroine walked home in "an agony of confusion. Old fears bred into me before I was born, taboos older than my father's memory, conflicts between the things I had learned and those I could not forget held me rigid."[59] While Yezierska rejected her father's faith, she could not forget the strict moral codes of Bernard Mayer's world.

Over fifty years later, Yezierska remarked that she did not have the "worldly wisdom to keep that friendship going. I was not able to give love. I was too frightened, too unsheltered."[60] "Unsheltered" is a strange word; we would expect its opposite. But Yezierska was not sheltered when it came to sex. On the contrary, conditions during her tenement childhood made the facts of life all too obvious to the growing girl. When she described the Dewey affair in *Red Ribbon* she wrote, remembering her childhood, "On the East Side there was no privacy, couples seized their chance to be together wherever they found it; they embraced in hallways, lay together on roofs." And Yezierska's response: "I had passed them all with eyes averted."[61] Yezierska tried to keep herself sheltered, but could not. The prospect of sexual love would, then, leave her feeling vulnerable, defenseless, alone—unsheltered.

Yezierska's daughter does not believe her mother's relationship with Dewey was ever consummated. She feels that though

Yezierska desired a consummation, it was also unthinkable because it was triply tabooed. It would have been incest (because
Yezierska saw Dewey as her father), irreverence (because she saw
Dewey as God), and plain adultery (because Dewey was married).[62] Though her daughter is right that Yezierska felt the ambivalence connected with deep feelings of taboo, the specific taboos
she cites probably would not have impeded a physical relationship. Yezierska had become close enough to Dewey to overcome
her hero worship, and by the time of their break she saw him
very much as a man. It is unlikely, given her feelings about religion, that she would have any compunctions about sleeping with
"God." And, too, it is unlikely that a woman who refused to
legalize her marriage after her child's birth would have had any
qualms about adultery; Yezierska was intellectually committed to
the idea of free love.

In fact, that seems to have been the crux of the matter. Yezierska believed in sexual freedom, but—in Deweyan terms—she believed with the head rather than the heart. Her ambivalence was
profound, and her sexuality extremely complicated. There is, for
example, her perplexing "companionate marriage" to Jacob Gordon in 1910, which she entered into while still professing igno-
rance of marital relations. She seems to have enjoyed the idea of
being a femme fatale, a "passionate Russian Jewess—a flame, a
longing" (as she more than once describes her heroines) but she
was never very good with the follow-through. Her inability to
find release from her passions may help explain the intensity of
her fiction and the fierceness she brought to her vocation, but it
remains puzzling in light of her devotion to the principle of sexual
freedom.

In another fiction, the sensationalist 1924 story "Love
Hunger!" Yezierska provides a clue to her sexual ambivalence. In
this story, she completely reverses her usual gender-assigned
roles and creates a heroine with a "cold, impersonal, Anglo-
Saxon quality"[63] who attracts an "Oriental" lover. The story is
revealing not only because it gives further evidence of the Dewey/
Yezierska relationship (the heroine curses the "six generations of
New England ancestry . . . holding me back with their fear of
emotion"[64]) but also because it suggests how Yezierska viewed
her own sexuality. The heroine has an "ideal of love" that she
worries cannot be matched in reality. The story closes as she asks,

"Can it be that I who so passionately hunger for love can't take it when it comes to me because it's so different from my ideal of love?"[65] There is no doubt that Yezierska believed in love and considered herself a passionate woman—one of her early poems is titled "I Am a Spendthrift in Love." But about the physical expression of love she was unsure.

Yezierska seems to have known something was wrong; at least once in her life she sought help. In 1923, at the height of her fame, she set out on a European tour, bearing an introduction to Havelock Ellis, the celebrated expert in abnormal sexuality, an introduction she had expressly sought from her publisher.[66] Whether she had an audience with Ellis is not known, but there is no indication that she reached any resolution about her sexual ambivalence. For the rest of her life this woman, outspoken on so many subjects, remained strangely silent about sex.

Yezierska's actual sexuality, then, was highly complicated. But certainly what Dewey regarded as her passion—which he had every reason to assume was genuine and physical—encouraged his initial attraction. Yezierska's daughter has written, "Dewey had a right to expect, from Anzia's volatile, emotionally direct temperament, her seeming honesty (and the fact that she was not 23 but 33, married and a mother as well), that she would virtually burst into flame at a touch." For, after all, "it was he who had always been reserved, disciplined, unwilling or afraid to act on emotional impulse."[67] Of course, this was part of the problem; Dewey had his own ambivalence about sexuality. In struggling with his conflicting emotions about his response to her, he must have assumed that she felt no such conflicts. A good part of Yezierska's appeal had to have been the promise of heightened responsiveness she held out to him. Once again, their misunderstanding of each other was profound. The two were locked in a fierce and mutual attraction and at the same time unaware of the other's sexual ambivalence. Moreover, Dewey's mistaken view of Yezierska as a sexual free spirit intensified the consequences of this misunderstanding.

For the ethnic woman suffers considerably from the consequences of being associated with the erotic. Just as surely as emotionality becomes associated with sexuality—passion immediately assumed to be physical passion—so too do warmth and emotionality become related to excess. To be emotional is to run the risk of being considered overemotional, as Yezierska knew only too well. Time and again, her Deweyan heroes accuse their immigrant lovers of excessive emotion. ''You're an emotional, hysterical girl and you have exaggerated my friendly interest,'' says John Morrow. ''Compose yourself.''[68] John Blair, rejecting not the heroine herself but one of her stories, tells her her mind is too ''chaotic,'' commenting, ''You Russians are full of interesting stuff. But you're so incoherent. You'd be no use to us unless you could learn to think clearly.''[69] John Manning, who calls his wife ''my beautiful maddening Jewess,'' constantly cautions her not to be ''overemotional,'' telling her at one point, ''You're insane, Sonya. . . . You've lost complete control of yourself.''[70] Henry Scott, who laughs at his beloved's ''Slavic seriousness''[71] scolds her repeatedly in the same vein: ''Fanya, aren't you being a bit hysterical today? Problems are solved by reason, not emotion.''[72]

It is a stock in the trade of sexism to accuse women of hysteria, overemotionalism. To accuse a Jewish woman of these traits is to traffic in anti-Semitism. Yezierska well knew the pattern: Her novels were first welcomed by native-born America, but as she continued to play the same tune the reviewers began to find her overemotional, hysterical, even—some reviewers were explicit— ''too Jewish.''[73] Too often, the native-born male who has called his immigrant beloved ''my passionate Russian Jewess'' reveals his ''hidden hate of the Jew.''[74]

What went on exactly, given these cultural circumstances, in Dewey's study of the community of Jewish Poles in Philadelphia, bankrolled as it was by Albert Coombs Barnes? Dewey and Barnes sometimes acted like two overgrown boys together; *Time* referred to Dewey as Barnes's ''frequent drinking companion,''[75] and Barnes is said to have remarked to his friend, ''Jack, do you know why I like you? It's because you remind me of a bartender I used to know.''[76] The professor and the collector: two old boys. Their ''study of the study'' was conducted in the spirit of aristocratic smugness that is conducive to jovial anti-Semitism. Dewey studied the study of the Polish immigrant, in fact, with a known anti-Semite.

The image of the two men's friendship is, on the surface, benign, and is supported by interpretations of Barnes's role in Dewey's life as that of another harmless crank. Journalists, who never knew what to make of a man of Barnes's viciousness, were

to call him things like "a combination of Peck's Bad Boy and Do-
nald Duck";[77] they learned better when Barnes retaliated with
lawsuits. Too many commentators looked the other way when it
came to Barnes's anti-Semitism. Barnes biographer Hart denies
that his subject hated Jews, but biographer Schack grudgingly
reports some chilling instances of it. Barnes approached Gilbert
Seldes of the *Dial* and complained of Seldes's magazine "that
there were too many Jews in it."[78] A lawyer named Robert Abra-
hams was repeatedly addressed as "Abie."[79] Barnes particularly
relished denying Jewish Americans admission to the collection.
To Helen B. Jastrow, the widow of a University of Pennsylvania
Hebrew professor and librarian, he composed a letter from an
imaginary "Rachel Cohen, Third Assistant Filing Clerk." In the
letter "Cohen" asserts that she has shown her boss Jastrow's re-
quest, and that he had responded that the movies were better
entertainment for Jastrow and her friends. And, "the boss"
added, "Her sense of the ethical significance of English seems to
be defective—so write her in Yiddish."[80]

Barnes was no "Peck's Bad Boy." When contacted by biographer Schack for a comment on the collector, one figure in the art
world would not let his name be used because of

> the rottenness of [Barnes's] actions. . . . I saw and heard such
> things about his treatment of art, his wife, his acquaintances . . .
> and all who did not toady to him. As one Philadelphia lawyer, who
> I am sure had no personal grudge against him, said, very simply,
> "He was evil."[81]

Dewey's relationship with a man like this reflects very badly on
him. And, whether or not Dewey cast aspersions on Yezierska's
ethnicity—and she clearly felt he did—he behaved very shabbily
toward her. On one level, his failure to rise to the occasion is
simply sad, showing as it does his emotional cowardice, his inability to take risks, and his sense of obligation to his family and
his public image. But his cavalier dismissal of a woman who for
a time meant a great deal to him—she was, let us remember, "the
promise of centuries to come"—suggests more than cowardice.
He extricated himself from what had become an impossible love
affair in a way that was totally out of keeping with his usual
gentleness. He simply withdrew, refusing to explain, refusing to

communicate—even, perhaps, entertaining without protest the boorish Barnes's jabs at the woman Dewey had once loved. Dewey knew Yezierska's vulnerability but chose, in the end, to overlook it. He dealt her the final indignity by refusing to discuss it, except to ask that she return his letters. He left Yezierska totally bereft. His encounter with the immigrant failed.

Finally, the encounter between the eminent representative of the Eastern establishment and the immigrant writer was a tragic one. Each misunderstood the other, endowing their relationship with extraordinary symbolic weight. If we accept their terms— that he represented Anglo-Saxon coldness, "thinking with the head," and she passion and eroticism, "thinking with the heart"—the conclusion is that the twain never *can* meet, that, in Dewey's terms, the split between mind and body is irreparable.

Moreover, the tragedy of their encounter is particularly resonant if we consider it in the context of American response to the immigrant. Dewey and Yezierska met and fell in love as the nation was moving into the 1920s, years marked by increasing nativism and distrust of the immigrant. The twenties would see the sensational trial of immigrants Sacco and Vanzetti, tight new restrictions on immigration, and the acceptance of genteel anti-Semitism among educated people. With the Russian Revolution and the "Red scare" at home, the specter of Jew as Bolshevik plotting global revolution poisoned the minds of the American public. These years also saw Henry Ford's *Dearborn Independent* feature reports of a cabalistic organization of Jewish bankers maneuvering for world rule, which eventually led to Ford's publicizing the viciously anti-Semitic tract *The Protocols of the Elders of Zion*. Though virulent anti-Semitism declined around 1925, Jews were still subject to widespread social discrimination as prejudice against them became culturally institutionalized.[82]

Dewey and Yezierska's union, however difficult and, finally, impossible, nevertheless held great promise. Its failure tolled a very real failure on the part of native-born America in accepting immigrant America. In Yezierska, Dewey saw the possibility of knowing the immigrant through experiencing her, which he rightly saw as the only true way of knowing. But in viewing her as an "experience" he failed, finally, to come to terms with the flesh-and-blood person. Their encounter represents America's own encounter with the immigrant—fraught with expectation, apprehension, and replete with misunderstandings. Dewey's "experience" of the immigrant was imperfectly integrated into his own life; so too was the immigrant, in slipshod, unpredictable fashion, integrated into American society, with resentments and anxieties on each side.

Seen in this light, Yezierska can be forgiven the melodrama with which she often described the "gap," or "chasm," between the immigrant woman's culture and that of the older American. In "Wild Winter Love," a typical story about an immigrant heroine who falls in love with an older, married, native-born American, the woman commits suicide when the affair ends unhappily. The narrator, observing neighborhood reaction to Ruth Raefsky's death, writes:

> How could they know the real Ruth Raefsky?. . . . How could they understand the all-consuming urge that drove her to voice her way across the chasm between the ghetto and America?
>
> A lonely losing fight it was from the very beginning. Only for a moment, a hand of love stretched a magic bridge across the chasm. Inevitably the man went back to the safety of his own world.[83]

In this elegiac story, Yezierska's heroine hopes her union with an American can bridge the gap between the ghetto and America. When it fails, she cannot continue, and falls into the very chasm she had so fervently hoped to bridge:

> In the fading of this dazzling mirage of friendship and love, vanished her courage, her dreams, her last illusion. And she leaped into the gulf that she could not bridge.[84]

The gulf between the immigrant and the American still yawns.

In the fall of 1918 Dewey went west. He was a visiting professor at the University of California, and in January 1919 he and his wife sailed for Japan. They would not return from the Far East until 1921, when Yezierska was at the height of her fame. In the meantime, Yezierska immersed herself in her writing, still reeling from the shock of her failed affair. She wrote about it obsessively and would continue to do so for the rest of her life. For a time she chose not to accept the absoluteness of Dewey's rejection. She included one of his poems in the manuscript of *Hungry Hearts* when she turned it in to Houghton Mifflin, but then, three weeks later, asked that it be returned, writing, ''I first must get Prof. Dewey's permission to use [the poem] in any way.''[85] Evidently she never did (though she published his ''Generations,'' of course, in her 1932 *All I Could Never Be*, presumably without his permission). When *Hungry Hearts* was brought out, Yezierska sent her publisher a list of those to whom she wanted copies sent. At the head of it was ''Prof. John Dewey, Young Men's Christian Association, Peking, China.''[86]

There is no record that Dewey responded, no evidence that he even noticed as Yezierska's overnight success made newspaper headlines. Her fiction yields few clues of any further exchange between them. Certainly there was some; he had to get back his letters. In *All I Could Never Be* the heroine very reluctantly returns the Dewey figure's letters. In *Red Ribbon on a White Horse*, her most autobiographical work, Yezierska describes herself as burning them. Certainly there is no trace of the letters, except as she reproduces parts of them in her fiction. Yezierska's daughter believes her mother committed their contents to memory.[87]

Yezierska may have sent Dewey her books or notices of her reviews; certainly they had some contact in the years to come. In *All I Could Never Be*, Fanya sends her first novel to Henry Scott and gets no response; finally, she makes an appointment with him and sees her book on his office shelves, its pages uncut. She invites him to the premiere of the movie made from her first book, but he is too busy. She goes to hear him speak at a dinner held in his honor, and he looks straight through her.

Surely Yezierska's path crossed Dewey's in the twenties and beyond. In the twenties, both were famous—public figures, eminent New Yorkers. In later decades Yezierska made her home in the shadow of Columbia University and, in her usual eager way, availed herself of its resources; there is no end to the possibilities of their meeting. But nowhere is there any suggestion that she received so much as a kind word from him—not even an acknowledgment of her existence. Dewey's zealous avoidance of her suggests that he came to see their involvement—once so fraught with promise—as imbued with danger, so much so that he could not even admit to knowing her.

For her part Yezierska worked the problem out in her fiction. She wrote obsessively about Dewey—not out of a desire for revenge, though there was that. With her new literary connections, for instance, she arranged an assignment to review Dewey's *Democracy and Education* for the *Bookman*. She knew that he would inevitably see what she wrote, and she launched a full-blown personal attack, complaining that Dewey's style (and, by implication, the man) "lacks flesh and blood." She asks disingenuously,

> Can it be that this giant of the intellect—this pioneer in the realms of philosophy—has so suppressed the personal life in himself that his book is devoid of the intimate, self-revealing touches that make writing human?

"He thinks so high up in the head that only the intellectual few can follow the spiraling point of his vision," she concludes.[88]

Yezierska's anger at Dewey surfaced in her choice of fictional names. (This is a woman, after all, who gave the hero of *Bread Givers* the distinctive name of Hugo Seelig, that of a former lover.) Her Deweyan heroes have names like Henry Scott, John Morrow, and John Barnes, all of which echo Dewey's in rhythm and tone. Of all her colleagues in Dewey's seminar she disliked Irwin Edman the most; so, with seeming glee, she named the psychology teacher on whom the heroine of *Bread Givers* has a crush "Mr. Edman." She took a swipe at Dewey's article on "The Reflex Arc Concept in Psychology" in the same book. The heroine complains about "Mr. Edman's" assigned reading: "At first, psychology was like Greek to me. So many words about words. 'Apperception,' 'reflex arc,' 'inhibitions.' What had all that fancy book language to do with the real, plain every day?"[89]

Yezierska's obsessive fictional re-creations of Dewey can, of course, be seen as attempts at revenge, but she returned again and again to the affair for more compelling reasons—for its symbolic weight. With *All I Could Never Be* she was not so much trying to "get at" Dewey as she was trying to exorcise her own personal demons, to satisfy her need to give her account of the Polish American study. By the time she wrote her fictionalized autobiography—in whose first drafts she used Dewey's real name and made no effort to conceal his identity—she simply felt that the public had a right to know about a significant incident in the public man's life—and surely she hoped as well that naming him would bring the book more attention.[90]

Yezierska wrote about Dewey in love because the idea of America in love with the immigrant was a compelling and vivid image for her, a vision of the immigrant's acceptance by the New World. She herself felt both alien and alienated, intensely drawn to "open up" herself and her culture to native-born America. She saw immigrant culture and America separated by a gulf, a gulf she could bridge in her writing and a gulf symbolically bridged by a "hand of love" across it. In her mind, immigrant and native-born America were fundamentally at odds, but she felt the very nature of their antagonism willed them together. A frankly auto-biographical essay in her *Children of Loneliness*, "Mostly About Myself," describes her disappointment at the icy reception the immigrant met in America. She compared it to a man and a woman in love:

> Sometimes a man and a woman are so different that they hate each other on sight. Their intense difference stabs a sharp sword of fear into each heart. But when this fear that froze each into separate oppositeness ever has a chance for a little sun of understanding, then the very difference that drew them apart pulls them closer together than those born alike. Perhaps that accounts for the de-vouring affinity between my race and the Anglo-Saxon race.[91]

Right about so many things—the "sharp sword of fear" that both immigrant and native-born American felt in confrontation, for ex-ample—Yezierska erred in setting the two cultures in a dichotomy so absolute that its only resolution could come in absolute union. In Dewey she met a man who bought in as fully as she to such a dichotomy, a man so repulsed by dualisms that he saw them everywhere he turned. In both cases, their insistence that the immigrant and the American had natures so fundamentally op-posed and so elementally attracted to each other made union between the two—acceptance of the immigrant by America—im-possible.

In creating such a dichotomy, Dewey and Yezierska reinforced age-old gender stereotypes about the differences between men and women, stereotypes that attribute impassivity and reason to the male and passion and emotion to the female. Under such terms, the man and woman are locked in mutual attraction and repulsion; just as oil and water cannot mix, neither can emotion and reason. In Dewey's terms, the American mind remained split from its body.

It comes as no surprise that two such imaginative people

should seize on one of the most central ideological paradigms in the American mind, amplify and celebrate it in their art, and act it out so compulsively in their lives. If America is male, represented by reason and the mind, and the immigrant female, represented by emotion and the body, Dewey and Yezierska took up their respective roles readily and vividly. He in his poetry and she in her voluminous stories relentlessly played out this central and tragic drama. Their encounter was as doomed as it was, for its time, inevitable.

# 7

# *Yezierska, 1917–1970:*
# *Hungry Heart*

John Dewey gave Anzia Yezierska her first typewriter. As she later remembered, too, "He made me realize that art is the climax of human experience. You don't know what happened to you until you create with it."[1] And he impressed one other important fact upon her: America was fascinated by the immigrant and very eager to hear what she had to say. That this fascination could easily shade off into morbid curiosity and even repulsion she did not foresee. She knew only that there was a public ready to read what she wrote and that she had a good deal to say. In fact, as she later stated, "I did not think I was writing. I was simply expressing myself." Writing was "an outlet for something inside me that could not communicate."[2]

Yezierska felt a need to communicate, and for a time the public listened eagerly. In 1919 she began her career as a professional immigrant, a writer whose work sounded one theme repeatedly: that of the immigrant misunderstood and betrayed by America. Initially, America was enchanted by this immigrant and the stories she told, and as the new decade opened Yezierska was hailed as the "queen of the ghetto" and the "sweatshop Cinderella."

Not that it had been easy for Yezierska to get into print. By 1919 she was no stranger to New York's magazine world. For several years she had apprenticed in the business of self-promotion, sometimes storming the offices of editors with a sheaf of manuscripts in her fist.[3] One story, "The Free Vacation House," appeared in *Forum* in 1915, and another, "Where Lovers Dream," appeared in *Metropolitan* in 1918, but it was not until Dewey brought her "Soap and Water and the Immigrant" to Herbert

Croly at the *New Republic* that her stories began appearing regularly.

Public relations, itself a fledgling profession at the time, built a whole new persona for Yezierska—that of the immigrant woman who triumphs over both a backward-looking family and the bigotry of the native-born on her way to achieving real American success. From a specimen studied by sociologists and university professors Yezierska became a specimen advertised to the public as a genuine immigrant fresh from the ghetto of New York's Lower East Side. It was Edward O'Brien's naming her "The Fat of the Land" as the best short story of 1919 that led to the 1920 publication of her first collection of stories, *Hungry Hearts.*[4]

"The Fat of the Land" was a representative piece—both of Yezierska's style and of what the public found appealing in the immigrant writer. The heroine is Hannah Breineh, an immigrant mother who is estranged from her successful Americanized children. Sumptuously ensconced on Riverside Drive, she sneaks off to Hester Street to eat herring and onions. The public responded to the vivid heroine and her "ghetto ways" as well as to her assimilated children. Of all Yezierska's writing, this single story remains the best known, most widely anthologized and reprinted.

*Hungry Hearts* received favorable reviews almost immediately; reviewers seized on the intensity of the narrative voice and the authenticity of the ghetto scenes. "These stories of the East Side reek with the aching passion of a lonely girl, and with the scent of herring and onions," wrote the *Bookman* reviewer.[5] But as many a young author knows, critical acclaim does not always sell books. In the autobiographical *Red Ribbon on a White Horse*, Yezierska depicts herself as still living in the ghetto after her book's publication. Critical acclaim, she felt, was the death of *Hungry Hearts:* "It had been praised by the critics, esteemed as literature. That meant it didn't sell. After spending the two hundred dollars I had received in royalties, I was even poorer than when I started writing."[6] *Red Ribbon* goes on to describe how she then received a telegram about motion picture rights and had to pawn her mother's wedding shawl for carfare to meet her agent.

In fact, her circumstances were quite different from those she describes. In 1919 and 1920, on the eve of her success, Yezierska was leading a comfortable life on East 101st Street, teaching night school and still attending classes at Columbia, where she earnestly participated in the writing courses offered by her friend and teacher Dorothy Scarborough. Yezierska always portrayed herself as untutored and crude, but actually she was an avid student of the craft of writing. "The Fat of the Land" was in fact a workshop piece, read and commented on repeatedly in Scarborough's class. *Red Ribbon* also misrepresents the timing of its events, for, after the publication of *Hungry Hearts*, Yezierska set forth on a rigorous and self-managed publicity campaign. Yezierska kept her teacher informed of the story's and then the book's progress, and asked her to pass along messages to the class. In November 1920, Yezierska wrote to Scarborough advising her to watch for an "editorial" by "Dr. Crane" in that week's *Globe*.[7]

The gospel of Anzia Yezierska was first spread by a minister-turned-syndicated-columnist, Frank Crane, an inspirational "man of letters" revered by American readers aspiring to culture. "Dr. Crane's editorial" was a public relations masterpiece. Yezierska, impatient with her publisher's publicity efforts, burst into Crane's office on November 26. Crane was impressed, and his column appeared the next day in the *New York Globe and Commercial Advertiser* as well as in papers across the country. It was her authenticity that struck Crane, and he described her metonymically as the Old World itself:

> I got a new slant on America from Anzia Yezierska. She walked into my office one day and brought the Old World with her. She had not said three words before I saw farther into the heart of Russia and Poland than I had ever been able to do by reading many heavy books.
>
> She was Poland.
>
> She was the whole turgid stream of European immigration. The waters of the stream laved my consciousness.

"From a sweatshop worker to a famous writer!" he exclaimed, thus helping to forge the myth of the girl from the ghetto.[8]

Crane's column brought Yezierska considerable attention. On December 5 she wrote a friend that after it appeared she had many offers from newspaper syndicates. And it caught the eye of an executive assistant who showed the story to his boss, Hollywood producer Samuel Goldwyn. Goldwyn offered Yezierska $10,000 for the film rights to *Hungry Hearts* and a three-year contract writing movie "scenarios" at $10,400 a year.[9] In January 1921 Yezierska boarded a train for Hollywood, and the sweatshop Cinderella's career was launched.

Newspaperman Crane was struck by the journalistic appeal of Yezierska's story. Indeed, he wrote that "she told her story, told it well, in a way to rejoice the heart of a newspaper person, in a few swift words, of keen beauty, redolent with individuality." Yezierska's experience as a specimen, taken up by wealthy patrons and curious academics, had taught her well how to present herself dramatically. She was the conscious author of her own life story, and she knew how to give it the dramatic turns and twists that would "sell" it to the American public. Yezierska created her own Cinderella story.

In the course of making her public self, Yezierska had to alter many of the facts of her life. This came naturally enough to the woman who had studied acting with such enthusiasm at the American Academy of Dramatic Arts ten years before. The record of her brief flirtation with the theater is in fact representative of Yezierska's readiness to alter facts as she wished. She studied acting with Marcet Addams Haldeman, who was later to marry Emanuel Julius, the publisher of a popular series of inexpensive reprinted classics, the Little Blue Books. The only record that remains of Yezierska's acting is in her correspondence with Marcet Haldeman-Julius—which tells us, among other things, that Yezierska told her friend that she was naming her baby girl Marcet, a tribute Haldeman-Julius remembered fondly in a letter to her own daughter fifteen years later.[10] But Yezierska, of course, had named her daughter not Marcet but Louise.

The skill with which Yezierska took to self-invention is astonishing. Her daughter remembers her mother "had a talent for dramatizing and enlarging her life for an appreciative listener."[11] Yezierska's mythmaking mostly involved, but was not confined to, her vital statistics. As noted, she was herself unaware of her own age, and, in fact, accounts of her age vary by as much as ten years. When a Hollywood publicist asked her age in 1921—when Yezierska was at least thirty-five—he speculated, "I'd say you were about thirty-five." She responded coolly, "I'll say I am about thirty."[12] Less a nod to vanity than to necessity, Yezierska's untruths about her age were meant to keep the Cinderella success story aesthetically intact. This necessitated that she present herself as fresh out of the ghetto in 1920—neatly erasing about twenty years of her own life. Her years as a teacher, her two marriages, her child—none of these important features of her life appeared in either her official or unofficial versions of herself. She always depicted herself as emerging straight from the sweatshops into Hollywood splendor, omitting her intervening years as a young working woman whose life was, if relatively cheerless, by no means squalid. So, in a 1920 *Good Housekeeping* interview, for instance, Yezierska talks as if the year were 1901 and she were just emerging from the ghetto.[13] In a 1920 review of John Dewey's *Democracy and Education,* she describes herself reading the book over a sandwich on her lunch hour at the factory—a charming picture indeed, but an unlikely one.[14]

Yezierska not only distorted the facts of her life to friends and interviewers but to the readers of her fiction, who are often misled by its autobiographical nature to assume that events she describes in her novels and stories always happened exactly as she described them. Facts simply did not matter to her; what she was after was the emotional truth, and if she could portray that by describing something that happened to someone else as her own experience, she did so without compunction. She freely appropriated her own or anyone else's experience to shape her plots. One of her sisters bore ten children and had to struggle to make ends meet; this sister's life was convenient for such fictions as *Bread Givers* and "The Free Vacation House" in *Hungry Hearts. Salome of the Tenements,* about a young immigrant girl who wins a millionaire WASP husband only to find the differences between them unbridgeable, might remind readers of Yezierska's relationship with Dewey. Certainly it is where she sets forth most clearly her stereotype of the cold Anglo-Saxon male. But *Salome* was based on the much-publicized contemporary event of the immigrant reporter Rose Pastor's Cinderella marriage to the millionaire Graham Stokes. Again, "Wild Winter Love" is about an immigrant woman writer who has a relationship with a Deweyesque hero, an affair that drives her to suicide. Yet Yezierska's daughter explains in a reprint of *Hungry Hearts* that the story was inspired by Yezierska's response to the attempted suicide of Rose Cohen, an immigrant writer whose *Out of the Shadows* did not meet with the same acclaim as Yezierska's work.[15] The emotional veracity of the immigrant girl in love with an unreachable American man was what she sought to convey.

In fact, her lapses in accuracy do not impugn Yezierska's honesty. She not only told what she saw as the emotional truth, but she did so in ways that revealed her own naïvetés and faults in a manner consistent with unflinching, almost compulsive truthfulness. Rather, her distortions of factual particulars show how well she took to the mythmaking process and the extent to which she could turn events to her advantage. Though Yezierska was in fact "made" by others, by the nascent public relations industry, she consciously participated in the process. It was *her* idea—not a Hollywood publicist's or a press agent's—to change her name back from the Americanized Hattie Mayer, the name she was given upon her arrival in America, to the difficult and foreign-sounding Anzia Yezierska. Records show that she was calling herself Anzia in 1910—a full ten years before she was "discovered." (Her surname generally remained "Mayer" or "Levitas" until her first appearance in print in 1915.) We cannot be sure whether by 1910 she had already rediscovered her Jewishness or was looking forward to reinventing it. The author of "We Can Change Our Noses But Not Our Moses" and "You Can't Be an Immigrant Twice" knew well the intricacies of reinventing oneself as a superethnic heroine, an Old World "specimen."[16]

So the sweatshop Cinderella was a creation of public relations, her own as well as others'. The phrase *public relations* was not yet in use in 1920, and in fact a whole range of influences created the "historian of Hester Street." The 1920s saw the birth of modern advertising, but the rise of public relations in a broad sense is at least as characteristic of the age and perhaps more significant.[17] The 1920s saw the rapid growth of the movie industry and an explosion in communications—phenomena at once conducive to and productive of public relations efforts. It is easy to see the need for public relations as a response to the sheer mass of society that the growth of communications and media revealed to American citizens. The "hordes of immigrants" were part of this mass, and a particularly frightening part. One writer of a public relations handbook attributes the rise of the industry to just this need: "Public relations started as publicity . . . because, as it became harder for people with different backgrounds to understand and know about each other, the first necessity was for one group to tell another about itself.''[18] Edward L. Bernays, an early publicist considered the "father" of modern public relations, attributes the growth of the industry to the work of the muckrakers and explicitly connects its real beginnings with the need for good Americanization publicity for immigrants during the war years.[19] By 1925, H. L. Mencken could poke fun at the profession, declaring, "Every politician, movie actor, actress, and prize fighter has a publicist," and likening the euphemism of "publicist" to that of "mortician.''[20]

Yezierska could not foresee the consequences of the invention of her Cinderella story. She had yet to encounter the fantastic public relations machine that was Hollywood, and to see how the "sweatshop Cinderella" myth would become a curse. For Hollywood presented Yezierska with another disillusionment, almost as wrenching as her entanglement with Dewey. Initially overwhelmed at the thought of working with such writers as Alice Duer Miller, Elinor Glyn, Gertrude Atherton, Rupert Hughes, and Will Rogers, she was soon put off by the crassness of Hollywood society: "The fight that went on at the pushcarts in Hester Street went on in [the] Hollywood drawing room.''[21] She had hoped that the film version of *Hungry Hearts* would mark a watershed in moviemaking; as she later commented, "Hollywood was still busy with Westerns and Pollyanna romances. The studios seldom bought stories from life.''[22] In those days Jewish culture was represented in Hollywood productions only by Montague Glass's sentimentalized and broadly comic *Potash and Perlmutter,* and Yezierska was dismayed to see *Hungry Hearts* given a happy ending and burlesque overtones. And she herself did not know why she was in Hollywood; her presence seemed needed only for publicity reasons. She fundamentally misunderstood Hollywood's Jewish culture and her place in it.

When Yezierska arrived in Hollywood early in 1921, it was as part of Goldwyn's recently initiated "Eminent Authors" series, itself a triumph of public relations. Annoyed by the growth of the "star system," which allowed the actors and actresses in his films to demand larger and larger salaries, Goldwyn hit upon the idea of billing the writer over the star. When the series began in 1919, the following statement appeared in the motion picture trade publications: "Eminent Authors Pictures, Inc., organized by Rex

Beach and Samuel Goldwyn, unites in one producing organization the greatest American novelists of today. It insures the exclu-
sive presentation of their stories on the screen and each author's
cooperation in production. The authors are—Rex Beach, Rupert
Hughes, Leroy Scott, Gertrude Atherton, Governeur Morris,
Mary Roberts Rinehart, Basil King." Goldwyn declared, "The
picture must pass the severest critic that it will ever meet—the
author of the story."[23] Not the greatest reader of all time—
the only book he ever read through was *The Wizard of Oz*—Goldwyn reportedly also wanted to get Washington Irving to do *The
Legend of Sleepy Hollow* as a vehicle for Will Rogers, until Rex Beach
informed him he was sixty years too late.[24] Undaunted, Goldwyn
tried to sign George Bernard Shaw, who declined (though Goldwyn did sign the equally eminent Maurice Maeterlinck, who
seems to have taken the studio for something of a ride[25]).

The "Eminent Authors" scheme was a publicity stunt, an attempt to cash in on the literary business. The attempt failed
(though the long tradition of writers "going Hollywood" can be
seen in a way as its stepchild), mostly because in the days of silent
films the script was not considered an element of primary importance. The Eminent Authors, it seems, were paid to come up with
ideas, which "scenario writers" then wrote into scripts. In reality, the authors were used as publicity dummies.

The rise of Hollywood was in symbiotic relation to the rise of
public relations. Even publicist Edward L. Bernays found the
business of "star-making" too heavy-handed. In his autobiography, he describes promoting Theda Bara in *Cleopatra* for Fox in
1917. Devising slogans like "The high cost of kissing the modern
Cleopatra is cheap compared with the price Caesar paid," Bernays not only tried to lure the general public but devised strategies to make the film appeal to high school principals by stressing
its educational qualities and to milliners and dressmakers as a
source of fashion inspiration. Bernays remarked wryly on the
packaging of Theda Bara, who was "sold" as an illegitimate
daughter of a French artist and an Arab woman. Though *Bara* is
*Arab* spelled backward, the invented superethnic star was actually Theodosia Goodman from Cincinnati.

Resolving never to work for the movies again, Bernays commented, "It was a crude, crass, manufacturing business, run by
crude, crass men." Bernays wrote that Goldwyn, who he met

three years later, reminded him of a "salesman in a perpetual rush."[26]

As Lary May and other film historians have pointed out, almost all the early movie moguls were immigrants, East European Jews, who had come out of the sales business. Carl Laemmle, the founder of Universal Pictures, was a clothing salesman who compared selling movies to selling clothes; Adolph Zukor sold furs; and Sam Goldwyn, né Goldfisch, sold gloves.[27] Their sales backgrounds shaped the great moviemakers' approach to their new enterprise. Goldwyn was so determined to stay on top of public opinion that he sometimes sat in movie theaters with his back to the screen, watching audience reaction. He once said,

> If the audience don't like a picture, they have a good reason. The public is never wrong. I don't go for all this thing that when I have a failure, it is because the audience doesn't have the taste or education, or isn't sensitive enough. The public pays the money. It wants to be entertained. That's all I know.[28]

Mary Roberts Rinehart and Gertrude Atherton, two of Goldwyn's original Eminent Authors, remembered their Hollywood experiences with some disillusionment. Rinehart remembered that she felt she had no place at the studio: "I was precisely as useful as a fifth leg to a calf." But both remembered their publicity functions. Goldwyn tried to send a blimp to greet Rinehart on her arrival in Hollywood; when she declined, he sent an open car filled with flowers instead. Rinehart wrote very little in Hollywood but was photographed constantly, in any variety of settings.[29]

With her up-from-nothing life and success, Anzia Yezierska was perfect fodder for a Goldwyn public relations triumph. As might be expected, she was glorified not for the stories she had written but for the story of her life. The Goldwyn publicity machine cranked out innumerable "sweatshop Cinderella" stories. In *Red Ribbon on a White Horse*, Yezierska describes a Goldwyn assistant's enthusiasm over selling her story to the papers: "A natural for the tabloids! Millions couldn't buy this build-up for the picture." She reflects, "As long as I remained with Goldwyn I was in a glass house with crooked mirrors. Every move I made was distorted, and every distortion exploited to further the sale of *Hungry Hearts*. The dinner parties, the invitations . . . , all that had seemed to be the spontaneous recognition of my book was but the merchandising enterprise of press agents selling a movie. Money and ballyhoo—the fruit of the struggle to write.''[30]

Yezierska was among Jews in Hollywood, but she felt a great gulf between herself and them. William Fox she liked well enough—with this most low-keyed of the big studio bosses she felt ''East Side had met East Side.''[31] But even Fox she found unsympathetic to her struggles with writing and ultimately turned down his offer of a lucrative writing contract. Of Paul Bern, the director of *Hungry Hearts,* she wrote, ''He had a dark Hester Street face, but slick as a picture on the cover of a movie magazine.''[32] She was enchanted with the stage sets of East European *shtetls* and Hester Street kitchens built for her film, and she felt the scenario writer had improved on her own material. But she was horrified to learn that Montague Glass had been hired to do the ''post-mortem''—to ''doctor''—the final version of the film. Yezierska described Glass, the author of the *Potash and Perlmutter* stories, as ''the man who made a living burlesquing Jews for *The Saturday Evening Post.* . . . Americans reading his Potash and Perlmutter stories thought those clowning cloak and suiters were the Jewish people.''[33] Glass was to provide ''laughs and a happy ending'' for the film,[34] which disgusted her. The entire Hollywood experience left her disillusioned. ''I had dreamed of Olympian gods and woke up among hucksters,'' she wrote.[35] Afraid that the turmoil would affect her writing, she fled Hollywood and eventually returned to New York.

Hollywood had made her feel cut off from her culture, ''as if I were part of a stage-set,''[36] and she found she had trouble writing. She had confided to Goldwyn her desire to write an ''expiation of guilt,'' a novel to be called *Children of Loneliness,* about children who lose their heritage in their struggle to become Americans. She explained:

> I had to break away from my mother's cursing and my father's preaching to live my life; but without them I had no life. When you deny your parents, you deny the ground under your feet, the sky over your head. You become an outlaw, a pariah.[37]

From this time forward, Yezierska commented obsessively about her alienation from her past, the alienation that resulted from the Americanization she so eagerly sought. In her ''Children of Loneliness,'' a college-educated character laments, ''I can't live with the old world and I'm yet too green for the new. I don't belong to those who gave me birth or to those with whom I was educated.''[38] Her attempt to mediate between two cultures left her suspended between them.

Yezierska was ready to leave Hollywood as early as a month after her arrival; by April she was back in New York. She returned to California one month later, but not to Hollywood; she oversaw the making of *Hungry Hearts* from her sister Fanny's home in nearby Long Beach. The film itself opened in 1922. Scenario writer Julian Josephson had taken a few of the love stories in her short story volume and conflated them into one sentimental rich-boy-meets-poor-girl yarn; the hero, played by Bryant Washburn, bails the immigrant family out of their rent trouble with the landlord and eventually marries the immigrant heroine, played by Helen Ferguson. The sets were appropriately vivid, and an authentic note was sounded by the performance of Rosa Rosanova, a star in the Yiddish theater, as the immigrant matriarch. But Yezierska took little interest in the film, and when Paramount Pictures undertook the filming of her next book, she merely signed away the rights and had little to do with the film's progress.

For Yezierska was writing again by the time she left Hollywood for good, and she returned to New York as something of a literary lioness. She was undisturbed by Houghton Mifflin's rejection of her next book, *Salome of the Tenements*. Albert and Charles Boni, the Greenwich Village bookstore owners of her ''new woman'' days, had teamed up with Horace Liveright in a new publishing house with a rising reputation for signing such exciting new authors as Jean Toomer and Ernest Hemingway. Boni and Liveright gladly took on Yezierska's new novel—the fictionalized version of the Rose Pastor Stokes saga—and Horace Liveright staged a full-blown New York literary event on her behalf. He gave a dinner party in her honor at the Waldorf Astoria, where much was made of the fact that she had applied at that very hotel years before for a job as a waitress or dishwasher.

In 1922 and 1923 Yezierska was part of the New York literary scene, a celebrity in her own right. She met and befriended such literary figures as Edward Dahlberg, Waldo Frank, William Lyons Phelps, Fannie Hurst, and Zona Gale—the last of whom was to become an important friend. She enjoyed lunches at the Algonquin and countless cocktail parties with this coterie of highly paid and popular writers, where they rubbed elbows with literary figures whose reputations were to be more lasting. Most importantly, she continued writing. *Children of Loneliness,* another volume of short stories, followed *Salome* in 1923.

Like many a twenties author, Yezierska sailed for a tour of Europe, where she made the usual literary rounds. Her 1923 passport describes a woman who was five feet five inches tall with brown hair and blue eyes. In Paris she visited Gertrude Stein, whom she described as "a very nice big cow."[39] As was her wont, she questioned Stein with intensity about what made a writer, and Stein responded with amused tolerance: "Why worry? Nobody knows how writing is written, the writers least of all." In London she met George Bernard Shaw, Israel Zangwill, and fellow Pole Joseph Conrad. Like Stein, Conrad took an interest in his intense visitor. Yezierska later described him "crippled with neuritis in his wheelchair, pointing to the clutter of manuscripts on his table" and confiding, "This, on which I have spent years of labor, will never see print because I won't live long enough to take out the knots."[40] She met John Galsworthy, the head of the international writers' group PEN. She was delighted to find that Galsworthy was among the passengers on her steamship back to America; in later years she was to hint at a shipboard romance between them. It was in keeping with her attraction to "the cold-blooded Anglo-Saxon" to imagine a relationship with an aristocratic Englishman, especially the author of the ultra-WASP *Forsyte Saga,* but it is unlikely that Yezierska and Galsworthy enjoyed more than a flirtation, given Mrs. Galsworthy's close rein on her once-wayward husband.[41]

Back in New York, Yezierska settled down to a rigorous writing schedule and made a semipermanent move to a three-room apartment at 249 Waverly Place. She stuck to farmers' hours, rising at five and writing until noon. Supper was usually a baked potato and milk, and she was in bed by 7 P.M.[42] She kept in close touch with her family, especially her sister Annie, and she set up a regular visiting schedule with her daughter. Though she never wrote with ease, the routine apparently helped her turn out her best work, the novel *Bread Givers,* in 1925. She published another competent novel, *Arrogant Beggar,* in 1927.

By then, however, Yezierska was severely troubled emotionally. Her sister's Annie's death at age fifty shook her badly. She sensed, too, that she was rehearsing familiar ghetto material in her work and, with characteristic drive (and energy—she was forty-seven), became a waitress at a local restaurant, Le Petit Patin, to enrich her writing with new experiences.[43] Money was growing scarce, and, for the first time in her life, she felt she had little to say.

In the coming years she sought help desperately, and turned in particular to two writer friends, Zona Gale and Dorothy Canfield Fisher, seeking help with what was fast becoming a spiritual crisis. As she shaped her novel about the Dewey affair and the Polish study, *All I Could Never Be*, old wounds were reopened, and she relived her determination to be accepted by native-born America. Tragically, her American public was at that very time abandoning her.

Yezierska met and became friends with Zona Gale in 1921 or 1922 when she was sent to interview the best-selling author by Clifford Smythe of the *International Book Review*. But as the twenties wore on and Yezierska's reputation declined, she came to see Gale as a savior. In a typical letter, she waxed urgent:

> Well at this moment, I swear, I *see you*—the *real you*. I see—not the Zona Gale the others see—but *the you*—the spirit—the message—the rock of refuge in the wilderness to whom the lost one [sic] from all the corners of the earth crowd for shelter.—And because I see you I feel that you too must see me—the real me—in spite of the unreasonable things I may do and say to shut myself out from you.[44]

There was something material as well that Yezierska wanted from Gale. In 1921, Gale had set up a scholarship fund at her alma mater, the University of Wisconsin at Madison. The fund was set up for struggling writers, who usually received about fifty dollars per month. As Yezierska later explained, a near cult was developing around this fellowship among young writers: "One rumor had it that any ambitious boy or girl could get a college education free, by merely writing to Zona Gale. The story started with a janitor's daughter who won a scholarship at Wisconsin."[45] The "janitor's daughter" was Marya Zaturenska; other recipients included Margery Latimer, Eric Walbrond, Eliseo Vivas, and Mark Shorer.[46]

Not surprisingly, Yezierska got a scholarship, which took her to the University of Wisconsin for two years. She took advantage of her Wisconsin residency to enroll her college-age daughter at the university in these years, and Yezierska was especially pleased to be near her. Glenn Frank, an editor at *Century* magazine, who had seen much of Yezierska's work, had been brought to Madison as the university's new president in 1925. He in turn had invited Alexander Meiklejohn to found his Experimental College there. The campus was a hotbed of activity, and unpublished chapters from Yezierska's *Red Ribbon on a White Horse* indicate that she was actively involved in college affairs. Denied a traditional college education herself—her Teachers College degree in domestic science represented four years of drudgery—it was as if she were finally getting the "coed's" college education that she had once dreamed of.

No explanation is recorded, but Yezierska left Wisconsin in 1930, and shortly thereafter she and Zona Gale seem to have had a falling out. The pattern of their relationship suggests that the inevitable occurred: Yezierska invested too much in her hope that Gale could "save" her, and Gale could not live up to her expectations. In fact, Yezierska suffered a breakdown of sorts at this time and was hospitalized at the New England Sanitarium and Hospital, a Seventh-Day Adventist institution in Melrose, Massachusetts. She wrote Gale that she was suffering from "anaemia" and was curious about receiving "radionic" treatment.[47]

Breakdowns were nothing new for Yezierska; she had long suffered from headaches and attacks of "nerves." Although there is no evidence that she was ever affiliated with Seventh-Day Adventism, interest in an alternative religion of this sort would not be unusual for Yezierska either. With her sister Annie, she had developed an enduring interest in Christian Science a few years before. She dabbled in all manner of mystical sidelines, attending the lectures of Krishnamurti, for instance, and reading and re-reading such spiritualist favorites as *The Little Locksmith* and Charles Morgan's *The Fountain*.[48] None of this is surprising; a woman of Yezierska's intensity experienced every day as a spiritual struggle, and the daily round often left her defeated and in search of solace from any source. It took remarkable courage, often, simply to continue.

In 1932, Yezierska thought, once again, that she had found salvation. She believed she had found a homeland—and it was, perversely, a small New England town in Dewey's home state, Vermont, peopled by provincial farming folk whose forebears had settled there centuries ago. Her spiritual savior this time was the novelist Dorothy Canfield Fisher, very much a New England writer and a chronicler of her beloved Vermont.

How Yezierska came to choose Arlington, Vermont, is not known. She was looking for a place where the cost of living was lower than in the city, for her finances were in very bad shape. She came to Arlington in very bad physical and mental shape as well, and Mrs. Fisher's warm welcome seemed to her a miraculous gift. Her early letters to Fisher are filled with gratitude for Fisher's help in getting her settled, and wonder at her immediate improvement in health. For the first time, she wrote Fisher, she slept dreamlessly the entire night through. "I came here a wreck in mind and body, unable to sleep, unable to digest the simplest food," she wrote. "What more can be said of Arlington than that it restores to the most hopeless, lost wanderer the gift of sleep?"[49]

The miraculous restoration of her health suggested to Yezierska that the town had more miracles in store. She wrote to Fisher that "God must have sent to you to show me the way out of the prison of self."[50] Indeed, Yezierska experienced some kind of mystical awakening in Arlington, although its nature was complex. Before it was over, her experience at Arlington wounded her deeply; in later years, she gained some insight from it.

Arlington becomes a fictional haven at the end of Yezierska's last two books, *All I Could Never Be* and *Red Ribbon on a White Horse*. In *Red Ribbon*, Fair Oaks and Marian Foster represent Arlington and Dorothy Canfield Fisher (with something of Zona Gale thrown in); the chapter that explains her time there is titled "Bread and Wine in the Wilderness." In Fair Oaks the narrator believes she has found home. Marian Foster cautions her not to expect too much from people so different from the heroine herself, but the heroine sees insistent similarities between her experience and that of the New England settlers. When Mrs. Foster invites her to the town's Thanksgiving pageant, the heroine is strangely moved, recognizing, "The Pilgrims had been dissenters and immigrants like me."[51]

But the heroine's bitter alienation surfaces, and she complains to her hostess, "Of course, it must have taken courage to travel to an unknown country, but what courage does it take for the descendants to carry on here? . . . I'd like to challenge Marian's words 'Christian traditions of justice and mercy' and tell her what's going on in the world."[52] She leaves the New England town, her inability to find solace there adding to her sense of isolation and alienation. Still, she clings to the "lesson" that Fair Oaks taught her, returning home to her father in the immigrant ghetto with a new sense of peace. She realizes she has been fleeing only from herself, and that she had asked too much from Fair Oaks and Marian Foster:

> The ghetto was with me wherever I went—the nothingness, the fear of my nothingness. Marian Foster had given me all that could be given a beggar—a house, chattels, milk, bread—while I resented her for withholding what she could not give, the understanding that I thought would make me secure.[53]

Yezierska fully came to terms with her Arlington experience only after twenty years had passed, when she was writing *Red Ribbon*. In that book she describes a Thanksgiving pageant similar to the one in *All I Could Never Be*, that led her to hope that she could learn from the life of the Vermont farmers. She wrote to Fisher that the rehearsal of the pageant had made a "very definite impression" on her: "You see I come from an uprooted race, uprooted people who've torn themselves away from their ancestors that is why your going back to your ancestors hits me so deeply."[54] But just as she had been disappointed in her much-inflated expectations of what John Dewey could offer her, so too had she been disillusioned by the New England town. Fisher later described how Yezierska had come to Arlington "weeping and distraught," hoping to make connections with the villagers:

> Her efforts to get in touch with the Vermonters of Arlington, their efforts to understand her enough to help her—all proved futile. The enormous psychological differences between them were impassable. Both sides really tried hard to read each other. Neither could understand a single impulse or thought, an emotion of the other. It was melodramatically complete. She presently, still weeping, still distraught, went away after having lived here, I think more than a year. No hostility against her here, simple stupefaction at the strangeness of her ways and tastes.[55]

The alienation Yezierska felt was a vestige of her experience with Dewey, and again she experienced it as evidence of a profound gulf between herself and native-born America. She sounds this theme—and her faint hope that the gap might not be unbridgeable—repeatedly in her letters to Fisher. On sending her *Bread Givers,* she wrote, "It will show how wide apart are the worlds from which we come. But for all the myriad differences— between your people and mine—deep within, the same heart beats in all."[56] Fisher read a draft of Yezierska's *All I Could Never Be* (1932) and objected strongly both to the depiction of the fictionalized Vermonters (she felt Yezierska had disguised real people too thinly) and to the morals of the heroine, who takes a neighborhood hobo into her bed. Yezierska stood firm, citing Fisher's inability to understand as an ethnic difference: "a Russian Jewess could never achieve the heroic power of restraint of an Emily Dickinson."[57]

Yezierska left Arlington, then, feeling once again that she could never be understood by those whose understanding she sought most desperately. In the same year *All I Could Never Be* appeared. It was a distinct critical failure. The most common complaint was that "Miss Yezierska has only one story to tell—her own—and so she tells it over and over."[58] As the *New York Times* reviewer wrote,

> Again it is the story she has told before, to no small degree her own story, the tale of the inarticulate but passionate Jewish young woman who seeks sympathy and understanding among those who, because of a more austere background, cannot or do not know how to give them. This has been her thesis over and over again; this has also been her plot.[59]

The reception of her early books had taught Yezierska that the immigrant story was one the public wanted to hear, and she believed she was giving her public what they wanted.

But by 1932 Yezierska was no stranger to the unsympathetic review. In the late twenties, critics had begun to respond to her ghetto fiction much as her Deweyan heroes responded to their ethnic lovers—initially attracted by the woman's vitality and fervor but ultimately repelled by these very qualities. Where they had once praised her openness and lack of inhibition, critics called her fiction overemotional and uncontrolled. W. Adolphe

Roberts, in a typical review of *Salome of the Tenements*, called her work "an orgy of the emotions," "sentimental, illogical, hysterical, naive," adding somewhat cryptically, "I have assumed this incoherence to be racial. Yet I would hesitate to call it Jewish."[60] Yezierska was faulted for vaguely expressed lapses of "taste" in a spirit of thinly disguised anti-Semitism. Scott Nearing found *Salome* "an unwholesome book."[61] Marya Zaturenska, who ought to have known better (she was an immigrant herself, a protégée of Zona Gale, and an acquaintance of Yezierska's) faulted *Arrogant Beggar* on similar grounds:

> Miss Yezierska has a fiery sincerity that is utterly moving, sometimes a simplicity of expression that reminds one of the minor Russians of the great period. But she lacks a real understanding of human nature, and has a complete and amusing ignorance of gentile minds, and somehow a faint lack of good taste.[62]

Yezierska battled this kind of response tirelessly, always pointing out to her critics what they were doing: condemning the person they themselves had helped create. In a portrait of her by Burton Rascoe in "A Bookman's Day Book," Yezierska explained how she tried to convince reviewers not to dismiss her work as hysterical:

> These people in the ghetto are high-strung, inarticulate. They are so hungry for little bits of sympathy, love and beauty; they are like children; what seems to be hysterical or overemotional to Anglo-Saxons in them is a natural state, because they feel so deeply and are not educated enough to articulate their emotions.[63]

Her desire to "open up her culture" to native-born Americans was thus reduced to a plea for sympathy.

The pain Yezierska felt at her public's rejection of her was considerable. Her rise from the ghetto, her inability to leave it behind, and her failure to find a place outside it left her feeling terribly divided. In another letter to Dorothy Canfield Fisher, she revives the conceit of her mysterious "difference," but she expresses it with real poignancy. She writes that she wants to discuss a book idea with Fisher,

> "the question of the establishment of people from different cultures in a society new to them." It is a subject that has been close to my heart for many years. Not only that house painter who had

found work in Arlington or Prof. Solveni—there's Lafcadio Hern
[*sic*] who was able to feel at home in Japan or D. H. Lawrence in
Mexico or Italy or T. S. Lawrence [*sic*] in Africa [*sic*]—These men
had found the center of their work in themselves and could go on
with their work in any part of the country. But there is also a Stefan
Zweig—a versatile novelist—who was driven to suicide because of
his uprootedness.[64]

Clearly, Yezierska identified with Zweig's "uprootedness."

Yezierska sounds these themes relentlessly. Her various sav-
iors—and her public—cannot be entirely blamed for eventually
tiring of her. Her reviewers, for instance, initially hoped that her
seemingly healthy vitality and fervor might bring out a new vitality and fervor in her readers. But the vitality and fervor revealed
themselves as no more than neurotic desperation. Her fascination
with the gulf separating the immigrant from native-born America
turned into an obsession. Friends like Fisher and Gale finally
found her temperament too volatile to sustain the intimacy she
sought. She was simply too demanding and too unforgiving
when she felt misunderstood. Rejection by her friends and public, unfortunately, fed Yezierska's sense of alienation still further,
which in turn made her more demanding, more desperate. This
pattern, initially set up in her relationship with John Dewey, was
doomed to repeat itself throughout her life. She never quite came
to terms with it, though in her old age she seems to have achieved
some degree of understanding and, thus, peace.

At the end of *Red Ribbon on a White Horse*, Yezierska reflects
on the immigrant woman's victimization by American consumer
culture, recognizing the falseness of that culture's terms:

> I saw that Hollywood was not my success, nor my present poverty
> and anonymity, failure. I saw that "success," "failure," "pov-
> erty," "riches," were price tags, money values of the marketplace
> which had mesmerized me and sidetracked me for years.[65]

For Yezierska, the "price tags" were high. Seduced and betrayed
by her public, by "the money values of the marketplace," she
was doomed to disillusionment. Her experience with John
Dewey, which she rightly saw as central in her life, she replicated
time and again. She had dramatically high hopes for realizing
herself and for finding her place in the world, hopes that were
almost always dashed. Yet she never stopped fighting. Will

Rogers once said to her, ''You're like a punch-drunk fighter, striking an opponent no longer there. You've won your fight and you don't know it.''[66] Given her high expectations, her daughter wrote, ''she was the loneliest person I knew.''[67]

In spite of difficult material circumstances and emotional turbulence, Yezierska never stopped writing. On her return to New York City from Arlington in 1932, in the middle of the depression, she found that her Hollywood success had backfired in another way—her legend dissuaded potential employers from offering her the often menial jobs she was forced to seek. When the Federal Writers' Project (FWP) opened its New York City offices in 1935, Yezierska rushed to its headquarters, eager, like scores of other depression-crippled artists, to earn money at her trade.[68]

*Red Ribbon on a White Horse* records the heady early days of the New York City FWP, when, under director Orrick Johns, a group of writers including Yezierska, Maxwell Bodenheim, Claude McKay, Harry Kemp, Ralph Ellison, and David Ignatow (as well as numbers of lesser-known newspapermen, poets, and fledgling writers) rejoiced in their fair pay, $21.67 a week, ''as hilarious as slum children around a Christmas tree.''[69] Yezierska details the problems that later beset the project—strikes, bureaucratic foul-ups, a scandal surrounding Orrick Johns caught with an FWP writer in a hotel fire—and her disillusionment under new director Travis Hoke, when she was put to work on the *WPA Guide to New York City*, cataloging trees in Central Park. By the time the FWP folded, it had fallen into such disrepute that Yezierska and her fellow writers had to, in Yezierska's words, ''make up a story to cover the time spent on W.P.A., and invent fictitious recommendations to get back to the honest, everyday working world.''[70]

In the years following her WPA experience, Yezierska lived in relative obscurity. She remained close to her daughter, who, along with Yezierska's niece Cecelia Ager, was writing for the new publication *PM*. In these years she worked on a play and a novel, both of which she seems to have destroyed. She also continued work on the highly fictionalized autobiography she had begun in the twenties, which was to appear in 1950 as *Red Ribbon on a White Horse*.

As usual, Yezierska found ''sponsors'' for her work, so that on June 24, 1950, the *New York Times* reported that the manuscript of *Red Ribbon* had arrived at Scribners with endorsements from Reinhold Niebuhr, Lloyd Morris, Jerome Nathanson, and W. H. Auden. How she had approached these worthies is not known. But she had charmed Auden, and he agreed to write an introduction for the book.

Auden's introduction was full of both praise and insight; he wrote warmly of Yezierska's "account of her efforts to discard fantastic desires and find real ones, both material and spiritual."[71] But, though he graciously allowed Yezierska to revise his introduction several times, she was not pleased with it and unleashed a steady stream of abuse in his direction. He "missed the point," she said years later. Again, a promising friendship ended in disappointment.[72]

Yezierska's book was well received. The eighteen years of silence intrigued her public, and the stories of the "sweatshop Cinderella" were fondly recalled. The *New York Times* reviewer celebrated "An Artist Unfrozen." The book did not sell well, however, and Yezierska's comeback was perhaps not as dramatic as the Hollywood veteran would have wished. But she was treated as a respected woman of letters; throughout the 1950s, the *New York Times* assigned her a steady stream of books to review.

By the 1960s, Yezierska's health had begun to fail. Yet these years saw some of her most sustained writing efforts, as she turned once again to her own experience for material. But this time she turned to another aspect of her plight, for now she had come to see herself as part of another minority, the aged. Stories like "Take Up Your Bed and Walk" and "The Open Cage" describe in forceful tones reminiscent of her earlier voice elderly heroines who struggle for autonomy and dignity in the face of poverty and prejudice. In a vivid 1964 sketch in *Commentary*, for instance, Yezierska takes on another professor, an unidentified sociologist who opened a "workshop on aging." Yezierska and several other elderly women attended the workshop dutifully and enthusiastically, only to become disillusioned when they realized that they had served as mere subjects for the professor's "thousand pages of research."[73] Fueled by the fires of experience, of repeatedly dashed hopes, Yezierska's fighting spirit never deserted her.

As her eyes began to fail, Yezierska needed assistance, and she turned to a succession of willing students whom she pressed into service as amanuenses and muses. Those who visited her in her small room on a topmost floor of a building at 113th Street and Broadway found a riveting presence, a vivid, white-haired woman wearing out-at-elbow sweaters and—in the summer— sneakers. As often as not Yezierska demanded that any visitors return to help her with her writing. Many eager students, trans- fixed by her intensity and stories of the palmy days of Hollywood and 1920s New York, found themselves returning again and again to Yezierska's aerie over the Hudson, where she would brew tea on a hot plate and curse the management of the single room occu- pancy hotel in which she lived. As often as not, Yezierska found fault with her visitors, but not without eking several weeks of (often unpaid) work from them.[74] She had lost none of her power to charm.

In 1963 a group of Michigan State University students rediscov- ered her work and began a persistent (but, because of her grow- ing infirmity, unsuccessful) campaign to engage her as a lecturer. She resurfaced in other quarters as well. In November 1962, at an ''Encounter with Creativity'' at the Theodor Herzl Institute on Park Avenue, she was honored as the ''Grand Lady of American Jewish Letters.'' In 1962 and 1965, through the help of writer Leon Edel and PEN director Marchette Chute, she received $500 grants from the National Institute of Arts and Letters. But Yezier- ska, nearly blind from cataracts, was unable to enjoy her mild renaissance. Late in life her daughter had married a younger man, and though Yezierska was deeply reluctant to become a presence in Louise's life, by 1964 her health forced her to move to Cleveland where her daughter could care for her. In 1968 she moved with Louise's family to California, living near them at a succession of residence and nursing homes. Yezierska died in the Ontario Nursing Home outside Los Angeles in 1970.[75]

# 8

## *"Old Men Dreaming Dreams"*

We must bridge this gap of poetry from science. We must heal this unnatural wound. . . . The same movement of the spirit, bringing man and man, nature and nature, into wider and closer unity, which has found expression by anticipation in poetry, must find expression by retrospection in philosophy. Thus will be hastened the day in which our sons and daughters shall prophesy, our young men shall see visions, and our old men dream dreams.

—John Dewey, "Poetry and Philosophy"

"I told you my diet should be prose," John Dewey had written to Anzia Yezierska in 1918. For the thirty-four years of life left to him, it was. Dewey never again took a risk as great as he had in his relationship with the immigrant woman writer, nor did he turn again to poetry to express emotions he had long suppressed. The record of Dewey's life is, after this moment, public and prosaic. Though he would show passionate commitment throughout his career to such causes as academic freedom and the defense of Leon Trotsky, there is no indication of any private passion in the life of this public man. Perhaps his encounter with the immigrant left him so vulnerable and exposed that he recoiled from it in horror. Once the moment had passed, he wished only to get his letters back and to put as much distance between himself and his experience with Yezierska as he could.

The Far East tour that John and Alice Dewey undertook in 1918 proved providential to the shaken philosopher. Though the visit to Japan and China was planned to last a year, Dewey welcomed the chance to extend it for another year. In the East he found his mind quickening again, but in a familiar, intellectual way. He regained some of his former vigor, writing enthusiastic letters to departmental colleagues about his fascination with the Orient. He had grown a little "stale," he wrote in a letter to be read by his department members at Columbia, and needed the infusion of energy that his experiences in the East provided him. He described his visit as "most interesting and intellectually the most profitable thing I've ever done." The new perspective gave him a sense of rebirth: "Nothing western looks quite the same any more, and this is as near to a renewal of youth as can be hoped for in this world."[1]

The sojourn in the East allowed Dewey to get back on track. He returned to the safety of family life, and he found fresh comfort there. No longer did his life seem the "sepulcher" his poems had juxtaposed to the "daily wonder" wrought by his new love; no more did the imagery of "miles of dull blur/[Stretching] out into the rut worn/Roads of Day" apply. Dewey's letters to his family back home—collected by his daughter Evelyn and published as John and Alice's *Letters from China and Japan*—reveal a warm family man, experiencing with his wife eager delight in the new world around him. It was a mere unhappy coincidence that a review of *Letters from China and Japan* appeared in the July 24, 1920, issue of the *Nation* on a page facing a poem, "Deported," by Anzia Yezierska; as she had predicted, oceans yawned between them.

This is not to suggest that Dewey never again experienced emotion, never felt passion. In fact, those around him knew how deeply felt were his responses to such events as his wife's death in 1927 and the untimely deaths of two of his grandchildren. And he made a bold emotional statement in 1946, in taking a second wife at the age of eighty-seven. Roberta Grant, at forty-two less than half Dewey's age, was an old family friend, and it is difficult to say whether Dewey sought love or companionship in marrying her. But it is significant that he did so, over the strong objections of his family and hers.[2] The marriage cost him his life interest in Alice Dewey's estate, which his first wife had left him on the condition he not remarry—in which case the estate was to go to the Dewey children. (In some circles the children were criticized for honoring these terms.)[3]

We have to assume Dewey led a normal emotional life in these years, relatively untroubled by the dualisms that had so plagued him in the past. His experience with Yezierska—and perhaps not least his poetic attempt to express it—seems to have had a cathartic effect. But what is striking is how guarded Dewey became over the years, how careful he was not to let anything of his personal life be revealed.

Dewey in these years left no traces of his private life. He saved no personal correspondence and seems to have destroyed any that was to any degree revealing. Though his life spanned the Civil War and the Cold War, and though he was aware of how much he had seen and experienced, he never felt an impulse toward the autobiographical. This would not be remarkable except that Dewey was fascinated by his own reactions to events, by how—to borrow from the title of one of his best-known works—his mind experienced nature. There are, of course, scores of explanations for his never attempting an autobiography—the most persuasive being his reticence about his private life—but it is noteworthy that the most "autobiographical" piece he left was an "intellectual autobiography," a statement provided for George P. Adams and William P. Montague's collection of philosophical life histories. There his life was dryly presented, as the piece's title indicates, as a journey "From Absolutism to Experimentalism," from one "ism" to another.[4]

But judgments about Dewey's autobiographical impulse must be amended in light of the discovery of his poetry, which is intensely personal and autobiographical, documenting his innermost feelings with no censoring mechanisms. He wrote his poetry in the belief that it would not be seen. He showed some of his early work to Alice, but he never intended it for public view. None of his children knew he wrote poetry, and he confided it to few friends. One of these was Waldo Frank, who wrote in a recent memoir about his experience as editor of *Seven Arts:*

> There was no demarkation between my contacts as an editor and as a man. For instance, I saw John Dewey not only at his office at Columbia University but in his New York apartment and his humble house on Long Island. . . . He confided; he wrote poetry of a sort. Oh, no! it was not to be seen.[5]

"Oh, no!" indeed. Dewey would have been horrified had he known his poems would ever be read. He thought he had disposed of them. Some he had literally thrown in the wastebasket—unaware of librarian Milton Halsey Thomas's "Boswellizing" instincts. Others, written on torn scraps of paper, he shoved back in the masses of paper crammed into the cubbyholes of his desk. The single sure time he gave anyone a copy of one of his poems—when he gave Yezierska "Generations"—proved disastrous; it was her sole shred of evidence of their affair, and she published it boldly in two different novels.

But, unknown to Dewey, his poems were "discovered" during his lifetime, as Dewey scholar Jo Ann Boydston learned when she undertook a definitive edition of the poems in the 1970s. The circumstances surrounding their "discovery" have all the earmarks of a detective story. Milton Halsey Thomas wrote to Boydston that he made many of his finds by "look[ing] in Dewey's wastebasket at the end of the day, particularly when it was full." In a 1928 diary entry Thomas recorded that Dewey was sorting through his papers and Thomas had "been gathering up the crumbs, as it were" of Dewey's housecleaning of books and papers the professor had packed up just before his 1918 trip to the East. Thomas added these to the cache of poems he had earlier gleaned from Dewey's wastebasket. More poems surfaced upon Dewey's retirement from Columbia in 1939, when Herbert Schneider took possession of Dewey's office. In Dewey's rolltop desk, he found "a mess of loose scraps of poetry"; he put them aside but fortuitously told Thomas what he had done. Thomas salvaged the poems and tucked them away with the others in the library's Columbiana collection.

"Curiously," writes Jo Ann Boydston in her dramatic account of the discovery, "no one asked Dewey himself about the poetry when it was discovered, neither in 1928 or 1939." But the circumstances are not curious at all. Thomas told Boydston that he and Schneider assumed Dewey "seemed to have no further interest in" these papers he had thrown out or overlooked.[6] This, of course, is unlikely. Thomas and Schneider had to have been fully aware of what Dewey's response would be if he knew that his assistant Thomas was in possession of this highly personal and revealing material. He would have reacted with horror and probably outrage, and certainly he would have seen to it that the papers were destroyed.

Family members and friends understood how Dewey would have felt, and the papers probably would have been destroyed or at least suppressed had not "rumors . . . circulated about the poetry'' among students of Dewey's life and work.[7] In 1957, when the poems still lay untouched and available among the Columbiana papers, a French Dewey scholar, Gerard Deladelle, hand copied the originals and applied to Roberta Dewey for permission to edit and publish the poetry. Roberta asserted her legal rights to the material and arranged for the university to transfer it to her. She had never seen the poetry before but, when she looked into it, found she rather liked it. She considered allowing the poems to be published but was dissuaded by family friend Agnes Meyer, wife of then *Washington Post* publisher Eugene Meyer and mother of current publisher Katharine Graham. Meyer told Roberta Dewey, ''I just have a hunch John wouldn't like it.''[8]

However correct Meyer's ''hunch''—and it was surely more than that—might have been, curiosity about the poetry ran too high for it to be suppressed for long. When the manuscript collection was turned over to the John Dewey Foundation after Roberta Dewey's death in 1970, the foundation directors knew publication of the poems was inevitable. They ''decided to postpone'' it, writes Boydston, until ''a thorough study could be made to verify Dewey's authorship and, if possible, to establish when [the poems] were composed.''[9]

In 1977, twenty-five years after Dewey's death, Boydston's edition of the poetry finally appeared. In her introduction, she stated,

> Dewey obviously did not intend to publish this poetry. Now, however, some twenty-five years after the death of an important figure like Dewey, it is appropriate that such a significant segment of his writing and life experience should become part of the published record.[10]

The highly private John Dewey, who had laboriously protected the most intimate details of his past and his emotional life, would not have approved this turn of events in the least.

During his lifetime Dewey the public man was hailed as a national hero, the philosopher of democracy. Sobriquets sprang up around him unchecked. Waldo Frank called him ''the most characteristic American mind of his generation''; A. H. Johnson, ''the philosopher of the common man''; Sidney Hook, ''a Yankee saint and an American Buddha"; W. I. Thomas, "America's medicine man"; Max Eastman, "the man who saved our children from dying from boredom, as we almost did in school."[11] The philosophical system he was thought to have fathered, pragmatism, was once synonymous with "American"; in 1950, Henry Steele Commager wrote that pragmatism "is almost the official philosophy of America."[12] Morris Cohen said that "if there could be such an office as that of national philosopher, no one else could properly be mentioned for it."[13]

Who was the man behind all these sobriquets? Dewey the private man remained elusive. He was presented as a "grey, gentle figure,"[14] a quiet, thoughtful man whose reticence was fondly ascribed to his New England childhood. Idealistic, yes, but "homespun" in his pragmatism. When Dewey turned seventy, eighty, then ninety—his birthdays were almost national holidays, occasions for the flowering of still more sobriquets—commentators rushed to find anecdotes that revealed his absentmindedness, gentleness, or humility. Among the old chestnuts were his loss of his hood at an honorary degree ceremony and his failure to recognize one of his own children passing him on the Columbia University campus. The all-time favorite was the "egg man" story: On his Long Island farm, when his handyman was not available, Dewey would deliver eggs to the farm's customers himself. On his entrance at a neighbor's cocktail party, the hostess was said to have blurted out, "Oh my God, the egg man!" In an incredible reach, on hearing this story, writer Horace Kallen ventured that this might have been the origin of the word "egghead."[15]

Egghead, indeed. The picture that emerges is curiously flat, one-dimensional, lifeless. It is a comfortable image because of its very flatness. Behind it is the sneaking suspicion that the man was boring. This impression is encouraged by the density of Dewey's writing, again a favorite target for posies of purple prose and bemused reminiscence. Max Eastman wrote that Dewey had "published 36 books and 815 articles and pamphlets—a pile 12 feet 7 inches high—but if he ever wrote one 'quotable' sentence it has got permanently lost in the pile."[16] Richard Hofstadter said his prose was

> of terrible vagueness and plasticity . . . suggestive of the cannonading of distant armies: one concludes that something portentous is going on at a remote and inaccessible distance, but one cannot determine just what it is.[17]

William James called his style "damnable; you might even say God-damnable"; Irwin Edman dubbed it "lumbering and bumbling." Quentin Anderson has compared Dewey to William Faulkner's Benjy, forever "trying to say."[18] Oliver Wendell Holmes eloquently summed up: "So, methought, God would have spoken had He been inarticulate, but keenly desirous to tell you how it was."[19]

Dewey was, indeed, often irritatingly vague. It is difficult to keep the heavily abstracted titles of his books straight: *Democracy and Education? Experience as Education? Art and Experience?* But there is something too easy in all this. In trying to express new ideas, one must struggle—as Dewey's contemporaries, the literary modernists, said—to "make it new": to find a new way of phrasing that is sometimes awkward but seeks to convey a new way of looking at things. The critics quoted above passed judgment after laboring in the fields of Deweyana, but we must be suspicious when Dewey is too readily dismissed as "unreadable"—the word might better be "unread." Dewey has been persistently misunderstood in part because few have taken the time to read him.

In 1926, Waldo Frank, writing as the *New Yorker's* "Search-Light," profiled John Dewey as "The Man Who Made Us What We Are." The piece is remarkably prescient in its understanding of what would become the official Dewey image; it presents a mild, cipherlike creature whose presence has nonetheless guided the currents of American life. Frank opens by addressing the reader, "You have probably heard of him—vaguely." The reader will probably have read some of his work, writes Frank, particularly if he has taken college courses, "and felt [his] brain grow maggoty after sixteen pages":

> No matter. You have certainly never seen his name in the headlines, nor his face in the pictorials. No matter, again. He has influenced *you*. He is the most influential American alive.

Dewey has influenced the reader of the *World* and the *New Republic* because he is the man behind the editors; he has influenced the reader whose child attends a progressive school; the reader who casts his vote for this senator over that one; the reader who believes the country is an experiment in democracy; the reader who believes in progress and science. "You may not know it," writes Frank, "but John Dewey is the living man that made you."[20]

Frank's comments on Dewey's huge influence were made in 1926; they have some resonance today. For Dewey was indeed a commanding figure in twentieth-century history. Between 1920 and his death he refined his philosophy with a series of monumental works, ranging from the broadest statement of his ideas, *Experience and Nature* (1925), to *Art As Experience* (1934) (which elaborated his philosophy of aesthetics), to *Logic: The Theory of Inquiry* (which formulated pragmatism's formalist method). Still more influential were his writings on social issues: *The Public and Its Problems* (1927), *Individualism Old and New* (1930), *Liberalism and Social Action* (1935), and *Freedom and Culture* (1939). These works became the handbooks of the administrators of the late 1920s and 1930s, years in which social planning became a new bureaucratic industry.

Dewey exerted influence in his actions as well during these years: through his long service for the League for Industrial Democracy (formerly the Intercollegiate Socialist Society); his involvement, with Salmon O. Levinson, in the outlawry of war movement that culminated in the Kellogg-Briand pact of 1928; his participation in setting up the New School's University-in-Exile to which refugee scholars, mainly German, flocked; his valiant defenses of academic freedom; and his participation in the Mexican trial of Leon Trotsky. From trips to the Far East, Russia, Turkey, and Mexico, Dewey returned with thorough and thoughtful analyses of conditions in those areas and their significance for the American future.

Moreover, Dewey continued to shape the course of American life in a familiar way, from behind the scenes, where, as Waldo Frank put it, he

> served as a kind of father-figure for a succession of movements and circles that needed the reassurance of linkage with American tradition; to have as an ally, John Dewey—morally earnest, with no evident animus against tradition as well—was almost like having Ralph Waldo Emerson himself on your side.[21]

Thus Frank in his profile cited among those who had felt Dewey's influence Herbert Croly, Horace Kallen, Walter Lippmann, Robert LaFollette, Max Eastman, Rabbi Stephen Wise, and

Clarence Darrow. Even those with whom Dewey differed—Bertrand Russell, most notably, or Morris Cohen—acknowledged that Dewey was at the center of the arena of debate.

Dewey's old age was marked by the same vigorous activity that characterized Anzia Yezierska's later years. Like her, too, he continued to write until the very last, most notably in collaboration with Arthur F. Bentley on problems of logic in the theory of knowledge. He enjoyed great public renown, accepting honorary degrees and prestigious speaking engagements. But, while Yezierska lived out her life in loneliness, Dewey had a new companion in his wife Roberta. On his death on June 1, 1952, Roberta decided on a "simple service," to which some five hundred people flocked.[22] And after his death he was repeatedly commemorated. The John Dewey Foundation was established in 1964. Several nations issued stamps in his honor.

Inevitably, John Dewey, the "grey, gentle figure," became a figure of controversy, which mounted in the years just before and after his death. In the 1950s he was blamed for everything from juvenile delinquency to the rise of the welfare state. In the same decade he came under vicious attack from various intellectuals for what Richard Hofstadter called his antiintellectualism.[23] In educational circles, he was strongly criticized by a group of traditionalist educators who included Robert M. Hutchins of the University of Chicago, Alexander Meiklejohn of the University of Wisconsin, Mark Van Doren of Columbia University, and Mortimer Adler, the "Great Books" founder. Most at issue was the "godlessness" of progressive education; a typical attack was Mortimer Adler's widely read "God and the Professors." In March 1952, just months before Dewey's death, a *Time* cover story on Adler contained a photograph of Dewey whose caption asked, "Worse than Hitler?"[24] In the 1960s, when his ideas about progressive education received renewed attention, Dewey was widely denigrated as an educational precursor of the counterculture. Most recently, E. D. Hirsch has cited him as the villain responsible for what Hirsch sees as America's nationwide cultural illiteracy.[25]

His politics were similarly misunderstood. On his return from Russia in 1928 he wrote glowingly of what he had seen in the schools there and was embraced by the American left; this and his involvement with the Trotsky investigation opened him to attack on all fronts. Conservatives saw in his political activities confirmation that his educational and social reforms were "godless" and "pagan," finding him responsible for widespread political permissiveness. For his criticism of Stalinism he was attacked as a "faithful lackey" of American capitalism and imperialism. In recent years, revisionist historians have criticized Dewey and his fellow Progressives as neo-Fascists for their efforts at social planning and, these critics argue, social control. On another flank, and in a more considered judgment, he has been criticized for his belief that problems of poverty and inequality can be solved through social reform.

At the center of this controversy was the mild Dewey, a man who allowed himself to be painted in colorless, vague tones. Behind this official image, of course, was a man whose emotional life was extremely complex. That he hid behind the image—even when it led to distortions and misunderstandings—is but another symptom of this emotional complexity.

Waldo Frank's profile, prescient in dubbing Dewey "the man who made us what we are," was apt in other ways as well, ways that can help illuminate how the elusive Dewey came to be so misunderstood. Frank wrote that the crux of Dewey the man and his work was accepting:

> He *accepts*. He has found life often cruel, often miserable. But his instinct drives him to accept. So he has elaborated an immensity of reasons why he should accept. He is not so far from his Puritan Christian ancestors, after all.[26]

There is something at once insightful and awry in this statement. Dewey *was* passive, in the sense that he was reactive, responsive to people and ideas around him; but "accepting" he was not always. And certainly he had—Frank was wrong here—traveled far from his "Puritan Christian ancestors." This is the same man who wrote the following lines to Anzia Yezierska on this very subject:

> *Then take me as I am,*
> *Partly true and partly sham*
> *Not from wilful chance*
> *But by too ready acceptance*
> *Of the constraining work of chance,*
> *Here a blow to shape, there a luring voice*

*To call.* If I have not wholly stood
Neither have I wholly bent.

("Two Weeks," 105–112, emphasis added)

Frank, who knew nothing of Dewey's involvement with Yezier-ska but did know of his poetry writing, was able to locate exactly the "crux" of Dewey but failed in understanding it. Note what is "partly true and partly sham" in the following passage from Frank's profile:

> He has a horror of emotional expression, equaled only by his re-spect for all men and women who express their emotions. *His* po-etry is unpublished; yet his driest work is builded [*sic*] on a mystic faith. But the faith he takes care to bury in intricate, methodological detail. Acceptance, again. If he had revolted too deeply from the world, he would have been a lyric poet. . . . But he could neither utterly rebel, nor utterly accept. So he swung his acceptance into the future: and, having done so, he found he could accept the present as the logical Cause of the good tomorrows.

The result, concluded Frank, was that Dewey had "turned his lyric energy into logical search" and set up "a Golden Calf called Progress. It justified for him the machines that racked him, the stupidities that flayed him."[27]

Frank was right on many accounts—he knew about Dewey's poetry and recognized Dewey's horror of emotion and his attrac-tion to those who expressed it. He was uncannily perceptive in tying this to Dewey's lyric impulse and the revolt from the world lyric poetry would entail. Meeting Anzia Yezierska, Dewey was transfixed by her emotional intensity; it drove him to rebel against the dualism in his own soul, the dualism that separated reason from emotion, the head from the heart. The result was an outburst of lyricism. When Dewey began a poem about "the silken web in which I'm bound" with the line "I wake from the long, long night," he began a short sweet aria of a sleeping giant awakened by passion in the form of a beautiful and vibrant red-headed woman. Finally, for a variety of reasons—her very emo-tional vibrance, the ties that bound him, and his own cowardice—he ceased his song and returned to the earthly "silken web."

For he could not, as Frank wrote, "entirely rebel." But neither could he "utterly accept." To Dewey's refusal to accept we can credit the great accomplishments of this vigorous man in the three decades following World War I, the years of his old age—for he turned the passion that drew him to poetry to a passion for logical inquiry, maintaining his faith in progress. What was lost in his final inability to rebel cannot be measured.

In 1936, at the age of seventy-eight, John Dewey was asked which books had been most important to him. The only fiction he named was *Tess of the d'Urbervilles.*[28] It is an interesting choice. In Thomas Hardy's 1891 novel, Tess is a charming naïf with an innocent wrong in her past. To Angel Clare, a romantic intellectual who has renounced his expected vocation in the church for the life of a farmer, she appears as a vision of purity, a rosy milkmaid possessed at once of healthy passion and a spotless mind. Tess tries to tell Angel of her past, but he cannot accommodate such a blot on her and does not listen. On their wedding night, when she finally tells him the truth, Angel turns from her in revulsion (though he has just confessed his own "experience" to her). Tess's response is heartbreaking. She pleads with him; she refuses to believe it. Her response, writes Hardy, "would have won round any man but Angel Clare." But Angel is very complex:

> Within the remote depths of his constitution, so gentle and affectionate as he was in general, there lay hidden a hard logical deposit, like a vein of metal in a soft loam, which turned the edge of everything that attempted to traverse it. It had blocked his acceptance of the Church; it blocked his acceptance of Tess. Moreover, his affection itself was less fire than radiance. . . . [29]

The results are tragic; Tess, Angel's wife "in name only," eventually returns to Alec d'Urberville, the relative who ruined her. When she sees Angel again, she murders d'Urberville, and Angel rejoins her for some scant idyllic days before she is finally caught on the plain at Stonehenge and hanged, "the President of the Immortals" having "ended his sport with Tess."[30] In Tess's universe, stars are worlds either blighted or splendid and sound. Ours is a blighted star.

Dewey's response to the grim determinism of Hardy's moral universe suggests that we need to reconsider the underpinnings of his much-celebrated pragmatism. It is indeed difficult to account for the importance *Tess* held for him. The answer must lie in the psychology of the thinly realized Angel Clare, whose emotional cowardice brings about Tess's real ruin. The generations of evangelical training that have made Angel Clare have made him unable to accept either a future in the church or the innocent delinquency of a woman as truly innocent as Tess and have made him averse to the claims of the body over those of the ascetic soul. Hardy writes that over Angel and Tess lay

> the shade of [Angel's] own limitations. With all his attempted independence of judgment this advanced and well-meaning young man . . . was yet the slave to custom and conventionality. . . . No prophet had told him, and he was not prophet to tell himself, that essentially this young wife of his was as deserving of the praise of King Lemuel ["Who can find a virtuous woman? For her price is far above rubies"] as any other woman endowed with the same dislike of evil, her moral value having to be reckoned not by achievement but by tendency.[31]

Hardy's portrait of Angel Clare disappoints, somehow, perhaps because his failure motivates the story's tragedy. He never attains the status of a villain; although he wrongs Tess, he is not the author of her tragedy. His sin is that of cowardice, hardly the stuff of heroes or villains.

Of course, John Dewey did not cite *Tess* as his most valued novel because he saw himself in Angel Clare. Dewey was free of the hypocrisy and puritanical priggishness that plagued Angel Clare. But, like Hardy's character, he suffered from the weight of generations of convention, and he too showed tragic emotional cowardice when confronted with Anzia Yezierska, his own vibrant Tess. Like Angel Clare, John Dewey felt with the head and not the heart. Like Angel Clare, John Dewey idealized and romanticized his lover to such a degree that she could never meet his expectations. Like Tess, Anzia Yezierska was not a disembodied idealization of Woman but flesh and blood, with real desires and limitations.

*Tess of the d'Urbervilles* is a monumental tragic work, and Dewey meant no revelation in citing it as his favorite novel, no indication that he read his own life in its terms. As we have seen, his interlude with Anzia Yezierska was just that—an interlude, a interval between two major stages of his own monumental life. But it was an interlude in which his innermost self was touched and revealed, and it colored his entire life no less than it did hers. His lifetime fondness for *Tess* suggests that his inner landscape may have resembled the Wessex of Thomas Hardy's blighted star. There remained in his nature chords of tragedy, emotion, and lyricism that were never played again.

That the discovery of Dewey's poetry has not seriously affected the official Dewey image is itself a comment on the monolithic quality of the common view of him. Today the image is largely intact. In academic circles Dewey is still revered as one of the great fathers of the twentieth-century university. Not inappropriately—he was the first president of the American Association of University Professors—he is invoked as part of the academic tradition. But that tradition is often called upon in the service of attempts to preserve so-called core curriculum courses that teach "traditional" values. John Dewey, these scholars would do well to remember, always preferred experiment to tradition.

Among philosophers, it seems to be considered wisest to let Dewey be. Certainly there are few "Deweyans" today, though many philosophers acknowledge their indebtedness to pragmatism. Richard Rorty is something of an exception. For the last decade or two he has vigilantly promoted Dewey's pragmatism as an answer to societal malaise and to what he sees as the inevitable death of philosophy. He places Dewey among a group he celebrates as "antiphilosophers": James, Nietzsche, Heidegger, Wittgenstein, and Foucault. Dewey lies, Rorty believes, at the end of Jacques Derrida's road, for he anticipated that structuralist's denial of the a priori existence of anything, of the notion of "truth" as accuracy of representation. Dewey offers human solidarity as a stay against the chaos such "antiphilosophy" insists on, argues Rorty. Most philosophers remain unconvinced, and many believe that Rorty simply misreads Dewey.[32]

Against those who invoke Dewey in the name of tradition are those who, following Adler and the critics of the 1960s, blame his educational innovations for undermining "traditional" values. Dewey has always been a villain to those who decry the secularity of our public schools, and it is once again fashionable, especially among the fundamentalist Right, to cast Dewey in a morality play on whose outcome our country's very future hinges. In setting the conditions for his 1988 presidential candidacy, fundamentalist leader Pat Robertson declared, ''We have taken the Holy Bible from our young and replaced it with the thoughts of Charles Darwin, Karl Marx, Sigmund Freud, and John Dewey.''[33] Here John Dewey is reduced to a tactical weapon in a very dangerous war, an occasion for a rhetorical flourish in a highly charged dialogue.

It is only among historians of education that Dewey's relationship with Yezierska has been duly noted, but for curiously motivated ends. They find in Dewey's Philadelphia study of Polish Americans in 1918 proof of what they take to be his paternalism and desire for social control, qualities it is fashionable in revisionist history to attribute to all Progressive reformers. These historians treat Yezierska's *All I Could Never Be* purely as further documentation of Dewey's formal study of the immigrant—one historian dismissed its literary value as rivaling that of *Jaws*[34]—failing to admit into the ''evidence'' Dewey's intimate involvement with an immigrant woman. Their effacement of Yezierska's existence echoes Dewey's attempt to expunge her from the record.

It is one of the many ironies in this story that today Anzia Yezierska's difficult name is in many circles more familiar than John Dewey's. For the slight resurgence of interest that she experienced in her later years has blossomed into a full-blown renaissance. When *Bread Givers* was reprinted in 1975, five years after Yezierska's death, it found an enthusiastic audience. The decade of Alex Haley's *Roots* saw a marked new interest in ethnic ancestry, and many second- and third-generation immigrant Americans found a distinctive voice in the novel. Women have found in Yezierska's fiction compelling portraits of female autonomy and independence. *Bread Givers* was so successful that other reprints followed: *Red Ribbon on a White Horse* in 1978, a collection of writings in 1979, and, in 1985, *Hungry Hearts*, the book that first won her fame. Sales are brisk; Yezierska once again has a loyal public, and her books are required reading in numerous college history and English courses. In academic circles, as the new social history looks to the experiences of those previously omitted from the historical record, Yezierska's fiction is considered a valuable document of an age. Her dream of ''opening up'' her culture to America seems to have been realized. Anzia Yezierska is in critical vogue.[35]

The irony of Yezierska's current popularity and Dewey's eclipse constitutes a cultural statement of sorts, but one whose meaning is difficult to decipher. Champions of the underdog may relish the irony, viewing Yezierska's recent rise as her revenge. But Dewey's star has not yet set, and Yezierska's shines at perhaps an unnatural height. It may be better to view this irony as the beginning of a redressing of balance. History is more than the record of great men, as the story of John Dewey and Anzia Yezierska shows. There is often a woman's voice in the background, persistent and insistent, if we listen carefully.

# Notes

*Introduction*

1. Corliss Lamont, ed., *Dialogue on John Dewey* (New York: Horizon Press, 1959), p. 49. Besides Lamont, those present were James T. Farrell, James Gutmann, Alvin Johnson, Horace Kallen, Harry W. Laidler, Ernest Nagel, John H. Randall, Jr., Herbert W. Schneider, Harold Taylor, and Milton Halsey Thomas. For Lamont's description of the evening, see *Yes To Life: Memoirs of Corliss Lamont* (New York: Horizon Press, 1981), pp. 82–83. Paul Levy, "A Philosopher's Love Songs," *Times Literary Supplement* (June 2, 1978), p. 611, draws attention to this significant moment.
2. Quoted in Jo Ann Boydston, "Introduction," in Jo Ann Boydston, ed., *The Poems of John Dewey* (Carbondale: Southern Illinois University Press, 1977), p. xi.
3. Louise Levitas Henriksen, "Afterword," in Alice Kessler-Harris, ed., *The Open Cage: An Anzia Yezierska Collection* (New York: Persea Books, 1979), p. 254.

*Chapter One   Dewey: The Making of the Philosopher*

1. On the closing of the frontier, see Henry Nash Smith, *Virgin Land: The American West as Symbol and Myth* (Cambridge, Mass: Harvard University Press, 1950). For a discussion of the significance of this social shift in relation to Dewey's generation, see, for example, Jean B. Quandt, *From the Small Town to the Great Community: The Social Thought of Progressive Individuals* (New Brunswick, N.J.: Rutgers University Press, 1970).
2. Corliss Lamont, ed., *Dialogue on John Dewey* (New York: Horizon Press, 1959), p. 89.
3. Dorothy Canfield Fisher, *Vermont Tradition: The Biography of an Outlook on Life* (Boston: Little, Brown, 1953), p. 383.
4. Dewey, "From Absolutism to Experimentalism," in George P. Adams and William Pepperell Montague, eds., *Contemporary American*

*Philosophy: Personal Statements,* vol. 2 (New York: Macmillan, 1930), p. 19.

5. Fisher, p. 369.
6. Ibid., p. 371.
7. Jane Dewey, ed., "Biography of John Dewey," in Paul Arthur Schilp, ed., *The Philosophy of John Dewey* (Evanston, Ill.: Northwestern University Press, 1939), p. 7.
8. George Dykhuizen, *The Life and Mind of John Dewey* (Carbondale, Ill.: Southern Illinois University Press, 1973), p. 6.
9. Dewey, "The Place of Religious Emotion," in Jo Ann Boydston, ed., *John Dewey: The Early Works, 1882–1898* (Carbondale: Southern Illinois University Press, 1969–1972), vol. 1, p. 91.
10. Robert C. Crunden, "Essay," in John D. Buenkher, John C. Burnham, and Robert C. Crunden, eds., *Progressivism* (Cambridge, Mass.: Schenkman, 1977), p. 93.
11. Elvirton Wright [Mrs. Jessie (Wright) Whitcomb], *Freshman and Senior* (Boston and Chicago: Congregational Sunday-School and Publishing Society, 1889), p. 309.
12. Max Eastman, *Great Companions* (New York: Farrar, Straus, and Cudahy, 1959), p. 250.
13. Fisher, p. 371.
14. Lewis S. Feuer, "America's Medicine Man" [review of Neil Coughlan's *Young John Dewey*], *Times Literary Supplement* (December 3, 1976), p. 1507.
15. Fisher, p. 370.
16. Fisher, p. 371.
17. Dykhuizen, *The Life and Mind of John Dewey,* p. 6.
18. Jane Dewey, p. 6.
19. Eastman, *Great Companions,* p. 254.
20. On moral philosophy, see, for example, D. H. Meyer, *The Instructed Conscience: The Shaping of the American National Ethic* (Philadelphia: University of Pennsylvania Press, 1972); Sidney Ahlstrom, "The Scottish Philosophy and American Theology," *Church History* 24 (1955), pp. 257–272; Raymond Jackson Wilson, *In Quest of Community: Social Philosophy in the United States, 1860–1920* (New York: Wiley, 1968); and Lawrence R. Veysey, *The Emergence of the American University* (Chicago: University of Chicago Press, 1965).
21. Dewey, "From Absolutism to Experimentalism," p. 15.
22. Neil Coughlan, *Young John Dewey: An Essay in American Intellectual History* (Chicago: University of Chicago Press, 1975), p. 8. See also Lewis S. Feuer, "John Dewey's Reading at College," *Journal of the History of Ideas* 9 (June 1958), pp. 415–421.
23. See, for example, Merle Curti, *The Growth of American Thought* (1943; 2nd ed., New York: Harper & Bros., 1951), and D. H. Meyer, "American Intellectuals and the Victorian Crisis of Faith," *American Quarterly* 27 (December 1975), pp. 585–603.

24. John Buckham was ordained a Congregational minister in 1888, was a pastor in New Hampshire churches until 1903, and then became a professor of Christian theology at the Pacific School of Religion in Berkeley, California. He was an exponent of Borden Parker Browne's "personalism," a movement that maintained that God was "personal." See J. C. Schwarz, ed., *Who's Who in the Clergy,* vol. 1, 1935–36 (New York: n.p.), p. 168, and various issues of the *Personalist,* a journal begun in 1920 that was the official voice of "personalism." James Buckham studied "religious journalism" at Andover Theological Seminary in 1891–1892, was associated with various literary and quasi-philosophical journals, and wrote a number of inspirational books about nature. The fates of the Buckham brothers are instructive, for they, like Dewey, had to "invent" their careers.

25. Charles Darwin, *The Autobiography of Charles Darwin,* ed. Nora Barlow (1887; reprint, New York: W. W. Norton, 1958), p. 87.

26. See Dorothy Ross's "The Development of the Social Sciences" in Alexandra Oleson and John Voss, eds., *The Organization of Knowledge in Modern America* (Baltimore: Johns Hopkins University Press, 1979), pp. 107–138, and her "American Social Science and the Idea of Progress" in Thomas L. Haskell, ed., *The Authority of Experts: Studies in History and Theory* (Bloomington: Indiana University Press, 1984), pp. 157–175.

27. Dewey, "Psychology and Social Practice," in Jo Ann Boydston, ed., *John Dewey: The Middle Works, 1898–1924,* vol. 1 (Carbondale: Southern Illinois University Press, 1976), p. 150.

28. Quoted in Dorothy Ross, *G. Stanley Hall: The Psychologist as Prophet* (Chicago: University of Chicago Press, 1972), p. 41.

29. Ross, ibid., p. 79.

30. Ross, ibid., p. 105–106.

31. Dewey, *German Philosophy and Politics* (New York: Henry Holt, 1915), p. 7.

32. Quoted in Burton J. Bledstein, *The Culture of Professionalism: The Middle Class and the Development of Higher Education in America* (New York: W. W. Norton, 1976), p. 159.

33. Quoted in Bledstein, p. 162.

34. Jane Dewey, p. 13.

35. Quoted in Dykhuizen, p. 25.

36. See Lawrence A. Cremin, *American Education: The National Experience 1783–1876* (New York: Harper & Row, 1980), p. 398, and Willard Emsbree, *The American Teacher: Evolution of a Profession in a Democracy* (New York, American Book Company, 1939), p. 199. See also Myra H. Strober and Audri Gordon, "The Feminization of Public School Teaching: A Cross-Sectional Analysis, 1850–1880," *Signs* 11 (Winter 1986), pp. 212–235.

37. Quoted in Sol Cohen, ed., *Education in the United States: A Documen-*

*tary History* (New York: Random House, 1974), vol. 3, pp. 1318–1319.

38. Quoted in Cohen, vol. 3, p. 1415.
39. See Bledstein for the most thorough study of professionalization; see also, for example, Roy Lubove, *The Professional Altruist: The Emergence of Social Work as a Career* (1965; reprint, New York: Atheneum, 1973). The most prominent critics of the progressives' "social engineering" have been Christopher Lasch, in *The New Radicalism in America (1889–1963): The Intellectual as a Social Type* (New York: Alfred A. Knopf, 1965), and Dorothy Ross, in the essays cited above.
40. Eastman, *Heroes I Have Known*, (New York: Simon & Schuster, 1942), p. 283.
41. Dewey, "From Absolutism to Experimentalism," p. 19.
42. Quoted in Coughlan, p. 16.
43. Dewey, "From Absolutism to Experimentalism," p. 16.
44. Coughlan, p. 67.
45. Dewey, "From Absolutism to Experimentalism," p. 25.
46. Ross, *G. Stanley Hall*, p. 146.
47. Dewey, "A College Course: What Should I Expect From It?" in Jo Ann Boydston, ed., *John Dewey: The Early Works*, vol. 3, pp. 52–53.
48. Jane Dewey, p. 21. For Alice Chipman Dewey, see Judy Suratt's entry in Edward T. James, ed., *Notable American Women 1607–1950* (Cambridge, Mass.: Harvard University Press, 1971), vol. 1, pp. 466–468. Lewis S. Feuer notes her study of Turgenev in "John Dewey and the Back-to-the-People Movement in American Thought," *Journal of the History of Ideas* 20 (October–December 1959), p. 548.
49. Eastman, *Heroes I Have Known*, p. 289.
50. Eastman, ibid., p. 293.
51. Lamont, p. 61.
52. Dykhuizen, *The Life and Mind of John Dewey*, p. 57.
53. Dykhuizen, "John Dewey and the University of Michigan," *Journal of the History of Ideas* 23 (October–December 1962), p. 517.
54. Lawrence Crunden, *Ministers of Reform: The Progressives' Achievement in American Civilization* (New York: Basic Books, 1982).
55. Dewey, "Christianity and Democracy," in Jo Ann Boydston, ed., *John Dewey: The Early Works*, vol. 4, p. 9.
56. Ibid.
57. D. H. Meyer, "American Intellectuals and the Victorian Crisis of Faith," *American Quarterly* 27 (December 1975), p. 602.
58. Coughlan, p. 96.
59. Quoted in Coughlan, p. 98.
60. Dewey, *Outline of a Critical Theory of Ethics*, in Jo Ann Boydston, ed., *John Dewey: The Early Works*, vol. 3, p. 239. On Dewey and the Ford brothers, see Coughlan, pp. 100–109; Feuer, "John Dewey and the

Back-to-the-People Movement in American Thought''; Willinda
Savage, "John Dewey and 'Thought News' at the University of
Michigan," *Michigan Alumnus Quarterly Review* 56 (May 27, 1950),
pp. 204–209; and Zena Beth McGlashan, "The Professor and the
Prophet: John Dewey and Franklin Ford," *Journalism History* 6 (Win-
ter 1979–1980), pp. 107–111, 123. For Dewey's comments on the
Fords to William James, see Ralph Barton Perry, *The Thought and
Character of William James* (Boston: Little, Brown, 1935), vol. 2, pp.
518–519.

61. Quoted in Coughlan, p. 96.
62. Corydon Ford, *The Child of Democracy: Being the Adventures of the Embryo State* (Ann Arbor, Mich.: John V. Sheehan, 1894), pp. 157–158.
63. Ibid., pp. 216–217.
64. Dewey, "The Ethics of Democracy," in Jo Ann Boydston, ed., *John
Dewey: The Early Works*, vol. 1, p. 237.
65. Ford, p. 217.
66. See Charles E. Rosenberg, *The Trial of the Assassin Guiteau: Psychiatry
and Law in the Gilded Age* (Chicago: University of Chicago Press,
1968). In view of the importance of Jane Addams to this story, it is
interesting to note that she was the best friend of Guiteau's half-
sister and was deeply upset by the assassination and Guiteau's exe-
cution. See James Weber Linn, *Jane Addams: A Biography* (1935; reprint, New York: Greenwood Press, 1968), p. 67.
67. Gary Bullert, *The Politics of John Dewey* (Buffalo, N.Y.: Prometheus
Books, 1983), p. 26.
68. Ross, *G. Stanley Hall*, p. 158.
69. Dewey, "The Sense of Solidity," in Jo Ann Boydston, ed., *John
Dewey: The Early Works*, vol. 5, p. 430.
70. Upton Sinclair, *The Autobiography of Upton Sinclair* (New York: Harcourt Brace, 1962), p. 135.
71. See Quandt, *From the Small Town to the Great Community*.
72. Quoted in Savage, "John Dewey and 'Thought News' at the University of Michigan," p. 207.
73. Quoted in McGlashan, p. 211.
74. See Robert H. Wiebe, *The Search for Order 1877–1920* (New York: Hill
and Wang, 1967).
75. Robert Ezra Park, *Race and Culture* (Glencoe, Ill.: Free Press, 1950),
pp. v–vi.
76. Quoted in Coughlan, p. 104.
77. David H. Burton, *Progressive Masks: Letters of Oliver Wendell Holmes,
Jr., and Franklin Ford* (Newark: University of Delaware Press, 1982),
p. 12. In a letter dated January 1, 1909, Ford tried to induce Holmes
to quit his job: "I think you should be asked to resign from the
Supreme Court and join the News Centre in New York. . . . We
cannot of course pay such salaries as, say, the steel Trust dispenses

with lavish hand, but we can do better than the present Supreme Court standards'' (p. 72).

78. Feuer, ''America's Medicine Man,'' p. 1507.

## Chapter Two  *Yezierska: The Making of the* Teacherin

1. Yezierska, *Salome of the Tenements* (New York: Boni and Liveright, 1923), p. 65.
2. *The Poems of John Dewey*, Jo Ann Boydston, ed. (Carbondale: Southern Illinois University Press), p. 4.
3. Naturalization records in the National Archives, New York Branch, vol. 85, p. 5, indicate that Bernard Mayer was naturalized in 1906; he gave his date of birth as September 1851. Yezierska's birthplace is usually given as Plinsk, a town to be found on no map. In a letter to the author, dated August 8, 1986, Victor Rubenstein suggested that ''Ploch'' is how the village appears on Polish maps, and that it was pronounced ''Plutzk''; he visited the town in 1924. But the exact name and location of Yezierska's birthplace remain, at this writing, difficult to pinpoint.

     The other Yezierska children were Bessie (who died in early childhood), Mayer, Helena, Isidore, Gustave, David, Felicia, Henry, and Bill.
4. Yezierska, *Children of Loneliness* (New York: Funk & Wagnalls, 1923), p. 9.
5. Yezierska, *Red Ribbon on a White Horse* (1950; reprint, New York: Persea Books, 1981), p. 49.
6. Yezierska, *Bread Givers* (1925; reprint, New York: Persea Books, 1975), p. 33.
7. Yezierska, *Hungry Hearts* (1920; reprint, New York: Persea Books, 1985), p. 261.
8. Ibid., pp. 261–262.
9. Ibid., p. 46.
10. See the naturalization records cited above for the date of arrival. The naturalization papers of Max Mayer, the eldest brother, indicate that he arrived earlier, in 1886 (bundle 561).
11. Jonathan Goldberg, interview with author, June 16, 1986. The sources for Yezierska's life range widely in accuracy. The correspondence of Louise Levitas Henriksen and Alice Kessler-Harris and of Henriksen and Jules Chametzky, in the author's collection, indicates that Yezierska's daughter Henriksen was not sure how many brothers and sisters her mother had—nor was Yezierska. Other plausible birthdates, according to Chametzky, Kessler-Harris, and Henriksen, are 1883 and 1885.
12. 1969 interview of Yezierska by Ralda Sullivan, quoted in Ralda Sullivan, ''Anzia Yezierska, An American Writer,'' Ph.D. Diss., University of California, Berkeley, 1975, p. 25.

13. Yezierska, *Bread Givers*, p. 16.
14. Ibid., pp. 9–10.
15. Yezierska described her brother-in-law's living as "precarious" to Sullivan, p. 35. The inscribed copy of *Bread Givers* is in the Haldeman-Julius Collection, Pittsburg (Kansas) State Library.
16. Yezierska, *Bread Givers*, p. 286.
17. Yezierska, *Red Ribbon on a White Horse*, p. 72.
18. Irving Howe, *World of Our Fathers* (New York: Simon & Schuster, 1976), p. 230.
19. Moses Rischin, *The Promised City: New York's Jews, 1870–1914* (1962; reprint, Cambridge, Mass.: Harvard University Press, 1977), p. 102.
20. Quoted in Moses Isaiah Berger, "The Settlement, the Immigrant, and the Public School: A Study of the Influence of the Settlement Movement and the New Migration upon Public Education," D.Ed. diss., Teachers College, Columbia University, 1956, p. 50.
21. Berger, p. 55, ellipsis in original.
22. Yezierska, *Hungry Hearts*, p. 57.
23. Ibid., p. 132.
24. *Alliance Review* 2 (January 1902), p. 311. (In the Jewish Division, New York Public Library.)
25. "The Clara de Hirsch Home for Working Girls," *New York Times*, May 23, 1899, p. 5. Further information about the Home was provided in a talk by Nancy Sinkoff, November 11, 1986, at the YIVO Institute, New York City, "Educating for Proper Jewish Womanhood: A Case Study in Domesticity and Vocational Training, 1897–1926."
26. Quoted in Sullivan, p. 42. A record of Hattie Mayer's application to the home is in the records of the Clara de Hirsch Home for Working Girls (at the 92nd Street Y Archives, box 4, folder 25, Record of Applications, 1887–1900); it is dated February 19, 1900.
27. Yezierska, *Arrogant Beggar* (Garden City, N.Y.: Doubleday, 1927), p. 56.
28. Ibid., p. 59.
29. Ibid., pp. 63–64.
30. Yezierska to Rose Pastor Stokes, September 28, 1916. Rose Pastor Stokes Papers, reel 3300, folder 101. The Yezierska/Stokes correspondence is in the Collection of American Literature, The Bienecke Rare Book and Manuscript Library, Yale University. References given here and subsequently are to the microfilms of that correspondence in the Tamiment Library at New York University.
31. Yezierska to Charles Olson, April 1, 1953. Charles Olson Papers, Literary Archives, University of Connecticut.
32. Clara de Hirsch Home for Working Girls, *Report of Officers* (New York: Press of Philip Cowen, 1901), p. 53.

     Mrs. Ollesheimer's obituary appeared in the *New York Times*, December 1, 1923; she also helped to establish the Manhattan Trade School for Girls, an institution with a similar purpose.

33. See Lawrence A. Cremin, David A. Shannon, and Mary Evelyn Townsend, *A History of Teachers College, Columbia University* (New York: Columbia University Press, 1954); on Grace Hoadley Dodge see Ellen Condliffe Lageman, *A Generation of Women: Education in the Lives of Progressive Reformers* (Cambridge, Mass.: Harvard University Press, 1979).

34. Yezierska, *Bread Givers*, p. 246.

35. Quoted in Emma Seifrit Weigley, "It Might Have Been Euthenics: The Lake Placid Conferences and the Home Economics Movement," *American Quarterly* 26 (March 1974), p. 82.

36. Quoted in Susan Strasser, *Never Done: A History of American Housework* (New York: Pantheon, 1982), p. 210.

37. Ava Milam Clark and J. Kenneth Munford, *Adventures of a Home Economist* (Corvallis: Oregon State University Press, 1964), p. 24.

38. Strasser, p. 210.

39. Quoted in Laura Shapiro, *Perfection Salad: Women and Cooking at the Turn of the Century* (New York: Farrar, Straus & Giroux, 1986), p. 139. With Shapiro and Strasser, see Margaret Rossiter, *Women Scientists in America: Struggles and Strategies to 1940* (Baltimore: Johns Hopkins University Press, 1982), and Ruth Schwartz Cowan, *More Work for Mother: The Ironies of Household Technology from the Open Hearth to the Microwave* (New York: Basic Books, 1983).

40. Weigley, p. 86.

41. Howe, p. 175.

42. Gale's two articles were "Shall the Kitchen in Our Home Go?" *Ladies Home Journal* 36 (March 1919), p. 35, and "Is Housework Pushing Down the Birth Rate?" (May 1919), p. 41. See also "One Kitchen Fire for 200 People," *Ladies Home Journal* 35 (September 1918), p. 97.

43. "Learning Home Arts," *New York Times*, October 31, 1909, part 5, p. 11.

44. Yezierska, *Arrogant Beggar*, p. 77.

45. *Teachers College Announcement, 1903–1904*, pp. 68–71.

46. Clara de Hirsch Home for Working Girls, *Report of Officers*, pp. 50–51.

47. Shapiro, pp. 6–7.

48. Yezierska, *Arrogant Beggar*, p. 66.

49. Yezierska to Zona Gale, August 3, [1930?]. Zona Gale Papers, State Historical Society of Wisconsin, Madison.

50. *Teachers College Announcement, 1903–1904*, p. 71.

51. Yezierska, *Hungry Hearts*, p. 166. "Soap and Water" was a particularly important story to Yezierska, perhaps because its subject matter touched her so deeply. In a letter to Ferris Greenslet, Yezierska asked him not to cut the story from *Hungry Hearts*: "This was the first thing I tried to write and it's more real to me than the other stories," April 20, 1920. Houghton Mifflin Records, Houghton Library, Harvard University.

52. Yezierska, *Salome of the Tenements*, p. 122.

53. Quoted in Sullivan, p. 42.
54. Teachers College, *Class of 1904, Proceedings* (n.p.). Department of Special Collections, Milbank Memorial Library, Teachers College.
55. Yezierska, *Bread Givers*, p. 212.
56. Teachers College, *Class of 1904, Proceedings* (n.p.).
57. Ibid.
58. Yezierska's teaching positions are documented in the Board of Education's *Directory of Teachers in the Public Schools*, published annually, and in the *Journal of the Board of Education* for these years.
59. Louise Levitas Henriksen, "Afterword," in Alice Kessler-Harris, ed. *The Open Cage: An Anzia Yezierska Collection* (New York: Persea Books, 1979), p. 258.

Chapter Three    *Dewey, 1894–1904*

1. Quoted in Cremin, *The Transformation of the School: Progressivism in American Education* (New York: Alfred A. Knopf, 1961), p. 116.
2. Edward Wagenknecht, *Chicago* (Norman: University of Oklahoma Press, 1964), pp. 18–19.
3. Dykhuizen, *The Life and Mind of John Dewey*, p. 105.
4. Henry Adams, *The Education of Henry Adams* (1918; reprint, Boston, Mass.: Houghton Mifflin, 1961), p. 343.
5. On the Chicago World's Fair, see David F. Burg, *Chicago's White City of 1893* (Lexington: University Press of Kentucky, 1976); Jeanne Madeline Weimann, *The Fair Women* (Chicago: Academy Chicago, 1981); and Reid Badger, *The Great American Fair: The World's Columbian Exposition and American Culture* (Chicago: Nelson Hall, 1979).
6. Jane Addams, *Twenty Years at Hull-House* (1910; reprint, New York: New American Library, 1960), p. 24. The best biography of Addams is Allen F. Davis, *American Heroine: The Life and Legend of Jane Addams* (New York: Oxford University Press, 1973); see also Lasch, *The New Radicalism in America*, pp. 3–37; and Jill Conway, "Jane Addams, An American Heroine," *Daedalus* 93 (Spring 1964) 761–80.
7. Crunden, *Ministers of Reform*, p. 18.
8. Addams, p. 32.
9. Addams, p. 59.
10. Addams, p. 137.
11. Allen F. Davis, *Spearheads for Reform: The Social Settlements and the Progressive Movement, 1890–1914* (New York: Oxford University Press, 1967), p. 31.
12. Emmett Dedmon, *Fabulous Chicago* (New York: Random House, 1953), p. 247.
13. The address was printed in Jane Addams, *The Excellent Becomes the Permanent* (New York: Macmillan, 1932).
14. Jane Dewey, p. 30.
15. On Harper's view of the school, see Richard J. Storr, *Harper's Uni-*

*versity: The Beginnings* (Chicago: University of Chicago Press, 1966), p. 297. The fullest account of the administrative conflicts surrounding the school can be found in Dykhuizen, "John Dewey: The Chicago Years," *Journal of the History of Philosophy* 2 (October 1964), pp. 227–253.

16. For the operations of the Laboratory School, see Katherine Camp Mayhew and Anna Camp Edwards, *The Dewey School: The Laboratory School of the University of Chicago* (New York: Appleton-Century, 1936). Mayhew was a vice-principal of the school, Edwards a history teacher and later special tutor there.

17. Quoted in Dykhuizen, *The Life and Mind of John Dewey*, p. 98.

18. Ibid., p. 51.

19. Dewey, "The New Psychology," in Jo Ann Boydston, ed., *John Dewey: The Early Works*, vol. 1, p. 58.

20. Dewey, "My Pedagogic Creed," in Jo Ann Boydston, ed., *John Dewey: The Early Works*, vol. 5, pp. 87, 95.

21. Joseph Ratner, ed., *The Philosophy of John Dewey* (New York: Henry Holt, 1928), p. 382. This talk also appears as the last chapter of Volume 1 of Dewey's *Philosophy and Civilization* (New York: Minton, Balch, 1931).

22. Starr, p. 298.

23. See Cremin, *The Transformation of the School*; David Nasaw, *Schooled to Order: A Social History of Public Schooling in the United States* (New York: Oxford University Press, 1979); R. Freeman Butts, *A Cultural History of Education* (New York: McGraw-Hill, 1947).

24. Dewey, *School and Society*, in Jo Ann Boydston, ed. *John Dewey: The Middle Works, 1898–1924* (Carbondale: Southern Illinois University Press, 1976), vol. 1, p. 17.

25. Dykhuizen, "John Dewey: The Chicago Years," pp. 245–246.

26. Ida Heffron, *Francis Wayland Parker: An Interpretive Biography* (Los Angeles: Ivan Deach, Jr., 1934), p. 131. On Parker's life, see also Jack K. Campbell, *Colonel Francis Parker: The Children's Crusader* (New York: Teachers College Press, 1967).

27. Heffron, *Francis Wayland Parker*, p. 135.

28. Dewey, *Characters and Events*, Joseph Ratner, ed. (New York: Henry Holt, 1929), vol. 1, p. 98.

29. Arthur G. Wirth, *John Dewey as Educator: His Design for Work in Education (1894–1904)* (New York: John Wiley & Sons, 1966), pp. 45–46.

30. Dewey, "The School as Social Center," *National Education Association Addresses and Proceedings* (1902), p. 381.

31. Addams, "A Toast to John Dewey," *Survey* 63 (November 15, 1929), p. 203.

32. Davis, *Spearheads for Reform*, p. 58.

33. Addams, *Twenty Years at Hull-House*, p. 76. On Davidson's life, see Kurt F. Leidecker, *Yankee Teacher: The Life of William Torrey Harris* (New York: The Philosophical Library, 1946); Leonora Cohen Rosenfeld, *Portrait of a Philosopher: Morris R. Cohen in Life and Letters* (New

York: Harcourt, Brace & World, 1948); and a contemporary account, "A Modern Wandering Scholar," *Current Literature* 29 (December 1900), p. 648.

34. Thomas Davidson, *The Education of the Wage-Earners*, Charles M. Bakewell, ed. (Boston: Ginn and Co., 1904), p. 101.

35. Morris Cohen, "Some Ideals and Characteristics of Thomas Davidson," *Alliance Review* 1 (December 1901), pp. 260–261.

## Chapter Four    *Yezierska, 1904–1917*

1. Abraham Cahan, "Foreword," *Selected Songs of Eliakum Zunser* (New York: Zunser Publishing Co., 1928). Yezierska cited Zunser, whom she likened to Bob Dylan, as a major influence on her work. See Sullivan, pp. 49–50.

2. Nahma Sandrow, "Yiddish Theatre and American Theatre," in Sarah Blacher Cohen, ed., *From Hester Street to Hollywood: The Jewish-American Stage and Screen* (Bloomington: Indiana University Press, 1983), p. 25.

3. Biographical information on Miriam Shomer Zunser is from Emily Wortis Leider, "Postscript," in Miriam Shomer Zunser, *Yesterday: A Memory of a Russian Jewish Family*, Emily Wortis Leider, ed. (1939; reprint, New York: Harper & Row, 1978), and from correspondence of Florence Zunser Saltz with the author. See also entries for Zunser and her husband Charles in *Who's Who in American Jewry 1928–1939*, John Simons, ed. (New York: National News Association, 1939), p. 1177. Zunser went on to write well-received Yiddish plays with her sister Rose and became an ardent Zionist, Hadassah leader, and a founder of MAILAMM, an organization supporting Jewish music in Palestine and America; she died in 1951.

4. Miriam Shomer Zunser, "The Jewish Literary Scene in New York at the Turn of the Century," *YIVO Annual of Jewish Culture* 7 (1952), p. 292.

5. Yezierska, *Salome of the Tenements*, p. 173.

6. For Stokes's life, see the entry by David A. Shannon in *Notable American Women 1607–1950* (Cambridge, Mass.: Harvard University Press, 1971), vol. 3, pp. 384–386; Cecyle S. Neidle, *America's Immigrant Women* (Boston: Twayne, 1975); and Ruth Sochen, *The New Woman: Feminism in Greenwich Village, 1910–1920* (New York: Quadrangle Books, 1972).

   For contemporary accounts, see, for instance, "A Ghetto Romance," *New York Tribune Illustrated Supplement*, April 16, 1905; "J. G. Phelps to Wed Young Jewess," *New York Times*, April 6, 1905, p. 1; and "Mrs. J. G. Stokes at Home," *Harper's Bazaar* 40 (September 1906), pp. 794–799.

7. Mabel Dodge Luhan, *Movers and Shakers*, vol. 3 of *Intimate Memories* (New York: Harcourt Brace, 1936), p. 143.

8. Quoted in Judith Schwarz, *Radical Feminists of Heterodoxy: Greenwich*

*Village 1912–1940* (Lebanon, N. H.: New Victoria Publishers, 1982), p. 1.

9. Carroll Smith-Rosenberg, *Disorderly Conduct: Visions of Gender in Victorian America* (New York: Alfred A. Knopf, 1985), p. 177. James R. McGovern, in "The American Woman's Pre-World War Freedom in Manners and Morals," *Journal of American History* 55 (September 1968), pp. 315–333, establishes definitively that, contrary to the views of such historians as Frederick Lewis Allen and William Leuchtenberg, the "new woman" was not a creation of the 1920s.

10. Peter Gabriel Filene, *Him/Her/Self: Sex Roles in Modern America* (New York: New American Library, 1975), p. 25.

11. Caroline Ticknor, "The Steel-Engraving Lady and the Gibson Girl," *Atlantic Monthly* 88 (July 1901), p. 106.

12. Robert E. Humphrey, *Children of Fantasy: The First Rebels of Greenwich Village* (New York: John Wiley & Sons, 1978), p. 23.

13. See "Dr. Grant Quits the Liberal Club," *New York Times*, September 12, 1913, p. 7; "Aided Mrs. Edgell, Married Herself," *New York Times*, March 19, 1913, p. 8.

14. *New York Times*, January 12, 1915, p. 1.

15. Gorham Munson, *The Awakening Twenties: A Memoir-History of a Literary Period* (Baton Rouge: Louisiana State University Press, 1985), p. 74.

16. Albert Parry, *Garrets and Pretenders: A History of Bohemianism in America* (1933; reprint, New York: Dover Books, 1960), p. 270. See also Sochen, *The New Woman*; Humphrey, *Children of Fantasy*; and Allen Churchill, *The Improper Bohemians: A Re-Creation of Greenwich Village In Its Heyday* (New York: E. P. Dutton, 1959). Elizabeth Gurley Flynn, *The Rebel Girl: An Autobiography, My First Life (1906–1926)* (1955; reprint, New York: International Publishers, 1973), p. 172, remembers Rodman as "a truly remarkable woman . . . who fought the school system on a dozen fronts." Bernadine Kielty Scherman, in *Girl From Fitchburg* (New York: Random House, 1964), p. 63, remembers "Henrietta Rodman, a high school teacher, a plain woman, but with powerful personality and influence, who after school hours donned sacklike garments as a protest against the still prevalent whalebones and corsets, and preached against the hypocrisy of the double standard and legal marital ties."

17. Quoted in Sullivan, p. 55.

18. Floyd Dell, *Love in Greenwich Village* (New York: George and Doran, 1924), pp. 17–18.

19. Harry Kemp, *More Miles: An Autobiographical Novel* (New York: Boni and Liveright, 1926), pp. 90, 106. Kemp also fictionally describes Rodman's controversial marriage.

20. Quoted in Sullivan, p. 54. Fisher's reference is written on a folder of correspondence with Yezierska in the Dorothy Canfield Fisher Papers at the Bailey/Howe Library, University of Vermont.

21. Mary A. Hill, *Charlotte Perkins Gilman: The Making of a Radical Feminist, 1860–1896* (Philadelphia: Temple University Press, 1980), pp. 295, 267.
22. Olive Schreiner, *The Story of an African Farm* (1883; reprint, New York: Penguin Books, 1971), p. 232.
23. William O'Neill, *Divorce in the Progressive Era* (New Haven, Conn.: Yale University Press, 1967), p. 138.
24. Ellen Key, *Love and Marriage,* trans. Arthur G. Chater, (New York: G. P. Putnam's, 1911), p. 359.
25. Quoted in Mari Jo Buhle, *Women and American Socialism, 1870–1920* (Urbana: University of Illinois Press, 1981), p. 294.
26. Quoted in Sullivan, p. 57.
27. Yezierska to Rose Pastor Stokes, September 28, 1916, Rose Pastor Stokes Collection, reel 3300, folder 101. Tamiment Library, New York University.
28. O'Neill, p. 255.
29. Quoted in Sullivan, p. 55. For the regimen of the academy, see Algernon Tassin, "The American Dramatic Schools," *Bookman* 25 (April 1907), 151–165. The American Academy of Dramatic Arts has no record of her attendance, but Yezierska described it in the 1969 interview with Sullivan, and Louise Levitas Henriksen confirmed it in a letter to the author, April 2, 1986. It is supported by Yezierska's friendship with Marcet Haldeman-Julius, who does appear in the Academy's records in 1909–1910, and to whom Yezierska gave an inscribed copy of *Love and Marriage* in 1911.
30. Frederic Cornell, "A History of the Rand School of Social Science, 1906–1956," unpublished D. Ed. dissertation, Teachers College, 1976, p. 65. The Board of Education's *Directory of Teachers in the Public Schools* for 1910 lists Yezierska's address as 112 E. 19th St., the location of the Rand School. The School's record in the years 1906–1911 indicate a category, "Rent from Lodgers"; see Cornell, pp. 228–9.
31. Humphrey, p. 5.
32. The articles in question are "Asks Separation from Spirit Wife," *New York American,* May 23, 1911, p. 3, and "Mental Bride's Views on Wedlock," *New York American,* May 25, 1911, p. 3.
33. Interview of Louise Levitas Henriksen with author, May 20, 1987. Levitas, according to Henriksen, was considerably gentler than Gordon.
34. Yezierska describes herself as an investigator for Hebrew Charities in Yezierska to Rose Pastor Stokes, September 28, 1916, Rose Pastor Stokes Collection, reel 3300, folder 101, Tamiment Library, New York University. In a letter to the author, April 2, 1986, Louise Levitas Henriksen said that Yezierska ran a model flat for the Charities.
35. Yezierska to Rose Pastor Stokes, [September 1916?], reel 68, folder 15, Socialist Collections in the Tamiment Library, New York University.

36. Quoted in Sullivan, pp. 64–65.
37. Yezierska to Rose Pastor Stokes, October 18, 1916, reel 68, folder 15, Socialist Collections in the Tamiment Library, New York University.
38. Ibid., [n.d.], reel 68, folder 15, Socialist Collections in the Tamiment Library, New York University.
39. Ibid., [n.d.], reel 68, folder 15, Socialist Collections in the Tamiment Library, New York University.
40. Mrs. Arnold Levitas, "Baby Garden," *Survey*, 30 (April 26, 1913), p. 151.
41. Ibid., pp. 150–51.
42. See Sullivan, p. 54.
43. "Feminists Design a New Home," *New York Times*, April 5, 1914, part 4, p. 4.
44. "Feminists Debate Plans for a House," *New York Times*, April 22, 1914, p. 12.
45. Ibid.
46. "Education for Motherhood," *Atlantic Monthly*, 112 (July-August 1913), p. 52. See also "Charlotte Perkins Gilman's Reply to Ellen Key," *Current Opinion*, 54 (March 1913), 220–1.
47. "Ellen Key's Attack on Amaternal Feminism," *Current Opinion*, 54 (February 1913), 138–9.
48. Quoted in Sullivan, pp. 63–4; manuscript in Louise Levitas Henriksen's collection.
49. Yezierska to Dorothy Canfield Fisher, May 31, [1932?], Dorothy Canfield Fisher Papers, Bailey/Howe Library, University of Vermont.
50. Yezierska, "America and I," in *The Open Cage*, p. 33.
51. Yezierska, *Hungry Hearts*, p. 230.
52. Dr. Henry Grinberg, in an interview with the author, June 7, 1986, reported that Yezierska told him of this incident. Yezierska's relatives have disputed it.
53. Yezierska, *Red Ribbon on a White Horse*, p. 61.

## Chapter Five   *Dewey, 1904–1917*

1. George Dykhuizen, *The Life and Mind of John Dewey* (Carbondale: Southern Illinois University Press, 1973), p. 180.
2. Jane Dewey, "Biography of John Dewey," in Paul A. Schilp, ed., *The Philosophy of John Dewey* (Evanston, Ill.: Northwestern University Press, 1939), vol. 1, p. 35.
3. Max Eastman, *Great Companions* (New York: Farrar, Straus, & Cuddahy, 1959), p. 280.
4. For an analysis of the two "generations" of intellectuals discussed see Paul Bourke, "The Social Critics and the End of American Innocence," *Journal of American Studies* 3 (July 1969), 57–72.
5. See John Dewey, "Industrial Education and Democracy," *Survey* 29 (March 22, 1913), 870–871. On the industrial education movement, see James B. Gilbert, *Work Without Salvation: America's Intellectuals*

*and Industrial Education, 1880–1910* (Baltimore: Johns Hopkins University Press, 1977), and Sol Cohen, "The Industrial Education Movement, 1906–1917," *American Quarterly* 20 (Spring 1968), 95–110.

6. John Dewey, "Introduction," in Henry Street Settlement, Committee on Vocational Education, ed., *Directory of the Trades and Occupations Taught at the Day and Evening Schools in Greater New York* (New York, 1916).

7. Quoted in Lawrence Cremin, *The Transformation of the School: Progressivism in American Education* (New York: Alfred A. Knopf, 1961), p. 34.

8. John Dewey, "Nationalizing Education," *National Education Association Addresses and Proceedings* 54 (1916), pp. 183–189.

9. Anzia Yezierska, "To the Stars," *Children of Loneliness* (New York: Funk & Wagnalls, 1923), p. 96, Yezierska quotes from Dewey's "Nationalizing Education," p. 187.

10. For a discussion of Dewey's involvement with the professional organization of teachers, see Dykhuizen, pp. 144–146 and 230–231. On the movement itself, see The Committee on Educational Reconstruction, *Organizing the Teaching Profession: The Story of the American Federation of Teachers* (Glencoe, Ill.: Free Press, 1955).

11. Quoted in John Joseph Carey, "Progressives and the Immigrant, 1885–1915," Ph.D. diss., University of Connecticut, 1968, p. 130.

12. Yezierska told this to Ralda Sullivan in a 1969 interview. See Ralda Sullivan, "Anzia Yezierska: An American Writer," Ph.D. diss., University of California, Berkeley, 1975, p. 50.

13. Lillian D. Wald, *Windows on Henry Street* (Boston: Little, Brown, 1934), p. 255.

14. See Arthur Wertheim, *The New York Little Revolution: Iconoclasm, Modernism, and Nationalism in American Culture, 1908–1917* (New York: New York University Press, 1976), pp. 19–28.

15. Randolph Bourne, *The Gary Schools* (Boston: Houghton Mifflin, 1916).

16. Dewey to Scudder Klyce, July 15, 1915. In the Scudder Klyce Papers, Manuscript Division, Library of Congress. Dewey scholar Jo Ann Boydston has written on Dewey's views on women in "John Dewey and the New Feminism," *Teachers College Record* 76 (February 1975), pp. 441–448, where, in this single study of Dewey's feminism, she pointed out the similarity between feminists' language and Dewey's description of himself as a "hog."

17. Dewey to Klyce, May 8, 1920.

18. Ibid., July 5, 1915.

19. Ibid., May 8, 1920.

20. Ibid.

21. "Mrs. Mackay Pleads for Equal Suffrage," *New York Times*, January 16, 1909, p. 18. See also "Suffrage Campaign Opens at Columbia," *New York Times*, July 27, 1909, which reports a speech given by

Dewey on "Some Educational Aspects of Equal Suffrage," in which he called for women to be appointed to the Board of Education.

22. Dewey, "A Symposium on Women's Suffrage," *International* 3 (1911), pp. 93–94.

23. Eastman, *Heroes I Have Known* (New York: Simon & Schuster, 1942), p. 317. For *New York Times* articles on Gorky's reception, see "Riot of Enthusiasm Meets Gorky," April 11, 1906, p. 6; "Gorky and Mark Twain Plead for Revolution," April 12, 1906, p. 4; "Gorky and Actress Asked to Quit Hotels," April 15, 1906, p. 1; "Gorky Is Now Hiding," April 16, 1906, p. 1.

24. Leon Harris, *Upton Sinclair: American Rebel* (New York: Thomas Y. Crowell, 1975), p. 95.

25. *Charities and the Commons* 17 (1906–1907), p. 185.

26. Michael Williams, *The Book of High Romance* (New York: Macmillan, 1951), pp. 144, 142.

27. Representative *New York Times* articles include "Sinclair Explains His Home Colony," July 18, 1906, p. 7 (which noted that three hundred people attended his lecture at the Berkeley Lyceum); "Upton Sinclair's Colony to Live at Helicon Hall," October 7, 1906, part 3, p. 2; "Helicon Hall Takes To Bloomers," February 14, 1907, p. 16; "Fire Wipes Out Helicon Hall," March 17, 1907, part 2, p. 1. Sinclair described the press coverage his venture received in his critique of the American press, *The Brass Check: A Study of American Journalism* (Pasadena, Calif.: 1920), pp. 62–67.

28. Upton Sinclair, *The Autobiography of Upton Sinclair* (New York: Harcourt Brace, 1962), p. 135. In writing about the effects of the press coverage on another philosophy professor from Columbia (presumably Montague), Sinclair indicated just how much Dewey risked criticism for his involvement in the venture: "Once or twice a week he had to give lectures to the young ladies at Barnard, and the Dean of Barnard was a lady of stern and unbending dignity, and after those articles had appeared our professor would quiver every time he saw her." *The Brass Check*, p. 64.

29. In Corliss Lamont, ed., *Dialogue on John Dewey* (New York: Horizon Press, 1959), pp. 74–75. James Farrell remembered an incident at a party when Tresca assured Dewey he could go ahead and get as drunk as he wanted as Tresca would "take care of" him; Dewey replied, "I'm being taken care of." "He liked Carlo very much," Farrell added. When Tresca was mysteriously shot down on a New York City street in January 1943 (Communist and Fascist plots were suspected), Dewey served on various memorial committees set up to investigate his murder.

30. Quoted in Richard Drinnon, *Rebel in Paradise: A Biography of Emma Goldman* (Chicago: University of Chicago Press, 1961), p. 88.

31. Dewey, "Introductory Word," in *Man's Supreme Inheritance: Conscious Guidance and Control in Relation to Human Evolution in Civilization* (New York: E. P. Dutton, 1918), p. xiii.

32. Ibid., p. xvii.
33. Eastman, *Heroes I Have Known*, p. 314.
34. Jane Dewey, pp. 44–45.
35. Dewey's second wife, Roberta, was very touchy on the matter of Alexander. When, during the discussion recorded in the 1959 *Dialogue on John Dewey*, Alvin Johnson said that Dewey was "enamored" of Alexander, Mrs. Dewey demanded that the comment be removed from any translations of the book. She even saw to it that an introductory note in the Japanese translation explicitly stated that Dewey never had any homosexual impulses. See Lamont, ed., *Dialogue on John Dewey*, p. 25. Lamont recounts Roberta Dewey's response in *Yes To Life: Memoirs of Corliss Lamont* (New York: Horizon Press, 1981), p. 83.
36. Lamont, ed., *Dialogue on John Dewey*, p. 47.
37. Henry Hart, *Dr. Barnes of Merion: An Appreciation* (New York: Farrar Strauss, 1963), p. 230. Hart edited the foundation's newsletter, and his book is essentially a memoir; far more complete is William Schack, *Art and Argyrol: The Life and Career of Albert Coombs Barnes* (New York: Thomas Yoseloff, 1960). At a public lecture years after his escapade Michener told Barnes what he had done, expecting an amused response; Barnes attacked him viciously. Barnes also sent carbon copies of all of his most nasty correspondence to various people; Schack notes in a (serious?) footnote that the foundation was by 1934 the second largest consumer of carbon paper in the United States.
38. Carl W. McCardle, "The Terrible-Tempered Dr. Barnes," *The Saturday Evening Post*, 214 (March 21, 1942), p. 11.
39. Lamont, ed., *Dialogue on John Dewey*, p. 46. The men who participated in the dialogue also remembered Dewey's disastrous efforts to get Bertrand Russell a position with the foundation.
40. Quoted in Schack, p. 241.
41. Schack, p. 191.
42. Hart, p. 64.
43. Klyce to Dewey, April 4, 1915.
44. Ibid.
45. Ibid., May 22, 1915.
46. Dewey to Klyce, April 22, [1915].
47. Ibid., May 6, 1915.
48. Ibid., April 16, 1915.
49. Ibid., May 13, [1915].
50. Ibid., November 9, 1927.
51. Ibid., June 20, 1928.
52. Klyce to Milton Halsey Thomas, March 24, 1929.
53. Dewey to Corinne F. Frost, September 1, 1941, John Dewey Papers, Rare Book and Manuscript Collection, Columbia University. Dewey maintained a long correspondence with Frost about philosophical matters; they seem never to have met. To Frost, Dewey nicknamed

himself Dr. Johnnie (Dewey to Frost, August 1, 1932); the nickname stuck.

54. Dewey, *Confidential Report on Conditions Among the Poles in the United States* (Philadelphia: 1918), p. 72.
55. Ibid., p. 45.
56. Ibid., p. 4.
57. It is impossible to document this debate in full. The revisionist attack was launched by Clarence J. Karier, Paul C. Violas, and Joel Spring, *Roots of Crisis: American Education in the Twentieth Century* (Chicago: University of Chicago Press, 1973), following Clarence J. Karier's "Liberalism and the Quest for Orderly Change," *History of Education Quarterly* 12 (Spring 1972), pp. 57–80. See also Walter Feinberg's "Progressive Education and Social Planning," *Teachers College Record* 73 (May 1972), pp. 485–505. Scholars answered these charges in *History of Education Quarterly* 15 (Spring 1975)—J. Christopher Eisele with "John Dewey and the Immigrants," pp. 67–85; Paul F. Bourke with "Philosophy and Social Criticism: John Dewey 1910–1920," pp. 3–16; and Charles L. Zerby with "John Dewey and the Polish Question: A Response to the Revisionist Historians," pp. 17–30. The revisionists in turn responded in *History of Education Quarterly* 15 (Winter 1975)—Walter Feinberg with "On Reading Dewey," pp. 395–415, and Clarence Karier with "John Dewey and the New Liberalism: Some Reflections and Responses," pp. 417–443.
58. Karier, "Liberal Ideology and Orderly Change," in Karier, Violas, and Spring, *Roots of Crisis*, pp. 92–93.
59. Feinberg, p. 496.
60. Dewey, *Confidential Report*, p. 2.

## Chapter Six   *John Dewey in Love*

1. Yezierska, *All I Could Never Be* (New York: Brewer, Warren, and Putnam, 1932), p. 28.
2. Yezierska to Dorothy Canfield Fisher, April 24, [1931]. In the Dorothy Canfield Fisher Papers at the Bailey/Howe Library, University of Vermont.
3. Yezierska to Mary Austin, April 12, [1921]. In the Mary Austin Papers at the Huntington Library.
4. Yezierska to Zona Gale, May 31, [1928]. In the Zona Gale Papers at the State Historical Society of Wisconsin (Madison).
5. Yezierska, "The Miracle," *Hungry Hearts* (1920; reprint, New York: Persea Books, 1985), p. 115.
6. Ibid., p. 133.
7. Ibid., p. 135.
8. Ibid., p. 136.
9. Ibid., p. 141.
10. Ralda Sullivan, "Anzia Yezierska, An American Writer," Ph.D. diss., University of California, Berkeley, 1975, p. 70.

11. *The Poems of John Dewey,* Jo Ann Boydston, ed. (Carbondale: Southern Illinois University Press, 1977), ''Autum,'' 11–15.

12. Dewey to Scudder Klyce, May 6, 1915. In the Scudder Klyce Papers at the Library of Congress.

13. Morton White, *Science and Sentiment in America: Philosophical Thought from Jonathan Edwards to John Dewey* (New York: Oxford University Press, 1972), p. 287.

14. Dewey, ''From Absolutism to Experimentalism,'' in George P. Adams and William Pepperell Montague, eds., *Contemporary American Philosophy: Personal Statements,* vol. 2 (New York: Macmillan, 1930), p. 19.

15. Yezierska, ''Prophets of Democracy,'' *The Bookman* 52 (1921), p. 497.

16. Lewis S. Feuer, ''The Standpoints of Dewey and Freud: A Contrast and Analysis,'' *Journal of Individual Psychology* 16 (November 1960), pp. 119–136.

17. Max Eastman, ''A Significant Memory of Freud,'' *New Republic* 104 (May 19, 1941), p. 694.

18. Sidney Hook, ''Materials for a Biography'' [review of George Dykhuizen's *The Life and Mind of John Dewey*], *New Republic* 169 (October 27, 1973), p. 28.

19. Florence Zunser Saltz, in a conversation with the author, October 15, 1986, remembered vividly her mother's vigorous opposition to Yezierska's making the affair public; it was the subject of a protracted quarrel between them.

20. Yezierska, *Red Ribbon on a White Horse* (1950; reprint, New York: Persea Books, 1978), pp. 111–112.

21. Yezierska, *All I Could Never Be,* p. 44.

22. See Boydston, ''Introduction,'' in *The Poems of John Dewey,* pp. xiv–xvii, for a definitive guide to the dates of Dewey's poems.

23. Dewey, ''Poetry and Philosophy,'' in Jo Ann Boydston, ed., *John Dewey: The Early Works, 1882–1898* (Carbondale: Southern Illinois University Press, 1969–1972), vol. 3, pp. 123–124.

24. *Memoirs of Waldo Frank,* Alan Trachtenberg, ed. (Boston: University of Massachusetts Press, 1983), p. 89.

25. Dewey, ''In a Time of National Hesitation,'' *Seven Arts* 2 (May 2, 1917), p. 3.

26. Yezierska, *All I Could Never Be,* pp. 60–61. In her 1969 interview with Ralda Sullivan, Yezierska used the same words in describing what Dewey said to her: ''You suffer from striving. You are already—you don't have to try to be—and perhaps I can have the happiness of making you realize you are and what you are.'' See Sullivan, p. 71. There is a strong indication that Yezierska had actually memorized his letters to her.

27. Yezierska, *Salome of the Tenements* (New York: Boni and Liveright, 1923), p. 51.

28. Yezierska, *All I Could Never Be,* p. 66.

29. Yezierska, *Red Ribbon on a White Horse,* p. 110.

30. Ibid., pp. 108–109.
31. Florence Zunser Saltz, interview with author, October 15, 1986.
32. Yezierska, *Red Ribbon on a White Horse*, p. 110.
33. Yezierska, *All I Could Never Be*, p. 63.
34. William Schack, *Art and Argyrol: The Life and Career of Albert Coombs Barnes* (New York: Thomas Yoseloff, 1960), pp. 122–123.
35. Yezierska, *All I Could Never Be*, p. 38.
36. Ibid.
37. Schack, p. 102.
38. Boydston, "Introduction," p. xlii.
39. Yezierska, *All I Could Never Be*, pp. 202–3.
40. See Schack, pp. 102–105, and Henry Hart, *Dr. Barnes of Merion: A Biography* (New York: Farrar Strauss, 1963), pp. 65–67, for the details of the study.
41. Yezierska, *All I Could Never Be*, pp. 84–5.
42. Dewey, *Confidential Report on Conditions Among the Poles* (Philadelphia: 1918), p. 2.
43. Hart, p. 66.
44. Yezierska, *All I Could Never Be*, p. 186.
45. The letter appears in William Lyon Phelps, *Autobiography with Letters* (New York: Oxford University Press, 1939), p. 905–907.
46. Yezierska, "Wings," *Hungry Hearts*, p. 5.
47. Hart, p. 66.
48. Yezierska, "Wings," *Hungry Hearts*, p. 9.
49. Christopher Lasch, *The New Radicalism in America (1889–1963): The Intellectual as a Social Type* (New York: Alfred A. Knopf, 1965), p. 83.
50. Yezierska, "Children of Loneliness," *Children of Loneliness* (New York: Funk & Wagnalls, 1923), p. 119.
51. Yezierska, *Arrogant Beggar* (Garden City, N.Y.: Doubleday, 1927), p. 204.
52. Ibid., pp. 208–209, 210.
53. Yezierska, "To the Stars," *Children of Loneliness*, p. 85.
54. Yezierska, "The Miracle," *Hungry Hearts*, p. 137.
55. See Mary V. Dearborn, *Pocahontas's Daughters: Gender and Ethnicity in American Culture* (New York: Oxford University Press, 1986), pp. 97–130, and Kristin Herzog, *Women, Ethnics, and Exotics: Images of Power in Mid-Nineteenth Century Fiction* (Knoxville: University of Tennessee Press, 1983), for the equation of the ethnic with the erotic.
56. Yezierska, *Bread Givers* (1925; reprint, New York: Persea Books, 1975), p. 297.
57. Sullivan, p. 73.
58. Yezierska, *All I Could Never Be*, p. 35.
59. Yezierska, *Red Ribbon on a White Horse*, p. 113.
60. Sullivan, p. 74.
61. Yezierska, *Red Ribbon on a White Horse*, p. 110.
62. Boydston, "Introduction," p. xlv.

63. Yezierska, "Love Hunger!" *Metropolitan Magazine* 58 (January 1924), p. 11.
64. Ibid., p. 12.
65. Ibid., p. 73.
66. Yezierska to Ferris Greenslet, May 27, [1923]. In the Houghton Mifflin Papers, Houghton Library, Harvard University.
67. Quoted in Boydston, "Introduction," p. xlv. Louise Levitas Henriksen, in interview with author, May 20, 1987, said she believed Yezierska severely misled Dewey, and that when he made an advance, she recoiled "as if he were a child molester."
68. Yezierska, *Red Ribbon on a White Horse*, p. 116.
69. Yezierska, "An Immigrant Among the Editors," *Children of Loneliness*, p. 62.
70. Yezierska, *Salome of the Tenements*, p. 238.
71. Yezierska, *All I Could Never Be*, p. 76.
72. Ibid., pp. 109–110.
73. See Babette Inglehart, "Daughters of Loneliness: Anzia Yezierska and the Immigrant Woman Writer," *Studies in American Jewish Literature* 1 (Winter 1975), pp. 1–10, for contemporary reviews of Yezierska's work.
74. Yezierska, *Salome of the Tenements*, p. 247.
75. "Russell Tussle," *Time* 41 (February 1, 1943), p. 56.
76. Carl W. McCardle, "The Terrible-Tempered Dr. Barnes," *The Saturday Evening Post* 214 (March 21, 1942), p. 94.
77. McCardle, p. 142.
78. Schack, p. 142.
79. Ibid., p. 367.
80. Ibid., pp. 185–186.
81. Ibid., pp. 17–18.
82. See, for example, John Higham, *Strangers in the Land: Patterns of American Nativism, 1865–1925* (New Brunswick, N.J.: Rutgers University Press, 1955).
83. Yezierska, "Wild Winter Love," *Hungry Hearts*, p. 335.
84. Ibid., p. 335.
85. Yezierska to Ferris Greenslet, April 3, 1920, and April 20, 1920. In the Houghton Mifflin Papers, Houghton Library, Harvard University.
86. Yezierska to Ferris Greenslet, October 25, 1920. In the Houghton Mifflin Papers, Houghton Library, Harvard University.
87. Louise Levitas Henriksen, interview with author, May 20, 1987.
88. Yezierska, "Prophets of Democracy," *The Bookman* 52 (1921), p. 497.
89. Yezierska, *Bread Givers* (1925; reprint, New York: Persea Books, 1975), p. 222.
90. Yezierska was convinced not to name Dewey only after considerable and sustained insistence on the part of her friend Miriam Shomer

Zunser. Conversation of Florence Zunser Saltz with author, October 15, 1986.
91. Yezierska, "Mostly About Myself," *Children of Loneliness,* pp. 19–20.

## Chapter Seven  *Yezierska, 1917–1970*

1. From a 1969 interview with Yezierska discussed in Ralda Sullivan, "Anzia Yezierska: An American Writer," Ph.D. diss., University of California, Berkeley, 1975, p. 73.
2. Sullivan, p. 51.
3. See Yezierska, "An Immigrant Among the Editors," in *Children of Loneliness* (New York: Funk & Wagnalls, 1923).
4. See Sullivan, p. 77, and Louise Levitas Henriksen, "Afterword," in Alice Kessler-Harris, ed., *The Open Cage: An Anzia Yezierska Collection* (New York: Persea Books, 1979), p. 260.
5. *The Bookman* 52 (February 1921), p. 551. See also M. C. in *Survey* 45 (January 15, 1921), p. 579, and the *New York Times,* December 5, 1920, section 3, p. 18.
6. Yezierska, *Red Ribbon on a White Horse* (1950; reprint New York: Persea Books, 1978), p. 26.
7. The Yezierska/Scarborough letters are in the Texas Collection, Baylor University, Waco, Texas.
8. Frank Crane, "Anzia Yezierska," [New York] *Globe and Commercial Advertiser,* November 27, 1920, p. 12.
9. Yezierska to Ferris Greenslet, December 17, [1920], Houghton Mifflin Papers, Houghton Library, Harvard University. She negotiated with Fox as well.
10. Anna Marcet Haldeman-Julius to Alice Haldeman-Julius, March 28, 1925, in the Haldeman-Julius Collection at the Leonard H. Axe Library, Pittsburg (Kansas) State University.
11. Henriksen, p. 256.
12. Yezierska, *Red Ribbon on a White Horse,* p. 80.
13. Yezierska, "The Immigrant Speaks," *Good Housekeeping* 70 (June 1920), pp. 20–21.
14. Yezierska, "Prophets of Democracy," *The Bookman* 52 (1921), pp. 496–499.
15. Louise Levitas Henriksen, "Preface," *Hungry Hearts and Other Stories* (New York: Persea Books, 1985), p. x.
16. "We Can Change Our Noses But Not Our Moses" is in the Anzia Yezierska Collection at the Mugar Memorial Library of Boston University; it is listed as part of the manuscript of *Red Ribbon on a White Horse.* "You Can't Be an Immigrant Twice," an interview of Yezierska by Richard Duffy, appears in Yezierska's *Children of Loneliness* (New York: Funk & Wagnalls, 1923).
17. For the rise of advertising and public relations, see, for instance, Stuart and Elizabeth Ewen, *Channels of Desire: Mass Images and the*

*Shaping of American Consciousness* (New York: McGraw-Hill, 1982); T. J. Jackson Lears, "From Salvation to Self-Realization: Advertising and the Therapeutic Roots of Consumer Culture," in Richard Wightman Fox and T. J. Jackson Lears, eds., *The Culture of Consumption: Critical Essays in American History, 1880–1980* (New York: Pantheon, 1983); and Daniel Pope, *The Making of Modern Advertising* (New York: Basic Books, 1983). Marion Marzolf, "Americanizing the Melting Pot: The Media as Magaphone for the Restrictionists," in Catherine L. Covert and John D. Stevens, eds., *Mass Media Between the Wars: Perceptions of Cultural Tension* (Syracuse, N.Y.: Syracuse University Press, 1984), pp. 107–125, analyzes the response of the press and the role of public relations as elements in the move for immigration restriction.

18. Philip Lesly, ed., *Public Relations Handbook* (New York: Prentice-Hall, 1950), p. 4.
19. See Edward L. Bernays, *Public Relations* (Norman: University of Oklahoma Press, 1952).
20. Quoted in Bernays, p. 93.
21. Yezierska, *Red Ribbon on a White Horse*, p. 62.
22. Ibid., p. 26.
23. Carol Easton, *The Search for Sam Goldwyn: A Biography* (New York: William Morrow, 1976), p. 51.
24. Arthur Marx, *Goldwyn: A Biography of the Man Behind the Myth* (New York: W. W. Norton, 1976), p. 98.
25. Alvin H. Morrill, in *Samuel Goldwyn Presents* (New York: A. S. Barnes, 1976), relates how Maeterlinck, hired at a weekly salary of five figures, turned in a screenplay based on his *Life of a Bee*. Goldwyn reportedly burst out of his office, exclaiming "My God, the hero is a bee!" No films were made from Maeterlinck's material. See also Marx, pp. 102–106.
26. Bernays, *Biography of an Idea: Memoirs of Public Relations Counsel Edward L. Bernays* (New York: Simon & Schuster, 1965), pp. 149–150.
27. Goldwyn did not change his name to disguise his background; his association with a partner, Edgar Selwyn, led others and then himself to conflate their two names. See Marx, Easton, and Philip French, *The Movie Moguls: An Informal History of the Hollywood Tycoons* (Chicago: Henry Regnery, 1969).
28. Quoted in Lary L. May and Elaine Tyler May, "Why Jewish Movie Moguls: An Exploration in American Culture," *American Jewish History* 72 (September 1982), p. 12. For Jews in Hollywood, see Lary L. May, *Screening Out the Past: The Birth of Mass Culture and the Motion Picture Industry* (New York: Oxford University Press, 1980); Patricia Erens, *The Jew in American Cinema* (Bloomington: Indiana University Press, 1983); Sarah Blacher Cohen, ed., *From Hester Street to Hollywood: The Jewish-American Stage and Screen* (Bloomington: Indiana University Press, 1983); and Lester D. Friedman, *Hollywood's Image of the Jew* (New York: Frederick Ungar, 1982).

29. Mary Roberts Rinehart, *My Story* (New York: Farrar & Rinehart, 1931), p. 294. See also Gertrude Atherton, *Adventures of a Novelist* (New York: Liveright, 1932).
30. Yezierska, *Red Ribbon on a White Horse*, pp. 80–81.
31. Ibid., p. 84.
32. Ibid., p. 44.
33. Ibid., p. 81.
34. Ibid., p. 82.
35. Ibid., p. 62.
36. Ibid., p. 69.
37. Ibid., p. 72.
38. Yezierska, "Children of Loneliness," in *The Open Cage*, p. 162.
39. Sullivan, p. 102.
40. Yezierska, "What Makes a Writer?" Ms. in the Anzia Yezierska Collection, box 1, folder 11, Mugar Memorial Library, Boston University.
41. Dr. Henry Grinberg, in an interview with the author, June 7, 1986, and Roberta Matthews, in a July 9, 1986 interview, recalled Yezierska's Galsworthy stories.
42. Sullivan, pp. 106–107.
43. Ibid., p. 107.
44. Yezierska to Zona Gale, May 31, [1928], in the Zona Gale Papers in the State Historical Society of Wisconsin, Madison. For Zona Gale's life and relation to Yezierska see August Derleth, *Still Small Voice: The Biography of Zona Gale* (New York: Appleton-Century, 1940); Harold Simonson, *Zona Gale* (New York: Twayne, 1962), and correspondence from Virginia Cox, Gale's present biographer, to the author, May 24, 1986, August 4, 1986, and August 13, 1986. Yezierska wrote a fictionalized account of her meeting Gale as a chapter in *Red Ribbon* that she later deleted; titled "Saint in Cellophane," it is in the Anzia Yezierska Collection, box 1, folder 1, Mugar Memorial Library, Boston University.
45. Yezierska, "Saint in Cellophane."
46. Simonson, pp. 55–56.
47. Yezierska to Gale, January 23, [1931], in the Zona Gale Papers at the State Historical Society of Wisconsin, Madison.
48. Sullivan, p. 122.
49. Yezierska to Dorothy Canfield Fisher, undated, in the Dorothy Canfield Fisher Papers in the Bailey/Howe Library, University of Vermont.
50. Yezierska to Fisher, undated.
51. Yezierska, *Red Ribbon on a White Horse*, p. 207.
52. Ibid., p. 208.
53. Ibid., p. 219.
54. Yezierska to Fisher, undated.
55. Dorothy Canfield Fisher's notes on the folder containing her corre-

spondence with Yezierska, undated. Dorothy Canfield Fisher Papers, Bailey/Howe Library, University of Vermont.

56. Yezierska to Fisher, April 7, 1931.
57. Yezierska to Fisher, April 7, [1932].
58. Selma Sable Parker, [review of *All I Could Never Be*], *Madison* [Wisconsin] *Times*, September 25, 1932.
59. "Thwarted Love" [review of *All I Could Never Be*], *New York Times*, August 21, 1932, section 5, p. 11.
60. W. Adolphe Roberts, "Hungry Souls" [review of *Salome of the Tenements*], *New York Tribune*, December 31, 1922, p. 26.
61. Scott Nearing, "A Depraved Spirit" [review of *Salome of the Tenements*], *The Nation* 116 (June 6, 1924), p. 676.
62. Marya Zaturenska, "The Melting Pot" [review of *Arrogant Beggar*], *New York Herald Tribune*, October 23, 1927, section 7, p. 7.
63. Burton Rascoe, "A Bookman's Day Book," *New York Tribune*, December 31, 1922.
64. Yezierska to Fisher, August 28, 1950. Dorothy Canfield Fisher Papers, Bailey/Howe Library, University of Vermont.
65. Yezierska, *Red Ribbon on a White Horse*, p. 219.
66. Ibid., p. 68.
67. Henriksen, "Afterword," *The Open Cage*, pp. 254–255.
68. For Yezierska's involvement with the Federal Writers' Project, see her *Red Ribbon on a White Horse* and also Jerre Mangione, *The Dream and the Deal: The Federal Writers' Project, 1935–1943* (Boston: Little, Brown, 1972), pp. 155–158, and Orrick Johns, *Time of Our Lives: The Story of My Father and Myself* (1937; reprint, New York: Octagon Books, 1973), pp. 341–350.
69. Yezierska, *Red Ribbon on a White Horse*, p. 161.
70. Ibid., p. 198.
71. W. H. Auden, "Introduction," *Red Ribbon on a White Horse*, p. 12.
72. Sullivan, p. 125. Yezierska's letters to Auden are in the Charles Scribner's Sons papers in the Princeton University Library. Louise Levitas Henriksen, in an interview with the author, May 20, 1987, said she made cuts in Auden's manuscript until it was minimally acceptable to her mother.
73. Yezierska, "One Thousand Pages of Research," *Commentary* 36 (July 1963), pp. 60–63.
74. Roberta Matthews and Henry Grinberg, in the interviews cited above, recalled working for Yezierska in the 1960s. Each remembered successfully "passing on" the job of working for her to another willing friend, and neither recalled being paid for the work.
75. An obituary appeared in the *New York Times*, November 23, 1970.

Chapter Eight    *"Old Men Dreaming Dreams"*

1. Dewey to John Jacob Coss, January 13, 1920. See also Dewey to Coss, November [1920]. John Jacob Coss Collection, Butler Library, Columbia University.

2. George Dykhuizen, *The Life and Mind of John Dewey* (Carbondale: Southern Illinois University Press, 1973), pp. 313–314.
3. See "Dr. Dewey Loses Estate," *New York Times*, June 19, 1947, p. 2. Sidney Hook, in *Out of Step: An Unquiet Life in the Twentieth Century* (New York: Harper & Row, 1987), p. 92, writes that the marriage caused an "abrupt and unhappy break" between Dewey and his children.
4. Dewey, "From Absolutism to Experimentalism," in George P. Adams and William Pepperell Montague, eds., *Contemporary American Philosophy: Personal Statements*, vol. 2, pp. 13–27.
5. Waldo Frank, *Memoirs of Waldo Frank*, Alan Trachtenberg, ed. (Boston: University of Massachusetts Press, 1973), p. 89.
6. Quotations and details from Jo Ann Boydston, "Introduction," *The Poems of John Dewey*, Jo Ann Boydston, ed. (Carbondale: Southern Illinois University Press, 1977), pp. xi–xii.
7. Boydston, p. x.
8. Ibid., p. ix.
9. Ibid., p. x.
10. Ibid.
11. Waldo Frank, *In the American Jungle [1925–1936]* (New York: Farrar & Rinehart, 1937), p. 35. Alvin H. Johnson, *The Wit and Wisdom of John Dewey* (Boston: Beacon Press, 1959), p. 8 (itself a remarkable volume); Sidney Hook, "Materials for a Biography," *New Republic* 169 (October 29, 1973), p. 29. W. I. Thomas in Lewis Feuer, "America's Medicine Man" [review of Neil Coughlan's *Young John Dewey*], *Times Literary Supplement* (December 3, 1976), p. 1507. Max Eastman, *Heroes I Have Known* (New York: Simon & Schuster, 1942), p. 277.
12. Henry Steele Commager, *The American Mind: An Interpretation of American Thought and Character Since the 1880's* (New Haven, Conn.: Yale University Press, 1950), pp. 18, 96–98.
13. Morris R. Cohen, *American Thought: A Critical Sketch*, Felix S. Cohen, ed. (Glencoe, Ill.: Free Press, 1954), p. 364.
14. Hook, p. 29.
15. Lamont, *Dialogue on John Dewey*, p. 80.
16. Eastman, pp. 251–252.
17. Hofstadter, p. 361.
18. William James quoted in Hofstadter, p. 361. Irwin Edman, *Introduction to John Dewey: His Contribution to the American Tradition* (New York: Bobbs-Merrill, 1955), p. 23. Quentin Anderson, "John Dewey's American Democrat," *Daedalus* 108 (Summer 1979), p. 147.
19. Mark de Wolfe Howe, ed., *Holmes-Pollock Letters*, vol. 2 (Cambridge, Mass.: Harvard University Press, 1941), p. 287.
20. "Search-Light" [Waldo Frank], "The Man Who Made Us What We Are," *New Yorker* 2 (May 22, 1926), p. 15.
21. Ibid., p. 16.
22. Dykhuizen, p. 320.
23. See Richard Hofstadter, *Anti-Intellectualism in American Life* (New

York: Alfred A. Knopf, 1963). Nineteen fifty-three, a representative year, saw such attacks as Albert Lynd's *Quackery in the Public Schools* (New York: Grosset & Dunlap); Arthur Bestor's *Educational Wasteland: The Retreat from Learning in Our Public Schools* (Urbana: University of Illinois Press); Robert Hutchins's *The Conflict in Education in a Democratic Society* (New York: Harper); and Paul Woodring's *Let's Talk Sense About Our Schools* (New York: McGraw-Hill).

24. "Fusilier," *Time* 59 (March 17, 1952), p. 77.
25. E. D. Hirsch, *Cultural Literacy* (Boston, Mass.: Houghton Mifflin, 1987).
26. Frank, "The Man Who Made Us What We Are," p. 16.
27. Ibid.
28. Lewis S. Feuer, "America's Medicine Man" [review of Neil Coughlan's *Young John Dewey*], *Times Literary Supplement,* December 3, 1976, p. 1507.
29. Thomas Hardy, *Tess of the d'Urbervilles* (1891; reprint, New York: W. W. Norton, 1965), p. 202.
30. Ibid., p. 330.
31. Ibid., pp. 221–222.
32. See, for instance, Rorty's *Consequences of Pragmatism: Essays 1972–1980* (Minneapolis: University of Minnesota Press, 1982); his *Philosophy and the Mirror of Nature* (Princeton, N.J.: Princeton University Press, 1979); and his "Philosophy in America Today," *American Scholar* 51 (Spring 1982), pp. 183–200. For representative responses, see Michael Levin, "Why Not Pragmatism?" *Commentary* 75 (January 1983), pp. 43–47; Richard H. King, "'In Other Words': The Philosophical Writings of Richard Rorty," *Journal of American Studies* 19 (1985), pp. 95–103; Anthony Quinton, "Dropping the Object," *Partisan Review* 51 (Summer 1984), pp. 467–473.
33. "Robertson Sets Conditions for Making a Run in 1988," *New York Times,* September 18, 1986, p. D29.
34. Walter Feinberg, "On Reading Dewey," *History of Education Quarterly* 15 (Winter 1975), p. 396.
35. Contemporary criticism includes Sam Girgus, "'Blut-und Eisen': Anzia Yezierska and the New Self-Made Woman," in *The New Covenant: Jewish Writers and the American Idea* (Chapel Hill: University of North Carolina Press, 1984), pp. 108–117; Joyce Carol Oates, "Imaginary Cities: America," in *The Profane Art: Essays and Reviews* (New York: E. P. Dutton, 1984), pp. 9–34; and three articles in *Studies in American Jewish Literature* 3 (1983): Rose Kamel, "'Anzia Yezierska, Get Out of Your Own Way': Selfhood and Otherness in the Autobiographical Fiction of Anzia Yezierska," pp. 40–50; Ellen Golub, "Eat Your Heart Out: The Fiction of Anzia Yezierska," pp. 51–61; and Susan Hersh Sachs, "Anzia Yezierska: 'Her words dance with a thousand colors,'" pp. 62–67. Yezierska was the subject of a *New York Times* "Hers" column by Vivian Gornick, April 6, 1978, p. C2.

# Index